'Cabbage Syndrome'

Acknowledgments

Special thanks to Geoff Mercer and Carolyn Baylies for their help, advice and support, Sarah Barnes for her computing skills and Andrew Scowcroft for the drawings.

'Cabbage Syndrome'
The Social Construction of Dependence

Colin Barnes

The Falmer Press
(A member of the Taylor & Francis Group)
London • New York • Philadelphia

UK   The Falmer Press, Rankine Road, Basingstoke, Hants RG24 0PR

USA   The Falmer Press, Taylor & Francis Inc., 1900 Frost Road,
            Suite 101, Bristol, PA 19007

First published 1990

British Library Cataloguing in Publication Data
Barnes, Colin
    Cabbage syndrome: the social construction of dependence.
    1. Great Britain, Day care centres for physically
    handicapped young persons
    I. Title
    362.40480835

    ISBN 1-85000-757-8
    ISBN 1-85000-758-6 pbk

**Library of Congress Cataloguing in Publication Data available on
request**

Typeset in 10/12 Garamond by
Chapterhouse, The Cloisters, Formby L37 3PX
Printed in Great Britain by
Redwood Burn Limited, Trowbridge, Wiltshire

Contents

To Hil

Preface

This is an empirical study which describes and evaluates the role of day centres with regard to young people with physical impairments aged between 16 and 30, describes and evaluates the interactions between users and staff within the day centre environment, outlines and assesses the level of user participation in the centres with reference to activities, the decision-making process and control, and suggests a set of policy recommendations which are applicable to both the service studied and day services generally for this user group.

Four ideal types of day centre for the younger physically impaired are identified. All are criticized on the basis that they are inherently segregative, emphasize difference and perpetuate stigma. Within this context day centres are perceived as the 'dumping ground' for those people who are excluded, because of physical impairment, from the normal social and economic life of society. Empirical evidence to support this view is provided firstly by the overtly negative features of the general organization and admission policies of the system studied, secondly by the degree of social and economic disadvantage experienced by the users interviewed prior to day centre use, and thirdly by the manner in which they were similarly labelled and 'directed' toward the centres. I argue that day centre use reinforces disadvantage because, although helper/helped relations within the system are viewed positively by both users and staff, user participation and control of services is low; and because, while the system provides a range of facilities which give many users a level of self-determination unavailable in the community at large, its capacity to extend those experiences beyond the day centre boundary is limited to only a few. Consequently attendance for the majority will be long-term.

I list a number of recommendations, including the formulation of a national policy clarifying the role of day services for this user group, which might help to alleviate this problem. I conclude that present policies which successfully disable young people with impairments are no longer simply socially unacceptable. They are also economically inept.

Colin Barnes
July 1989

List of Tables and Figures

Chapter 1
Introduction

Background

The initial impetus for this study stems from three distinct but related factors. The first is my interest in the general economic and social disadvantage associated with disability, in particular the experience of young people with physical impairments (highlighted by Anderson and Clarke, 1982; Brimblecomb *et al.*, 1985; Cantrell *et al.*, 1985; Hirst, 1984, 1987; Hurst; 1984; Kuh *et al.*, 1988; Lones, 1985). A second is the substantial critique directed toward those people who are employed, professionally or otherwise, in the rehabilitation or caring industries. In broad terms these arguments suggest that professional intervention compounds disability because it inhibits individual adaptation and induces dependence (see, for example, Davis, 1984; Finkelstein, 1980; Oliver, 1983a; and Scott, 1970). In conjunction with these censures there has emerged from some sections of the 'disabled' population an increasing demand for self-advocacy and self-determination in institutional settings which cater for people with impairments (Crawley, 1988; Dartington *et al.*, 1981; Davis, 1985, 1986; Oliver, 1983a, 1986, 1987a; Sutherland, 1981; and UPIAS, 1976, 1981).

While the positive effects of this movement are undoubted in terms of consciousness-raising, I believe it is essential that these developments are situated within an appropriate context to prevent their lending weight to those who would justify the erosion of state-sponsored welfare provision within the logic of utilitarian individualism and economic rationality. In order, therefore, to offer informed comment upon these debates with any degree of authority, it is important to conduct research located within an environment where the impaired and their accredited 'helpers' interact on a regular daily basis.

Probably the most obvious and arguably the easiest location for a study of this nature, if only because of its convenience, would be the archetypical residential institution specifically catering for a particular group of impaired people in which the avowed ideology is unequivocally therapeutic and rehabilitative and where there is a clear line of demarcation between the helper and the helped in terms of both role and function. Since the 1950s there has been increasing attention focused on this type of establishment by both social scientists and inmates.

Writers focusing on the incarceration of the physically impaired include Battye (1966), Hunt (1966) and Miller and Gwynne (1972), notwithstanding that the majority of this work has been concerned with institutions serving the mentally ill and handicapped (see, for example, Barton, 1959; Bloor, 1987; and Goffman, 1961).

While these studies have made an invaluable contribution to the understanding of the interdependence of the helper and the helped within residential settings they are limited in that their conclusions may only be applicable to the experiences of those who live and work in closed systems. It can be argued that they have little or no bearing upon the realities of daily life for the countless thousands of individuals with impairments who live within the local community, nor for that matter for the service providers upon whom they are said to depend.

This is particularly relevant to the experience of disability in Britain in the 1980s since 93 per cent of people with impairments now live in their own or their family's home (Martin, Meltzer and Elliot, 1988). This trend is partly due to the media exposure of the harsh realities of life in many residential institutions, the innumerable public outcries over conditions in some long-stay hospitals (Brown, 1980), the development of sophisticated drug therapies and a realization by policy-makers generally that prolonged incarceration for large numbers of the population does not make sound economic sense (Jones *et al.*, 1983). Consequently successive government statements on this issue since the 1950s have underpinned the idea of care within and/or by the community (Bulmer, 1987).

In response to this growing awareness by central and local government there was a large expansion during the 1960s and early 1970s of an assortment of services designed to facilitate independence and care in the community for people who hitherto had been confined to an institution (Parker, 1985). These services include increased numbers of general practitioners, district nurses, home helps, sheltered housing schemes, hostels, training centres, workshops and day centres. Despite this growth, provision has not been able to keep pace with consumer demand (Jones *et al.*, 1983) and the quality and allocation of services was, and remains, subject to regional variation (Griffiths, 1988). Moreover, due to the emphasis placed on financial constraints by the present Conservative government there is a very real danger that some of these services might disappear without proper evaluation (see Redding, 1989). One of the services increasingly under threat is the day centre run by the Social Services Department of the local authority.

Day centres are a relatively new phenomenon and as such have received little or no attention from social analysts, with the notable exceptions of Carter (1981, 1988), Kent *et al.* (1984), Jordan (1986), Symonds (1982) and Tuckey and Tuckey (1981). It is often stated that there is a particular need for this type of service for young people with impairments who have finished formal education and are unable to find work.

Much of the literature, however, is critical of the existing systems of day centre provision with regard to the needs of this particular user group. Most centres emphasize care rather than promoting young people's control over their own lives and their participation in ordinary adult society. Moreover, many day centres for the physically impaired are used predominantly by elderly people with chronic disabilities and offer little scope to young adults for peer contact and stimulation (Kent *et al.*, 1984). In short, for young people with physical impairments, most day services are criticized as precluding rather than promoting personal development, independence and self-esteem. This is particularly alarming since young people with physical impairments generally expect to establish an independent life of their own in much the same way as their non-impaired contemporaries (Parker, 1985).

This climate of opinion provides the starting point for the present study. It highlights the necessity for investigating how day centre provision is understood by both users and providers as a basis for furthering the limited knowledge of its dynamic, commenting upon the critique concerning the interactions between the helper and the helped, and formulating policy recommendations towards the system's improvement. I believe the latter to be a principal concomitant for all social analysis and broadly in line with the traditional view of social science recently elaborated by Heller (1987). In order to avoid what may be termed a theoretical vacuum, it is important that this research encompass both the empirical and the theoretical dimensions of the issues at hand by locating the empirical within the theoretical. Hence, it is essential to explore initially the principal sociological approaches to the subject of disability.

A preliminary task is to clarify the terminology used in the subsequent discussion. The following typology was developed during the 1970s and adopted by the World Health Organization in an effort to minimize the complexities of definition. It distinguishes impairment, disability and handicap.

Impairment

This refers to an anatomical or psychological disorder which is defined symptomatically or diagnostically. Impairments may affect locomotion, motor activities or sensory systems and be medically based or of psychological origin. They may involve any loss of physiological, psychological or anatomical structure or function. Such limitations can be permanent or temporary, present at birth (congenital impairments) or acquired later in life (adventitiously). Impairment is generally regarded as a neutral term.

Disability

This normally refers to the impact of impairment upon the performance of the basic elements of everyday living such as walking, negotiating stairs, getting in and out of bed, dressing, feeding, communicating with others, holding down work, etc. The term disability is used when an impairment is objectively defined and constitutes a restriction on mobility, domestic routines, occupational and communication skills.

Handicap

A term which has widely come to represent the most profound effects of impairment and disadvantage which implicate the whole person and not merely selective incapacities. Handicap in children has been seen as an impairment or disability which for a substantial period effects, retards, disturbs or otherwise adversely affects normal growth, development and adjustment to life. In adults, handicap constitutes a disadvantage for a given individual in that it prevents or limits the fulfilment of a role that is normal (depending on age, sex, and social and cultural factors) for that individual. The designation of handicap involves a value judgment.

The relationship between these three concepts is not direct but related to a number of ill-defined notions which, for reasons discussed later, are beyond the scope of the present study. However, they may be expressed diagramatically as shown in Table 1.

Table 1 Disablement Experience Summarized

Impairment	Intrinsic situations exteriorized as functional limitations
↓	
Disability	Objectified as activity restrictions
↓	
Handicap	Socialized as disadvantage

Source: Bury, 1979

Sociological Approaches to Disability

When discussing sociological perspectives on disability it is generally regarded as fruitful to begin with the work of Parsons and his analysis of sickness-related behaviour. This is because the Parsonian paradigm has been principally responsible for two distinct, but interdependent, approaches which have implicitly or explicitly influenced all subsequent analyses. They are the relevance of the 'sick role' in relation to disability and its association with social deviance, and the notion of health as adaptation (Bury, 1982). In short, Parsons' model suggests that at the onset of illness the sick person adopts the sick role. Rooted in the assumption that illness and disease impede physiological and, to some degree, cognitive abilities, the individual concerned is automatically relieved of all normative role expectations and responsibilities. S/he is not accountable for the malady, nor is s/he expected to recover through an active decision of free will or subjective action alone. Hence, s/he is expected to seek help, invariably professional medical help, in order to regain her/his former status. The sick person is encouraged to view her/his new-found status as undesirable and abhorrent (Parsons, 1951).

The Parsonian model is limited in the sense that it assumes that regardless of the nature and type of disease, or the subjective socio/psychological factors involved, everyone will behave in exactly the same way at the onset of illness. Moreover, since the model pays little heed to subjective interpretations, it articulates only the views of the representatives of society credited with the responsibility for recovery, namely, the medical profession. It does not accommodate sick role variation (Twaddle, 1969) nor the distinction between illness and impairment (Gordon, 1966) nor sickness expectations related to the illness and not the actor (Kassebaum and Baumann, 1960).

Occupation of the sick role is intended to be temporary. But for the chronically sick or for a person with an impairment there is little scope for recovery in terms of being restored to her/his former physical state, and because the 'disability' is part of her/his existence, the disabled person begins to accept the dependence prescribed under the sick role as normal. The sick role, therefore, removes from the impaired individual the obligation to take charge of her/his own affairs and sustains this on a more or less permanent basis (De Jong, 1979).

These general criticisms are elaborated within the context of the 'impaired role' as discussed by Gordon and by Sieglar and Osmond. Their alternative construct is applied to the actor whose condition is unlikely to improve and who therefore is unable to comply with the first prerequisite of the sick role model, that is, to try to recover as quickly as possible. It is claimed that those who accept the impaired role have abandoned all thoughts of rehabilitation and have largely accepted the notion of dependency as permanent. Thus

> a person who fails to maintain the sick role may find himself in the impaired role, unlike the sick role the impaired role is easy to maintain and difficult to leave for it is meant to be permanent, but it carries with it a loss of full human status. It is true that the impaired role does not require the exertions of co-operating with medical treatment and trying to regain one's health but the price for this is a kind of second class citizenship (Sieglar and Osmond, 1974, p. 116).

De Jong (1979) has suggested that the impaired role is not a normal role, but one that a disabled person is allowed to slip into as the passage of time weakens the assumptions of the sick role.

A further variation in the this train of thought is the 'rehabilitative role', as articulated by Safilios–Rothschild (1970). This model implies that once the impaired actor becomes aware of her/his new condition, s/he should accept it and learn how to live with it. This can be achieved, it is claimed, through the maximization of her/his remaining abilities. Thus the actor is obligated to assume as many of her/his previous normative roles as quickly as possible. S/he is therefore not exempt from social expectations and responsibilities but is expected to 'adapt' accordingly. Moreover, it is also assumed that not only will the impaired actor co-operate with the rehabilitative professions but will innovate and ameliorate new methods of rehabilitation.

In accord with this construct, the locus of responsibility rests squarely upon the shoulders of the impaired individual and, again, s/he is evidently dependent upon others, notably the rehabilitation professionals, for at least two specific functions — the initiation of rehabilitation programmes designed to return the impaired actor to 'normality' and assistance in the psychological adjustment to the new (disabled) identity. Some writers have suggested that the psychological adjustment to the realization that one is impaired can best be understood as a number of psychological stages, including 'shock', 'denial', 'anger' and 'depression', which the impaired actor must pass through before s/he can accept her/his new-found status. Movement is generally seen as only one way and as sequential. Passage through each stage is usually determined by an 'acceptable' time frame according to professionally agreed criteria (Albrecht, 1976).

In ideal typical form, all psychological theories of adjustment can be criticized on at least three different levels. The first is that they are essentially determinist. Behaviour is only viewed as positive if it is compatible with the consensual view of professional reality. Secondly, they pay little heed to extraneous economic, political or social factors. Thirdly, they ignore subjective interpretations of impairment from the perspective of the actor concerned. They are the products of what one critic has referred to as the 'psychological imagination', constructed on a bedrock of able-bodied assumptions of what it must be like to become impaired (Oliver, 1983a). Moreover, impairment is presumed to involve some form of loss, or personal tragedy. Consequently recent literature dealing with the traditional, medical or individual model of disability, has begun to refer to these formulations as 'personal tragedy theory' (Oliver, 1986).

An important factor which must be considered when assessing the logic behind the ideological hegemony of personal tragedy theory is its professional expediency, both at the individual and at the structural level. For example, if an impaired person fails to achieve the anticipated professionally determined rehabilitative goals, then that failure can be explained away with reference to the impaired actor's perceived inadequacies, whether they be physiologically or psychologically based. The 'expert' is exonerated from responsibility, professional integrity remains intact, traditional wisdom and values are not questioned, and the existing social order goes unchallenged.

The relationship between disability and deviance can be understood with reference to the freedom from social obligations and responsibility, explicit in the sick role model and subsequent derivatives and in the negative views of illness, disease and impairment that continue to hold sway throughout all modern industrial capitalist societies. Because such societies are founded upon an ideology of personal responsibility, competition and paid employment, any positive associations with sickness or disability, such as the exemptions outlined above, must be discouraged, particularly since they may appear attractive to those already disadvantaged, both economically and socially, by their structural location.

Indeed, the analysis of social reaction toward disadvantaged minority groups such as the disabled became a central focus for sociologists working within the traditions of symbolic interactionism during the 1960s. With their emphasis upon meaning, identity and the process of labelling, interactionists explored the relationship between disablement and socially proscribed behaviour. Initially theorists working within this perspective were interested in the areas of crime and drug addiction, but after substantial ethnographic research turned their attention toward the mechanisms by which these and other forms of human activity were shown to be socially unacceptable. Becker, for example, stated that

> Deviance is not a quality of the act a person commits, but rather a consequence of the application by others of rules and sanctions to an 'offender'. The deviant is one to whom the label has successfully been applied, deviant behaviour is behaviour that people so label. Deviance is not a quality that lies in behaviour itself but in the interaction between the person who commits an act and those who respond to it (Becker, 1963, p. 9).

Lemert (1962) made a further distinction between 'primary' and 'secondary' deviance, the former having only marginal implications for the actor in question and the latter relating to the ascription by others of a socially devalued status and a deviant identity. Secondary deviance for Lemert becomes a central facet of existence for those so labelled, 'altering psychic structure' and producing specialized organizations of social roles and self-management. Goffman (1968) developed the idea further with his use of the concept 'stigma', a term traditionally used to refer to a mark or blemish that is reputed to denote 'moral inferiority'. Goffman suggests that the stigmatized, such as 'the dwarf, the blind man, the disfigured, the homosexual and the ex-mental patient' are viewed by society at large as not quite human. The application of a stigma is the outcome of situational considerations and social interactions between the 'abnormal' and the 'normal'.

Within the context of these developments, impaired writers, first in America and then Britain, began to challenge the orthodox wisdom that underpinned the traditional approaches to rehabilitation and social provision in general. Scott (1970) questioned the type of 'deviance creation' that resulted from the interactions between the impaired and the acredited expert. In his study of 'blindness workers' in the USA Scott claims that these workers make 'blind men' out of people who can't see by imposing blindness-related behaviour patterns and attitudes which conform to the expert's view of blindness on people with sight problems. For Scott this represents a form of socialization in which the impaired individual is coerced into accepting a dependent subordinate role, concomitant with 'normal' perceptions of disability.

Throughout this period other writers adopted a more conventional approach to the study of disability. Haber and Smith (1971) argued that we should focus rather on the elaboration of behaviour alternatives within existing role relationships, rather than the proliferation of 'specialised role repertoires'. In this way the behaviour of the disabled may be normalized. It may not therefore, constitute secondary deviance.

This idea was developed further, although within the rubric of American radicalism, by Anspach (1979), but more in keeping with the work of Merton (1957) than Parsons, Anspach developed a four-dimensional model titled 'Strategems of Disability Management', which he claims typifies the modes of adaptation generally used by impaired individuals in response to society's overtly negative attitudes toward disability. The first he calls the 'normalizer', where the actor labelled 'disabled' accepts and concurs with societal estimations of her/himself, and behaves accordingly by seeking acceptance at any price. The second is 'disassociation', where the individual accepts the wider cultural interpretation of disability but is unwilling, or unable, to accept it with regard to her/himself. As a result s/he has a lowered perception of self. Social interaction is avoided since it only serves to reinforce negative self-concepts. The third, 'retreatism', is almost identical to the Mertonian concept of the same name. Consonant with negative perceptions of society and self, the individual rejects the wider cultural views of disability and has little or no self-esteem. Withdrawal, from all social activity is, therefore, the preferred pattern of behaviour. The fourth is the 'political activist', which is the construct favoured by the author. He writes:

> like the normalizer the activist seeks to attain a favourable conception of self, often asserting a claim to superiority over normals. But unlike the normalizer the activist seeks to relinquish any claim to an acceptance which s/he views as artificial (Anspach, 1979, p. 770).

Although orthodox in its construction, Anspach's formulation does serve to highlight the radicalization of some factions of the disabled population within American society during the late 1960s and early 70s. What became known as the Movement for Independent Living (ILM) emerged partly from within the university campus culture and partly in consequence of the efforts of some enlightened professionals to influence American legislation with regard to issues pertinent to people with disabilities. One of the movement's principal protagonists, De Jong, challenged the validity of the medical model, notwithstanding that he gave tacit approval to Safilios–Rothschild's construct, the rehabilitation role, arguing that disability was in large part a social construct and that environmental factors were at least as important as impairment-related variables in the assessment of the degree to which a person is able to live independently. De Jong claimed to be establishing a new paradigm in the celebrated tradition of Kuhn, by which the current body of knowledge and thinking on disability would be rendered obsolete. De Jong's paradigm shift heralds what later became known as the 'social model of disability' as opposed to the traditional perspectives associated with the medical model, psychology and the sick role variations (De Jong, 1979).

This approach and the activities of the ILM are, however, firmly entrenched within the philosophical and political traditions which De Jong refers to as 'radical consumerism'. In his estimation this was the driving force behind other major political movements which swept the USA during the same period. It is not surprising, therefore, that the ILM is wedded to the principal assumptions that form the ideological cornerstones of capitalist America, such as economic and political freedom, consumer sovereignty and self-reliance. The movement's avowed aim is to facilitate the reclamation of disabled people's subjective autonomy through opposition to what they see as the professionally dominated, bureaucratically inert state monopoly of welfare provision (in the American Federalist sense), through rational and competitive pursuit of the interests of the disabled in the political and economic marketplace.

Writers working within this paradigm tend to heap all their polemic upon the rehabilitation professionals and what they consider to be excessively bureaucratic administration. Whereas personal tragedy theory over-emphasizes subjective physiological and cognitive limitations through the professionally determined functional definitions of impairment, 'social reaction theory' challenged the authenticity of those definitions, but generally ignored the structural factors which may have necessitated or precipitated their application. While much attention is directed toward professional ineptitude and maladministration, little is paid to the structure itself. Such a position tends to ignore history and the stark inequalities of the free market economy.

State-sponsored welfare systems emerged as a necessary response to the fact that in the free expression of the market, people's needs were not being met through no fault of their own. Because the ILM is wedded to the notion of free competition it tends to favour particular sections of the disabled population, namely, young, intellectually able, middle-class white Americans (Williams, 1984). In addition, it is particularly suited to an achievement and self orientated culture which may allow for society the further disavowal of any responsibility (Blaxter, 1984).

Whereas personal tragedy theory lends itself to what has come to be regarded as unacceptable levels of paternalistic control and welfarism, social reaction theory implies a return to a free market economy which favours only the most able. While it may be argued that the latter marks something of an advance on the former, since it shifts the onus of responsibility for disability away from the individual and acknowledges the social construction of the disability category, it offers little by way of an explanation as to the reasons for its creation.

An attempt to resolve this problem can be found in the work of Stone (1985), who argues that all societies function through a complex system of commodity distribution, the principal engine of which is labour. Since not everyone is able, or willing, to work, a second system of distribution comes into play, a system based on perceptions of need. She maintains that disability assessments are not made on medical or clinical judgments alone, but on political considerations also. Thus the disability category is a social construct. The medicalization of disability is explained with reference to the accumulation of power by the medical profession and the state's need to restrict access to the state-sponsored welfare system.

A more radical approach has been adopted by a number of writers who are themselves impaired (notably Abberly, 1987; Finkelstein, 1980, 1990; and Oliver, 1983b, 1986). By utilizing an essentially materialist evolutionary model, Finkelstein contends that for Britain at least, history within the modern epoch can be divided into three distinct sequential phases. The first broadly corresponds to the feudal period immediately prior to industrialization where economic activity consisted primarily of agrarian or cottage-based industries. This mode of production, he claims, did not preclude the impaired from participation in the economic life of the community. But in phase two, when the process of industrialization took hold, the impaired were systematically excluded from the new production methods on the grounds that they were unable to keep pace with the 'disciplinary power' (Foucault, 1977) of the factory. Disabled people were therefore segregated from the mainstream of social life and incarcerated within large-scale institutions and asylums, which also appeared throughout this period (Scull, 1978, 1984). Finkelstein's third phase, which is only just beginning, will see the eventual liberation of the impaired from this form of discrimination through the development and eventual widespread utilization of modern technology, and the working together of the impaired and the rehabilitative professionals toward commonly held goals (Finkelstein, 1980).

For Finkelstein, disability is a paradox involving the individual with an impairment and the restrictions imposed upon her/him because of that impairment by society. Through the adoption of this three-stage historical model he demonstrates how this paradox only emerged during the period of industrialization in phase two. In phase one the impaired were dispersed throughout the community as part of the underclass, but in phase two they became segregated. Disability became a special category and as such was understood to involve individual impairment, and social restriction (Finkelstein, 1980).

It has been noted that available historical evidence does not substantiate this scenario in graphic detail, but temporal accuracy was not Finkelstein's prime concern. He used this model as a heuristic device to demonstrate the social nature of disablement and focus attention on both the economic and political considerations which contributed to contemporary British attitudes toward impairment and the meaning in which professional attitudes and those of the impaired themselves are shaped by these considerations (Oliver, 1986).

It is 'professional/client' interaction, referred to as the helper/helped relationship, which, he contends, plays a crucial role in structuring the consciousness of the individuals concerned.

The existence of helpers/helped builds into this relationship normative assumptions 'if they had not lost something they would not need help' goes the logic, and since it is us the representatives of society doing the help, it is society which sets the norms for the problem solutions (Finkelstein, 1980, p. 17).

For Finkelstein the rise of 'able-bodied' assumptions in phase two represents a major transformation in which relations with the impaired were conducted. Personal tragedy theory is built into these relations. It is suggested that when helpers take on board the normal assumptions of the helper/helped relationship, it is inevitable that they will inculcate the helped with these assumptions. Therefore, for Finkelstein, disability is defined as a specific form of social oppression that is faced by people who are in some way impaired.

While in broad agreement with this view, Oliver (1986) has pointed out that it is difficult to see why oppression with regard to disabled people is special. Since all social relations in capitalist society are synonymous with oppression, one class oppresses another and disabled people are nothing if not part of the oppressed class. But such contentions are difficult to substantiate since it is unequivocal that disability is 'no respecter' of race, sex or class (Thomas, 1982) and apart from one or two notable exceptions, such as Townsend's *Poverty in the United Kingdom* (1979), analyses which establish the links between disability and social class are few and far between. There is also considerable variation in the degree of oppression experienced by different elements within the disabled population, some of whom are more disadvantaged than others. Moreover, some people with impairments consider themselves neither oppressed (Goldsmith, quoted in Oliver, 1983b) nor disabled (Blaxter, 1984).

Oliver does, however, take up a theme which is clearly visible throughout the bulk of the literature associated with this subject when he asks why most social provision to date has tended to reinforce the dependency of people with disabilities rather than make them more independent. This is one of the main questions I hope to answer in this study, particularly with regard to day services for the younger physically impaired.

General Outline of the Study

Because of the relative absence of detailed empirical accounts of the daily interactions between helpers and helped within the context of the day centre environment, the temporal constraints of the research design, and a subjective preference for the ethnographic method of enquiry, the choice of methodology for this study was mainly interactionist. It is often pointed out that because of its consistent failure to link interpersonal relations with the material base upon which they occur, this type of investigation can never provide anything other than descriptive, but colourful, accounts of a given sequence of events or particular phenomenon. This type of research should, and invariably does, however, form the basis upon which much sociological theory is constructed. This study, therefore, is intended as an implicit, if not explicit, plea for the further development of the social oppression theory of disability. A detailed discussion of the methodology used in this study appears in Chapter Three.

Before proceeding, it may be appropriate to reiterate the primary objectives of the study. They are, firstly, to describe and evaluate the role of the day centre within the local community with regard to provision for young adults with physical impairments; secondly, to describe and evaluate the interactions between the users and staff within the context of the day centre environment; thirdly, to outline and assess the level of user participation within the centres with regard to activities, the decision-making process and control; and lastly, to formulate a list of policy recommendations based upon the findings of this research.

In order to fulfil these objectives I discuss in Chapter Two the socio/economic origins of societal oppression of people with impairments and their systematic segregation and incarceration during the nineteenth century and the first half of the twentieth century. Due to the rapid growth in the numbers of people termed 'disabled' in the 1950's, coupled with the rising cost of institutional care, a number of policies, including day centres, were developed to help people with impairments stay within the community and remain independent. Although day centres became fairly common in Britain in the following two decades there is no consistent or coherent national policy regarding their primary role.

Using Dartington, Miller and Gwynne's (1981) analysis of interactions between the impaired and the non-impaired, four ideal types of day centres for the young disabled are identified. They are the 'warehouse', 'horticultural', 'enlightened guardian' and 'disabled action' models. All are criticized on the basis that they are inherently segregative, emphasize difference and perpetuate stigma. Within this context day centres are perceived as the 'dumping grounds' for people who are excluded, because of impairment, from the normal economic and social life of society.

Empirical evidence to support this view is provided, firstly, by the overtly negative features of the general organization and admission policies of day centres; Secondly, by the degree of social and economic disadvantage experienced by the users interviewed prior to day centre use; and thirdly, by the manner in which they were similarly labelled and 'directed' toward the centres, despite the diversity of their individual impairments. In addition, I shall argue that day centre use reinforces disadvantage because, although helper/helped relations within the centres are generally viewed positively by both users and staff, user participation and control of services is low; and, while the system provides a range of facilities which give many users a degree of self-determination unavailable in the surrounding area, its capacity to extend those experiences beyond the day centre boundary is limited to only a few. Consequently for most attendance will be long-term.

The argument is substantiated with reference to the relatively recent and ad hoc evolution of provision for the younger physically impaired which was known as the Contact group in relation to day services generally. The data in Chapter Four show that Contact developed as a result of the protracted and complex interactions between external and internal forces, including the established traditions of day services in the local community, the limited resources available for younger users, the social characteristics of both Contact users and staff and the subsequent relations between the two groups within the Contact framework.

The three centres in which the Contact groups was located were well established and catered for a number of other disadvantaged groups, predominantly the elderly impaired. The service generally had evolved along 'traditional' lines, incorporating an ideology of 'care' and explicitly social activities, exemplified by the phrase 'tea and bingo', broadly in keeping with the 'warehouse' model discussed in Chapter Two. Contact emerged in response to locally perceived need. There was relatively little direction from the local authority social services department or other agencies concerned with disability regarding what facilities the new service should provide. As a result Contact developed along different lines from those of existing provision. For example, it provided a five-day service, used three day centres rather than one and had its own permanent staff. These factors led to higher levels of social and professional interaction between users and staff which are generally regarded as positive by both groups.

In contrast to earlier studies concerned with day services it was evident that the level of professional qualification and experience among senior day centre personnel was relatively high, but that this level of training was not apparent with reference to the care assistants (CAs), most of whom were on or had been recruited through government-sponsored youth training schemes. Although the lack of training and experience was considered a problem by some older day centre users and workers with respect to discipline and general aptitude, their introduction into the service was welcomed by both users and staff, since they offered a unique opportunity for the younger impaired to interact on a regular basis with non-impaired peers.

The data in Chapter Four suggest that the general ethos which evolved within the Contact format was almost solely a consequence of the protracted interactions between users and staff rather than coming from external sources. The aims of the group were to provide both social and, in the non-medical sense, rehabilitative activities within an explicitly voluntarist framework, consonant with the more progressive 'enlightened guardian' model of care. This approach has the advantage of accommodating the needs of the dependent as well as those of the not so dependent within one framework, but because these needs are often contradictory it tends to inhibit user participation and control. This is clearly evident in Chapters Five and Six.

Chapter Five focuses on the users and user relations within the context of the Contact group. Despite the relatively high level of homogeneity among Contact members in terms of age, class, social and economic disadvantage, there were significant disparities in terms of degree of impairment and attitudes regarding dependence, day centre staff and day centre use. I identify four distinct subdivisions or reference groups based on degree of impairment, observed dependence and friendship groupings. The first includes users who were almost entirely dependent on staff for their social activity, due mainly to the severity of their subjective impairments. The second is probably best understood with reference to the concept 'conformity', since its members appear to have adjusted to their dependent status. They tend to view the day centre and day centre staff in an overtly positive light. Members of the third subdivision are conspicuous by their non-alignment to any of the other factions within Contact. They are floaters and/or loners, and adapt to or 'innovate' in respect of the circumstances in which they find themselves. The principal characteristic of the fourth and final group in this typology is 'ritualism'. They reject the consequences of their disabled identity and as a result have devalued conceptions of self. This is manifest in their general ambivalence toward day centre attendance. They use the system because they feel they have no choice. These attitudes and frustrations are underpinned by their statements concerning the centres and their covert and occasionally overt animosity toward other users, particularly the conformists.

These differences are explained with reference to differential socialization and association theories, since the conformists were all congenitally impaired and had similar biographies before their day centre use began. I shall argue that they have been socialized into a dependent status by their life experiences prior to day centre attendance. Those in the fourth grouping, on the other hand, were relatively less impaired, had experienced either a separation from the conjugal home or were educated in 'normal' schools for the whole or a large part of their school career, or were adventitiously impaired. As a result all were imbued with perceptions of normality, 'able-bodied' normality. These contentions are substantiated with data from the statements of the users themselves and from those of the staff.

An awareness of the different life experiences and attitudes of users is sometimes evident in the practices of staff when they are attempting to 'encourage' user involvement in educational and vocational activities discussed in Chapter Six. Although environmental factors are important in explaining the relatively low level of user involvement in these activities, attention is drawn toward the limitations of policies which advocate structured didactic activity within an unreservedly voluntarist atmosphere such as that in the Contact group, as well as in the day centres generally. In addition, I shall suggest that for over two-thirds of the Contact users the notion of 'rehabilitation' in its literal sense is inappropriate, due primarily to their previous experiences, and that for those with moderate impairments the rehabilitative facilities provided are incompatible with their needs. As a result the majority of users view the centres as a site for social, rather than rehabilitative, activity.

The limited user involvement in formal mechanisms of policy formulation, such as user committees and group meetings, are explained with reference to factionalism and misrepresentation within the Contact group. As a result staff authority remains unchallenged. Formal controls within the day centre system were kept to a minimum, and are generally governed by 'common sense' usually determined by senior staff in the collective interest of the users, rather than some formal constitution or rule book. Although such a system is open to abuse there was no evidence of any during the study period. Control within the three centres studied was generally considered a non-issue. This is explained by staff with reference to the voluntarist nature of the day centre service and the advancing years of the day centre population as a whole.

The principal area in which control was exercised over Contact users was related to the restrictions on mobility outside the centres. Their statements demonstrate an acute awareness of the external constraints on their movements due to parental influence and the environment. Considerable discretion was exercised by senior Contact staff in this area. In spite of official policy to the contrary they adopted policies which apparently allowed users to leave the buildings at will in the interests of user freedom and independence. However, because some users were more able than others to take advantage of this right, this policy tended to exacerbate the social divisions within the group.

Control within Contact was subject to the normative power relations inherent to the division of labour within the centres. Authority rested in the superordinate status of senior personnel and was dispensed through a subtle combination of 'orchestration' and, when necessary, supervisory control. Discipline was not considered a problem by day centre staff and this is explained by them with reference to users' socialization and their relative independence within the centres, when compared with their dependence in the domestic sphere and the community at large. I note, however, that staff's use of power is limited in the sense that the imposition of punitive sanctions has negative implications for all concerned.

These arguments are further endorsed by the data presented in Chapter Seven which draws attention to the environmental, social and economic barriers to normal integration encountered by users outside the centres (Bowe, 1978). The evidence presented takes the form of observed examples of both individual and group interactions, highlighting the changes in behaviour patterns of the Contact users when outside the centres, and users' statements concerning their experiences and attitudes toward society generally. The importance of the day centres as a nexus of social activity for Contact members is underpinned by reference to their social activities outside the day centres, their general social isolation other than in the domestic sphere and their aspirations and expectations for the future.

In Chapter Eight I report the changes which occurred in the day centres during the eighteen months after the main study was completed. Although the Contact group had ceased to exist in this form the majority of Contact members were still using the system on a regular basis. In addition, there was an expansion of facilities and services specifically for the younger physically impaired, including a large well-equipped day centre located a considerable distance away from the centre of the local community. In view of the fact that the new unit fulfilled a similar role to that of the Contact group, that its extensive facilities will probably discourage users from using those used by the non-impaired, and that its location effectively removes people with disabilities from the local community, I suggest that these developments are likely to make users more dependent on the day centre service rather than less.

In the final analysis this study demonstrates that for many young people with disabilities day services represent an alternative to the debilitating social isolation of the domestic sphere and the harsh realities of life in contemporary Britain. At the same time it also demonstrates how all too frequently the cost to the individual of accepting that alternative results in a dependent status being reinforced. Moreover, given the degree of 'alienation, depression and pessimism' experienced by those excluded from the mainstream of economic and social activity (Willis,

1985) in 'yuptopian' Britain and the limited resources allocated to provision for the young disabled by the present government, it is difficult to see how this situation could be avoided. In Chapter Nine, however, I put forward a number of policy recommendations with regard to day centres which might go some way toward achieving this and conclude that due to the unprecedented demographic changes predicted for Britain in the next two or three decades, involving a rapidly expanding elderly population and the subsequent shortage of labour in the lower age groups, the time for a completely new approach to existing social policies concerned with children and young people with impairments has never been more appropriate or necessary.

Chapter 2
The Emergence of Day Centre Provision for the Younger Physically Impaired

It is often said that in Britain we have a tradition of welfare policies which separate dependent minority groups such as the physically impaired into segregated institutions (Manning and Oliver, 1985). It is a tradition, which although evident in the Middle Ages, became more widespread as a result of the Poor Law reforms of the nineteenth century. This tradition remained unchanged until the 1950s when 'community care' emerged as an official policy objective in government statements. In the following decades a number of services, including day centres, were developed to achieve this end.

My primary objective in this chapter is to draw attention to the principal similarities and distinctions between two particular forms of provision for the physically impaired. They are the 'traditional' residential institutions and the modern day centres. To complete this task the rest of the chapter is divided into four separate sections. The first focuses on the origins of English social policy for this group of people. The second covers the rise of institutional segregation and the differentiation of 'disability' during the nineteenth century. The third outlines the shift toward 'community care' and the establishment of day services for adults. The fourth section chronicles the emergence of the day centre, identifies its principal types, and discusses the major criticisms levelled at these structures from the perspective of the perceived needs of the young physically impaired. The chapter concludes with an assessment of day centres for the disabled in relation to previous forms of provision. It is contended that like that of their precursors, the residential institutions, their development can be best understood as a social and political response to the growth in the number of individuals who, because of impairment, are excluded from the world of work, though this increase is partly a result of the social construction of disability.

The Origin of Social Provision for the Disabled

How a society treats individuals with impairments is closely related to the meanings it assigns the causes of those impairments (Miller and Gwynne, 1972).

In all societies the impaired, particularly the physically impaired because of their visibility, are perceived as abnormal in the purely statistical sense of belonging to a minority group. And although it may be argued that our attitudes to abnormality are coloured by deep-rooted psychological suspicion of the unknown, it is generally accepted that our perceptions of normality are partially if not wholly determined by others through the process of socialization and the transmission of ideology or culture. For Mary Douglas, culture

> in the sense of the public, standardized values of the community, mediates the experience of individuals. It produces in advance some basic categories, a positive pattern in which ideas and values are fully ordered. And above all it has authority, since each is induced to assent because of the assent of others (Douglas, 1966, p. 39).

While it may be correct that individuals' perceptions of normality vary slightly, at the structural level cultural values are invariably more rigid.

Although there is evidence to suggest that in some non-occidental societies the meanings attached to the causes of impairment were arbitrary and those affected were fully integrated into the community (Hanks and Hanks, 1948), in the cultural and historical precursors to our own society there has been a consistent bias against impairment and disability. Examples are found in religion, Greek philosophy and European drama and art since well before the Renaissance. In the Old Testament, much of Leviticus is an articulation of the physical perfection deemed necessary for participation in Christian ritual (Douglas, 1966). While the ancient Greeks and the Romans placed a high precedent on the care of those disabled in battle, they were enthusiastic advocates of infanticide for deformed or sickly infants (Tooley, 1983). Shakespeare's depiction of Richard III clearly demonstrates the perceived association between physical deformity and evil. In the England of the Middle Ages, the impaired were viewed with a number of attitudes ranging from, at worst, fear and degradation to, at best, paternalism and pity. They were excluded from the mainstream of economic and social activity and were dependent on the benevolence of others.

Until the seventeenth century the impaired, along with such other dependent groups as the sick, the aged and the poor, relied almost exclusively on the haphazard, and often ineffectual, traditions of Christian charity and alms-giving for subsistence. Although disenfranchising them from religious ceremony, Christianity, like the other leading western religions, has traditionally acknowledged responsibility for the care of the disabled. During this period, however, as in the rest of Europe, the authority of the English clergy was greatly diminished by a series of confrontations between the church and the monarchy. These led to a decisive subordination of the former to the latter, which reduced the church's role in civil society. Monastic land was seized and redistributed and in consequence its ability to provide for the indigent classes was radically reduced.

The responsibility for provision shifted toward the emerging class of landowning gentry whose power replaced that of the feudal lord and the ecclesiastical elite (Trevelyan, 1944). But neither the monasteries nor private individuals made any serious attempt to match aid with need, or to provide an organized response to specific areas of dependency. It was generally accepted that this form of calculated, measured response was alien to a society where the urge to give to others was subject to the individual's felt need to ingratiate her/himself with God and thus ensure salvation (Scull, 1984). Impaired people were rarely lumped together under one roof, notwithstanding the probability that the most severely disabled were admitted to one of the very small medieval hospitals in which were gathered the sick, the bedridden and other 'honest folk' who had fallen into poverty. The ethos of these establishments was ecclesiastical rather than medical. They were devoted to care rather than cure (Scull, 1984). Throughout this period, however, there was a general increase in the numbers of people cut off from 'normal' economic activity.

Between 1500 and 1700 England experienced a dramatic growth in the general population following a century and a half of stagnation and occasional depletion due to plagues. At the same time commercialization of agriculture and the spread of the enclosure system meant that employment opportunities in the countryside were diminishing. Successive poor harvests were also blamed for unemployment. As food prices went up, people had less to spend on manufactured goods and therefore jobs in the textile and manufacturing industries were reduced. There was also an influx of immigrants from Ireland and Wales. Wars, too, were cited for the increase in vagrancy, although accounts of the effect of war were often contradictory. Some theorists argue that a decline in local conflicts eliminated one of the principal social mechanisms for soaking up large numbers of restless males. Others suggest that too much war caused large numbers of injured and jobless soldiers to be released into the general population without financial support (Stone, 1985). All through the early Tudor period the fear of 'bands of sturdy beggars' preyed on the minds of local magistrates (Trevelyan, 1944). This inevitably stimulated a political response from the central royal authority.

Prompted by the need to maintain order, secure allegiance, and establish a more secure foundation for the newly heightened monarchical power, the Tudor monarchs came under increasing pressure to make some sort of economic provision for the poor. The passage of the Poor Law Act of 1601 marks an initial official recognition of the need for state intervention in the affairs of the destitute and the disabled. Parishes were now empowered to levy taxes to provide funds for the relief of the poverty-stricken. And although it is clear that Section 1 of the Act makes explicit reference to providing special facilities for the lame, the infirm and the blind, it is generally accepted that little effort was made to separate and define the various classes of the needy considered deserving of aid (Stone, 1985). Provision was also hampered by bureaucratic constraints concerning eligibility. Notably, there was already an institutionalized suspicion of those claiming to be unable to work and seeking alms. This was legally expressed in the statute of 1388 which mandated local officials to discriminate between the legitimate recipients of charity and those suspected of feigning impotency to avoid work.

In consequence of the traditions of restricting aid to people within the parish boundaries, a practice enforced by law in 1622, as many as 15,000 separate local administrations were involved in the management of the dependent (Scull, 1984). Although there was much scope for local discretion, there was a high degree of uniformity in the way the problems posed by impairment were dealt with at the local level. Every effort was made to keep the senile, the blind and the infirm within the community. The largest resources were directed toward 'household relief' for individuals confined to the home. So intense were the pressures to achieve this objective, that funds were frequently provided to those willing to take on the responsibility for others unable to care for themselves. Major changes in this essentially non-institutional approach to the treatment of the impaired did not begin to be discussed or implemented until the nineteenth century.

The Shift Toward Institutional Care

Throughout the eighteenth century the practice of segregating the most severely disabled members of the community into hospitals and similar establishments was gradually extended to other sections of the indigent classes, until there was a general tendency to segregate them all into institutional settings (Stone, 1985). Consequently there was an unprecedented growth in the construction of institutions. Jones and Fowles have defined an institution as

> Any long term provision of a highly organized kind on a residential basis with the expressed aims of 'care', 'treatment' or 'custody' (Jones and Fowles, 1984, p. 297).

These included hospitals, asylums, workhouses and prisons.

One explanation for the incarceration of the disadvantaged links it to the breakdown of earlier forms of poor law relief in the face of urban industrialization and the huge problems of poverty that ensued (Mechanic, 1964). It has been shown, however, that the impetus to build institutions was not associated in time and place with the expansion of English cities. It invariably preceded it and was frequently most pronounced in rural communities (Ingelby, 1983). A variation on this theme is posited by others, who see the incarceration of the impaired as a direct result of the transition from traditional agriculture and/or cottage-based industries to the factory system.

> The spread of factory work, the enforced discipline, the time keeping and the production norms, all these were a highly unfavourable change from the slower, more self determined and flexible methods of work into which many handicapped people had been integrated (Ryan and Thomas, 1980, p. 101).

These accounts tend to play down or ignore the general moral ambivalence concerning disability that existed before the industrial revolution.

A more radical approach looks specifically to the relations of production, in particular the spread of wage labour. Firstly, a family dependent on wage earnings could not provide for its members in times of economic depression, so that large numbers of dependents were created by the new system. Secondly, the Elizabethan system of parochial relief was directly at odds with the ascending liberal market economy.

> To provide aid to the able-bodied threatened to undermine in radical fashion and on many different levels the whole notion of a labour market (Scull, 1978, p. 37).

Wage labour made the distinction between the able-bodied and non-able-bodied poor crucially important, for parochial relief to the able-bodied interfered with labour mobility. Segregating the poor into institutions had several advantages over domestic relief: it was efficient, it acted as a deterrent to the able-bodied malingerer, and it could actually create labour by instilling good work habits into the inmates (Ingelby, 1983). These considerations are reflected in the conclusions of the Report of the Poor Law Commission and the Poor Law Amendment Act of 1834 which succeeded it.

The 1834 Poor Law reforms introduced three new principles in welfare policy: national uniformity in welfare administration, denial of relief outside the workhouse, and deterrence as a basis for setting welfare benefit levels (Stone, 1985). However, these three principles were not implemented immediately and never fully.

At the beginning of the nineteenth century the administration of services varied radically at the local level. Centralization was, therefore, deemed necessary to discourage movement by workers in search of better welfare benefits or more generous treatment by Poor Law officials in other parishes. It was also believed that this policy would encourage labour mobility. Because aid was set at subsistence level only, and the treatment of the poor was to be universal, workers would go where the work was in search of higher wages. But Parliament set the minimum of guidelines and the policy was submitted to local officials by the Poor Law Commission through a series of circulars and orders. Consequently a high level of disparity between parishes continued.

As early as 1722 Parliament had granted local authorities the right to deny provision to anyone refusing to enter a workhouse, but the Amendment of 1834 went further by expressly prohibiting the provision of 'outdoor relief', or provision outside a workhouse. Stone (1985) has shown that this instruction was never strictly implemented. Until 1870 fewer than one-fifth of all adult able-bodied male paupers and no less than 15 per cent of all the destitute were on indoor relief, that is, confined to an institution.

Deterrence was evident in the principle of 'least eligibility', which stipulated that a pauper's situation should be less comfortable than that of an 'independent labourer of the lowest class' before relief could be granted. The workhouse was intended to be as unpleasant and unattractive as possible so that no one would enter it voluntarily. Families were broken up, inmates were made to wear special uniforms, there were no recreational facilities and socializing was strictly forbidden during working hours. Routines were rigidly enforced and food was limited to what was considered necessary for survival and work.

Stone (1985) has argued that these conditions were mitigated for certain groups since a number of regulations which succeeded the 1834 Act show there was a deliberate policy of exempting specific groups of the indigent from the principle of 'least eligibility'. Moreover, from the outset the Poor Law Commission suggested that workhouses should separate the incarcerated into four distinct groupings, namely, able-bodied males, able-bodied females, children and the 'aged and the infirm'. It was intended that the aged and infirm were to be housed in separate buildings and accorded separate care. In the following years these categories were refined still further, first, in order to determine who should be exempt from the prohibition against outdoor relief and, second, to establish separate facilities for different groups of paupers once they had entered the workhouse. The Poor Law officials developed five categories for dealing with those claiming aid. These were the sick, the insane, the aged and infirm, children, and the able-bodied. If an individual did not fall within one of the first four categories s/he was deemed able-bodied. There was some variation in the treatment of each group.

The term 'sick' was applied to those suffering from acute, temporary and infectious diseases. Chronic or permanent conditions were normally submerged within the category 'aged and infirm'. And although the position of the latter with regards to the granting of outdoor relief was often unclear, in terms of formal policy the rights of the acutely ill were quite specific. They automatically qualified for outdoor relief. Unfortunately there was much local variation of interpretation. In some areas the sick were granted medical aid, while in others they were subject to stringent means tests and forced to sell all their possessions before relief was provided. The central authority, however, encouraged local officials to provide aid in the home rather than in the workhouse. If admission was unavoidable separate facilities were to be provided, although here again conditions in different institutions and areas varied markedly.

Whether this group was to be subject to the principle of least eligibility and deterrence was never fully resolved. Some officials felt the sick 'were not proper objects' for such a system. Others took the opposite view, on the grounds that if the sick were exempt, it could discourage self-reliance or making provision for this type of misfortune through membership of friendly societies and insurance schemes. Official policy vacillated between the two. Eligibility for outdoor relief on the basis of acute illness was frequently, and increasingly as the nineteenth century progressed, left to the discretion of the local medical officer in conjunction with Poor Law administrators. If paupers were admitted to the workhouse as a result of sickness they were normally the responsibility of the medical officer. Doctors were generally considered by both inmates and administrators as more lenient than Poor Law officials (Stone, 1985).

Insanity was singled out for particular attention earlier than any other group. Despite the growth of public policy in this area during this period, insanity was never formally defined in official documents. The terms used varied from idiots, lunatics, the mad and the mentally infirm to 'persons suffering from diseases of the brain' (Stone, 1985). Consensus as to their meaning was not evident in the newly established psychiatric profession. For every treatise published on the subject claiming to set specific criteria for definition, another appeared rejecting it. As Scull (1978) observed, the definition of insanity involved a subtlety more easily accomplished in books than in practice.

There was, however, a universal recognition of the problems posed by mental illness, and there were two major strategies for dealing with it. The individual so labelled could be admitted to an asylum or other institution or boarded out on contract to families willing to be responsible for them. Several private asylums had been established during the seventeenth century. But public outcries over the atrocious conditions in many establishments, brought to light by a number of energetic and compassionate Benthamite and evangelical reformers, prompted the implementation of a public system in 1845, although the cruelty meted out to the insane in some institutions was often no worse than that afforded them in the community (see, for example, Roth and Kroll, 1986).

In terms of Poor Law policy the insane were exempt from the prohibition against outdoor relief. If admitted to a workhouse their special category status disappeared. Unlike other inmates they were subject to the jurisdiction of another body, the Lunacy Commission, whose influence in the workhouse was minimal. A further difference concerned the civil rights of the insane. Until 1871, Poor Law Officials had no authority to detain citizens within an institution against their will. But this did not apply to those labelled mad. During the seventeenth and eighteenth centuries the certification of insanity was the duty of the local lay officials, but after the 1845 Lunacy Legislation confirmation of mental illness was only valid if a doctor was involved. This has been attributed to the medical profession's successful struggle for control within private and public asylums, the general acceptance that mental illness was physiologically based and the view that it was responsive to medical treatment (Scull, 1984). Once defined as insane, an individual could be detained by both doctors and Poor Law officials, and transferred from one institution to another against her/his consent.

The term 'defectives' was used to describe those suffering from sensory deficiencies such as blindness, deafness or the inability to speak. This category later included the lame, the deformed and, after 1903, epileptics and mental defectives. This last label referred to children considered mentally subnormal. Like the above, members of this group were not prohibited from relief outside institutions but were singled out for special provision concerning vocational training and education. Although there is evidence of segregated structures providing these facilities, notably in the voluntary sector, their treatment within the workhouse was no different to that of other inmates. This was also true for the oldest of the categories used in Poor Law legislation to denote all those with serious incapacities, the aged and infirm.

Little controversy raged over their eligibility for aid in the community or in hospitals but once committed to the workhouse, their treatment, like that of the sick, posed problems. The provision of separate and better facilities within these structures conflicted with the principle of deterrence. The idea of the workhouse, or institutions generally, as a 'paupers' palace' was seen as giving little incentive for the young and healthy to plan for the future. As the nineteenth century progressed the pressures to commit more and more people to these establishments increased.

In 1871 welfare policies were tightened when Parliament disbanded the Poor Law Board and transferred its duties to a newly created Board of Local Government with the status of a Cabinet department. This new authority set about implementing the principles of the 1834 Amendment Act with renewed vigour. Particular attention was directed to a campaign against outdoor relief. The demand for welfare cutbacks followed a lengthy period of economic depression, rising unemployment and a rise in welfare expenditure. The severe winter of 1860–61 and the rise in unemployment due to the cotton shortage because of the American civil war meant that many more people were claiming aid (Stone, 1985). In an effort to reduce costs the Local Government Board officials decided on a more stringent and universal application of workhouse confinement, even to those hitherto recognised as exempt, the physically and cognitively impaired.

The campaign against outdoor relief was more eagerly supported by the employees of the new department than it was by the central authority. Despite recommendations to the contrary by Local Government Boards, official policy concerning exemptions never changed. But pressure on local officials to reduce the numbers of claimants was exerted in a number of ways. For example, information concerning the ratio of paupers to the general population, and the ratios of people on both indoor and outdoor relief in each local area were regularly published and circulated in order to embarrass local dignitaries in parishes with large numbers of claimants. Because these lists contained no data showing the different categories of paupers, their publication placed implicit pressure on local authorities to reduce aid across the board. Much emphasis was made by the inspectorate on applying the 'workhouse test' to all claimants in order to separate the incapacitated from the indolent. Hitherto there had been little pressure to validate eligibility for those classified under one or other of the categories of exemption. Even after 1885 when the initial fervour of the new regime died down and a more humanitarian approach was adopted, local officials were still instructed to scrutinize carefully those seeking aid, so that help should only be given to those of 'good character'. The net result of these policies was to further separate the impaired from the rest of the community.

The limited data available show that the numbers of people consigned to the workhouse did begin to fall and continued to do so until the turn of the century. Also the numbers of individuals receiving outdoor relief declined markedly after the implementation of these policies. The numbers of people claiming aid was lower in 1878/9 than at any other time since 1841. It is impossible, however, to say which group of recipients bore the brunt of this reduction, as the figures available do not differentiate among the pauper population. But there was an expansion of separate facilities for the non-able-bodied poor during this period due to a number of public scandals and subsequent government enquiries exposing the extreme conditions in some workhouses. These

> created pressure on local governments to establish separate schools for pauper children or board them out to local families. Similarly separate infirmaries for the sick and separate sick pavilions attached to workhouses became more common (Stone, 1985, pp. 51–52).

It is highly probable, therefore, that the decline in the provision of relief is partly due to the fact that an increasing number of paupers with disabilities were directed toward specialist institutions rather than the workhouse. For while it is true that the numbers entering the workhouse declined this was not the case for other institutions. There followed a general shift toward institutional care for the disabled, which only began to recede in the 1950s (Schull, 1984). The welfare policies of the nineteenth century established a pattern of provision for individuals with impairments which increasingly moved toward categorization and segregation from the rest of the community. In many respects this pattern remained unchanged until the emergence of the modern welfare state and the advent of the community care movement. These developments are the subject of the next section.

The Return to the Community and the Arrival of the Day Centre

Although community care did not become official policy until the 1950s a number of similar measures had previously been introduced. In the general area of disability there were limited efforts to provide facilities outside institutions from the 1870s onwards. For example, the Town and Country Association for Teaching the Blind in the Homes was founded in 1879 (Blaxter, 1981). A number of welfare schemes were also set up to provide training facilities, sheltered and home employment for their blind, the deaf and disabled ex-servicemen before, and during the 1914–18 war. As a result of the serious shortage of labour and the moral obligation felt toward the war casualties, the Tomlinson Committee Report of 1941 recommended that a national interim and post-war scheme of rehabilitation and resettlement should be provided for individuals suffering from any type of disablement, whether congenital or acquired (Schlesinger and Whelan, 1979).

In the field of mental impairments, the Mental Deficiency Act of 1913 contained provision for voluntary and statutory supervision of the mentally handicapped within the community. The Mental Treatment Act of 1930 recognised a growing movement for the provision of out-patient clinics. And although the National Health Service Act of 1946 accepted that hospitalization was the principal form of treatment, it acknowledged the need for policies which were geared for what was termed 'after care' and 'pre-care' (Jones *et al.*, 1983).

The official origins of the use of the phrase 'community care' can be traced back to the report of the Royal Commission on Mental Illness and Mental Deficiency of 1954–57, which considered in detail the problems arising from outdated mental hospitals and the considerable stigma attached to in-patient treatment. And although there was no precise definition given, subsequent government documents and statements concerning welfare policies for disabled people increasingly used the term, though the phrase has different meanings for different groups of people (Jones *et al.*, 1983).

Parker (1981) has identified three key components inherent to the concept of care in the context of community care. They are: (a) physical tending, with the most intimate kind of care relating to such physical needs of dependent people as toileting and bathing, (b) material and psychological support not involving physical contact, of which counselling is a good example, and (c) more generalized concern for others which may or may not lead to the other two types of help. Contributions to charity are a good example of this type of concern. To provide these three elements within the community, provision must invariably involve a combination of formal and informal, statutory and non-statutory services. Walker (1981) has suggested that the principles underlying community care include support by a dependent person's own family, friends and neighbours, an emphasis on care in non-institutional settings, the presence of support in the home from statutory services and preventative measures to prevent re-admission to an institution.

The move toward community care as a policy objective took a more prominent turn in 1961 when the British government announced its intention to halve the number of mental hospital beds. Titmus questioned the motives behind this announcement, arguing that they were primarily economic. It was his belief that while hospital facilities would be reduced, little would take their place. He maintained that patients would be transferred from the care of the trained to the care of the untrained (Jones *et al.*, 1983). Although Titmus challenged the government to refute his contentions, there was no official reply. The economic rationality of the policy was later reiterated by Jones who drew attention to the cost of maintaining large institutions.

> Many of our hospitals had been built in the mid Victorian period when an expanding empire meant expanding exports. The same degree of capital outlay could not be envisaged in the 1960s — particularly by a government dedicated to cutting public expenditure (Jones *et al.*, 1983, p. 105).

Some writers maintain that this new policy was based on a series of spurious statistics and an apparent blind faith in the positive effects of psychotropic drugs, recently developed during and after the 1939–45 war. The benefits of this form of treatment have been seriously challenged by several observers and psychiatrists themselves are divided as to their value (Jones and Sidebotham, 1962).

In 1962 the Ministry of Health published 'A Hospital Plan'. This was followed one year later by 'Health and Welfare, the Development of Community Care', generally referred to as the 'Community Care Blue Book'. Between them these two documents provided a sketchy outline of plans for care in the community including proposals for increases in the numbers of general practitioners, home helps, district nurses and health visitors, sheltered housing and sheltered workshops. Provision was intended for four specific groups, namely, mothers and children, the elderly, the mentally disordered and the physically handicapped. Services were to be

> so organized and administered as to meet more precisely the varying needs of special groups and even of different individuals (Jones, 1982, p. 73).

A major difficulty in implementation resulted from the fact that local authorities were autonomous from central government with regard to how they spent their resources. At the local level there was no consensus as to what was required or what it would be possible to provide. Consequently as with previous policies there was a disparity between central policy and local implementation.

Around this time there emerged a plethora of investigations into institutional life by a number of social scientists, nearly all of them condemnatory. The definitive study was Goffman's (1961) analysis of the 'total institution', which described the dehumanizing effects of life inside such organizations. Relatively cut off from the outside world, these structures were said to create pathological conditions for the inmates. Through the use of concepts such as 'binary management' (the division between staff and inmates), 'batch living' and the 'institutional perspective' (whereby the aims of the institution take precedence over those of the individuals it was designed to serve), Goffman developed an ideal type model and a theoretically universal framework which was applicable to all forms of institution ranging from mental hospitals to army barracks. A principal weakness of his study, however, is that while drawing attention to the similarities in these structures, it neglects the differences (Jones and Fowles, 1984).

There followed a number of investigations which corroborated Goffman's findings in various residential settings.[1] For example, Barton (1959) suggested that mental patients in long-stay hospitals developed a secondary illness due to their incarceration which he termed 'institutional neurosis'. Townsend (1967) utilized Goffman's approach for his study of old people's homes. Pauline and Terence Morris (1962) elaborated the personal and social deterioration experienced by prisoners in Pentonville jail. King, Raynes and Tizard (1971) studied the administration of homes for mentally handicapped children and developed the concept of 'normalization'. They showed that given the same individual care and attention accorded 'normal children', mentally handicapped children in residential homes improved in individual and social capacity as opposed to those kept in an institutional environment.

With regard to analyses specifically concerned with institutional care for the physically impaired, researchers have tended to view the effects of institutional care on residents in less negative terms than Goffman. On the basis of his study of life inside a residential home run by the Leonard Cheshire Foundation[2] Musgrove (1977) concluded that the conditions therein bore little resemblance to those of the total institution. The home was not a closed system, regimentation was minimal and residents were able to retain their individuality.

Miller and Gwynne (1972) studied both voluntary and local authority institutions and drew attention to the 'warehouse' and 'horticultural' models of institutional care.[3] The former refers to those structures in which the impaired individual is simply put away in storage. The function of these establishments is to perpetuate the distance between 'social death', the point when the individual enters the institution, and physical death as long as possible. The 'horticultural model' emphasizes the unique qualities of each inmate and the importance of subjective responsibility, and seeks to cultivate unfulfilled ambitions and capacities. The latter is not without its problems, however. The authors themselves expressed concern over the overvaluing of independence, the denial of disabilities and the general tendency toward the distortion of staff/resident interactions, where the realities of impairments are played down or ignored (see Chapter Four).

Studies of institutional care for the physically impaired have not been restricted to voluntary or local authority provision. In a national survey of long-term hospital services, Bloomfield (1976) stated that although many inmates of Young Chronically Sick Units require extensive help with personal care, hospitals were not the appropriate environment for this service. She contends that,

> by focusing on the one aspect of the inmate's requirements, the younger chronic sick units systematically robs the individual of the opportunity for achieving satisfaction and purpose in the life remaining to him. The unavoidable emphasis on his physical dependence on authoritative personnel frequently leads all but the strongest individuals to an accepting apathetic state with little interest in life and even less initiative (Bloomfield, 1976, quoted in Oliver, 1983a, p. 89).

Similar views were expressed by Battye (1966) after spending a large portion of his life in a chronic sick unit and a residential home run by the Cheshire Foundation.

Organizations claiming to represent the young physically impaired have also been vociferous in their critique of residential care. For example, the Union of Physically Impaired Against Segregation (UPIAS) have consistently called for the abolition of all segregated and segregative institutions, their ultimate objective being the complete integration of all impaired people into the community. This would necessarily involve the gradual phasing out of all institutional provision whether run by voluntary agencies or the state. And although to date they have not demanded the immediate shutdown of all existing structures they have opposed the construction of new ones (UPIAS, 1981).

It remains the case that for many there is little choice whether or not to opt for residential care in an institution, since there are relatively few alternatives available, such as sheltered housing. Although official figures in this area are much disputed, Topliss (1979) has shown that during the 1970s there were approximately 343,000 people with disabilities in residential institutions, 76,000 of whom were under the age of 65. Of these, 55,000 were accommodated in hospitals for the mentally ill and around 20,000 resided in institutions for the physically impaired. The most common reason for entry into residential care is family breakdown or the refusal of the principal carer to continue with her/his 'responsibilities'. A summary of the extensive literature detailing the economic, physical and emotional pressures on informal carers can be found in the work of Parker (1985). This underpins Goffman's assertion that institutions do not exist solely for the benefit of the inmates.

> If all the institutions in a given region were emptied and closed down today, tomorrow parents, relatives, police, judges, doctors and social workers would raise a clamour for new ones; and here the true clients of the institution would demand new institutions to satisfy their needs (Goffman, 1961, p. 334).

At a general level the arguments against institutions became more intense in the late 1960s and early 1970s when there was a spate of sensational public expositions of cruelty and harsh conditions manifest in some institutions for the elderly and the mentally ill. In 1967 the findings of an investigation by the Association for the Elderly in Government Institutions (AEGIS), into the treatment of old people in a London hospital was published and constituted a powerful indictment of institutional provision (Robb, 1967). There followed several publications and newspaper articles directing similar accusations toward a number of hospitals for the mentally handicapped. All were subsequently investigated and in at least one case, the Ely enquiry, the charges proved accurate and criminal proceedings against some hospital personnel ensued (Jones *et al.*, 1983).

As a result of these enquiries, public, and in some cases professional, confidence in the services provided by long-stay hospitals and similar establishments was seriously undermined. Local authority services, on the other hand, remained relatively unscathed. Consequently the pressure to reduce the numbers of patients in large institutions, generally hospitals run by the health service, intensified while local authorites were encouraged to expand their facilities.

There was little agreement as to what services should be provided or where the money to fund the expansion should come from. Extensive variation characterized provision at the local level and budgets were already stretched due to two main factors. The first was the heightened expectations of the general public since the inception of the welfare state, and the second, a steady increase of dependent groups after the 1939–45 war. These included children, the elderly and the disabled.

Published estimates of the numbers of people with impairments in the general population taken during the last three decades vary between just over 3.1 million (Harris, 1971), 9.9 million (Townsend, 1979) and 6.2 million (Martin,

Meltzer and Elliot, 1988). This disparity is due to the different definitions of disability used by the researchers. The Harris and Martin studies were sponsored by central government and both used functional evaluations of disability based on a series of questions regarding people's ability to care for themselves, for example, to wash, dress and use the toilet. The differential between the two estimates, according to Martin *et al.* (1988), are explained by the fact that the 1988 study, unlike its predecessor, included people who were mentally ill and/or handicapped and those whose disability was judged 'marginally less severe'. The Townsend (1979) study used a broader-based assessment covering individuals' capacity to care for themselves, share relationships and fulfil social roles analogous to those of others of a similar age range.

The available data show there are more disabled women than men, although within the age structure there is considerable variation. Up to the age of 50, both in numbers and prevalence, more men are impaired than women. Two likely explanations for this are (a) that more men work and risk disablement through accidents and work based illnesses, and (b) that more males indulge in dangerous sports and leisure activities. Hence these estimates reflect the sexual divisions in society and the fact that both work and leisure are dominated by men. After the age of 50 there are more disabled women but their prevalence in the population is also greater (Oliver, 1983a). This is a reflection of the fact that women live longer than men, coupled with the fact that the incidence of a significant number of disabling conditions increases with ageing.

At the other end of the age range the figures are less precise. The two government surveys did not take account of children and Townsend collected information only about children aged 10 or over. No data showing the prevalence of children with impairments among the general population have yet been published.[4] Estimates based on the work of the National Children's Bureau, Family Fund's records of children with severe disabilities, the Isle of Wight study and information from the 1974 General Household Survey indicate numbers of children with severe impairment ranging between 89,000 and 126,000, with a prevalence rate of approximately 6.2 children per thousand population. All indications are that the population of children with impairments has increased as more have survived infancy in consequence of medical advances in technology, but it is not clear whether this increase will continue due to developments in pre-natal screening etc. (Parker, 1985).

There is substantial literature available documenting the extensive material disadvantage suffered by people with disabilities. Townsend's (1979) study, for example, paints a picture of low pay, longer working hours, worse working conditions and poor housing, coupled with a higher likelihood of unemployment. A more recent government study found that people with impairments tend to be badly off financially and that three-quarters are reliant on state benefits for their main source of income (Martin and White, 1988). The problem of unemployment is particularly acute amongst young physically impaired adults (Parker, 1984).

In an effort to develop and rationalize provision at the local level the government set up a committee of enquiry which published its findings in 1968.

The Seebohm Report is generally considered a watershed in the development of services in and by the community for physically handicapped people.[5] Among its principal recommendations was that local authorities should accumulate data relating to the size and nature of the problems resulting from physical impairment, develop and/or expand existing services including day centres, and acknowledge the need for specific services for young people.

> Substantial development is particularly required in the services for handicapped school leavers, and more thought and experiment is required to determine the best timing and method of giving guidance on careers to physically handicapped children and young people (Seebohm, 1968).

Based on the Seebohm Report, the Local Authority Social Services Act 1970 established social services departments in their present form. The committee's recommendations on provision for people with physical impairments were incorporated into the Chronically Sick and Disabled Persons Act of 1970. But for a variety of reasons including the fact that legislation was passed at a time of organizational upheaval at local government level, the pressure of demands by other client groups, and inadequate resources, the new departments were never able to provide all the services envisaged. Moreover, any optimism regarding finances for expansion were dashed in 1973 because of the effects of the global oil crisis on the national economy. Despite this there was an unprecedented growth in the provision of day centres for adults throughout the country. What form they took and how they have been perceived in relation to the needs of young people with physical impairments is dealt with in the next section.

Day Centres for the Younger Physically Impaired

On the basis of data from the National Survey of Day Services conducted between 1974 and 1978, Carter (1981) estimated that in 1959 there were just over 200 day centres in England and Wales. In the following ten years, which Gough (1979) termed the 'golden age of the welfare state', the number increased fourfold. Carter contends that in 1976 there were 2,600 day units operating each week up and down the country. In order to find out who provides which services, she selected thirteen areas in England and Wales at random for investigation and found that local authority social services departments provided 47 per cent. Area health authorities were the second most important, combining to support 26 per cent, voluntary agencies such as Age Concern or MIND (The National Association for Mental Health) provide 23 per cent of the total and there is a residual group of units, approximately 4 per cent, supported by other statutory bodies such as the probation service or education departments.

Carter (1981) found that most day centres were situated outside city centres in suburbia and that four out of every ten were located in the grounds of residential institutions, usually hospitals, residential homes or long-stay hospitals. A number of critics have drawn attention to the stigma attached to this practice, particularly when the buildings normally used fall into one of two types, either large gymnasium-type structures, or the modern purpose-built variety. Both are accused of advertising their difference from the rest of the community (Durrant, 1983). When considered with the fact that most units cater exclusively for relatively, and often overtly, disadvantaged minorities, this adds further weight to the assertion that day centres are inherently segregative.

Most units are like schools and hospitals in that they are part of a larger bureaucracy, but are fairly small in comparison with most contemporary organizations. An average day centre has forty-eight places with a staff/user ratio averaging one to eight (Carter, 1981). Day centres are not governed by one unitary body and different units have differing objectives, meet in a variety of buildings and provide a range of services for various groups of people. They are subject to a variety of management structures although common strands are detectable in most if not all. Despite the obligation by central government to provide day services for disabled people and their families at the national level as specified in the Seebohm Report, day centres have generally been opened in response to locally perceived need. Hence there is much variation in provision from area to area (Kent *et al.*, 1984). There is no subsequent evidence of a comprehensive or coherent national policy on the development of day centres or what roles they should perform.

These considerations make the problem of definition somewhat difficult. Carter defined a day centre as

A non-profit making personal service which offers communal care and which has care givers present in a non-domicilliary and non-residential setting for at least three days a week and which is open at least four or five hours a day (Carter, 1981, p. 5).

Her analysis included day centres, sheltered workshops, adult training centres, drop-in centres, and family and community centres covering a variety of user groups. Table 2 shows Carter's estimates of the categories of users of day centres in England and Wales.

Table 2   Categories of Day Centre Users in England and Wales

The Elderly	39%
The Mentally Handicapped	19%
The Physically Handicapped	19%
The Mentally Ill	14%
The Elderly Confused	4%
Mixed	2%
Families	2%
Offenders	1%

Source: Carter, 1981

It is highly probable that although only 19 per cent of these units were designated for use by the physically impaired, there were considerable numbers of people with physical disabilities in centres for the elderly since the likelihood of impairment increases with age. Carter reported that there were slightly more women users than men than would be expected in relation to the general population and that more people who lived alone used these facilities. The percentage of those aged between 36 and 64 corresponded roughly to the numbers in the general population. But those in the 16 to 19 age range and those past retirement (60 for women and 65 for men) were proportionately over-represented.

Most day centre users were at the unskilled or unqualified end of the employment market. Half, excluding the elderly, had left school at 14 or before. And 79 per cent had no qualifications of any type or any marketable skills whatsoever. Carter also claimed that only 4 per cent of day centre users had any kind of work to return to, if and when they left the centres. She stated that

> users of day centres start at the bottom of the skill pile. Given that most have a disability, by reason of a labelled mental disorder or extant bodily infirmity, the combination of lack of skills plus disability leaves many day centre users as a difficult employment prospective (Carter, 1981, p. 5).

Since the Carter study there is evidence to suggest that there has been a growth in 'mixed' centres catering for different user groups at the same time. The Community Care Centre in West Wiltshire provides a good example of this type of establishment. It can accommodate twenty elderly, fifty psychiatrically ill, thirty impaired users and a playgroup and creche for twenty children daily (Foreshaw *et al.*, 1981). Of the 291 centres Carter studied only 6 were mixed. In a slightly later survey of 65 centres, Symonds (1982) found that 18 had adopted this policy. Commenting on this practice Tuckey and Tuckey pointed out that

> While it may be that helping or working alongside the mentally ill, the mentally handicapped or the socially inadequate would be beneficial to some disabled people it is not likely that the majority of disabled people, any more than the majority of non-disabled people would choose to spend their time in this way, even if paid to do so (Tuckey and Tuckey, 1981, p. 48).

It is clear from the Carter study and the few that have succeeded it that there is little, if any, provision specifically available for young adults with physical impairments. In general they are mixed with others considerably older. However, there is limited but conclusive evidence to show that many younger individuals with impairments do not wish to spend their time with those substantially older than themselves and that they would prefer centres which cater for those nearer their own age (see, for example, Anderson and Clarke, 1982; Jowett, 1982; and Kent *et al.*, 1984).

While there is some information relating to those individuals who already use these services, there is hardly any concerning those who, for whatever reason, choose not to. One of the few studies that addressed this issue clearly indicates that many young impaired people do not use day services because they would have to mix with the elderly (London Borough of Hammersmith, 1979). Kent *et al.* (1984) maintain that this point is hidden from policy-makers due to the high demand for day centre services generally. Until recently, within social services departments as in health authorities, individuals were classified as young if they were below the statutory retirement age. Since only 9.8 per cent of impaired people are less than 45, a terminological amendment has been made to the most recent literature with those previously termed 'young' being renamed 'younger' (Abberly, 1987).

The internal organization and staffing of day centres depends on the type of unit and the services it offers. At the general level Carter found that while day centres bear witness to the lack of jobs available for users, their very existence was a clear indication of the expansion of employment in the service sector during the 1960s and 1970s. Her analysis revealed that nearly a quarter of day centre personnel represented people who had transferred from blue collar and manual trades occupations. Many of the staff were as unqualified as the users. Half had left school at the age of 15 or before. A higher proportion of women than men were employed in day centres and the middle age group was over-represented in relation to the general population (Carter, 1981). This situation has prompted some observers to argue that there is an urgent need for higher levels of training for day centre staff, in accordance with the recommendations of the CCETSW (Central Council for the Education and Training of Social Workers) report of 1974 which looked in depth at this issue.

In their report on day services for the young physically impaired Kent *et al.* (1984) defined day centres as

A place where physically disabled people under the age of retirement meet on two or more days a week and where care is available and activities are arranged by or for the users. A day centre caters primarily for those who are permanently excluded, by reason of disability from the formal employment market (Kent *et al.*, 1984, p. 9).

The principal functions of day centres for people with physical impairments below retirement age can be understood with reference to the four models of care identified by Dartington, Miller and Gwynne (1981). Although these models were originally discussed with regard to institutional care they are equally applicable here. They are the 'warehouse', the 'horticultural', the 'enlightened guardian', and the 'disabled action' constructs. They were developed ten years after Miller and Gwynne's (1972) study of residential care which included the 'warehouse' and 'horticultural' models mentioned earlier.

The 'warehouse' construct corresponds with the traditional negative views of impairment. Subjective limitations are translated into total dependence. The 'horticultural' model is rooted in the liberal view that disability is relative. Professional energy is directed toward the denial of difference and rehabilitation. The 'enlightened guardian' construct recognizes the inadequacies of both the former and incorporates elements of each. Thus a model emerges which explicitly provides for both sets of needs — the dependent and the independent. The final paradigm disregards the others on the grounds that they are each based on able-bodied assumptions of impairment which are considered inappropriate, the first, because it encourages apathy and passivity in the impaired individual, the second, because it is seen as unrealistic and the third, because it allows the professional to vacillate between the assumptions of both the former. Disabled action refers to the situation in which the disabled themselves control or at least participate fully in the policy and decision-making processes of services which concern them. The theoretical basis on which these models were developed is discussed in Chapter Four.

The declared aim of many day centres is simply to provide a facility which enables people with impairments to leave their homes for a few hours a day once or twice a week. This is an extremely important function for both the impaired individual and her/his relatives or carers. It is one of the few instances where to date the state welfare system has provided assistance for the growing army of informal carers. And there is ample eivdence to show that these services are wanted by the general public. For example, a study by West *et al.* (1984) showed that the most preferred care arrangements were community-based services, particularly day units. The danger is, however, that many centres see providing relief for carers as their primary task. This is evident in the general tendency to refer to day centres as day 'care' centres, emphasizing the caring role. Hence this type of centre is in keeping with the 'warehouse' model. It is generally accepted that care alone is not acceptable for the young physically impaired, especially those now termed younger.[6] 'Tea and sympathy' achieves little in terms of promoting young people's control over their own lives or their participation in ordinary adult activity. These units provide little or no stimulation and induce passivity and dependence (Kent *et al.*, 1984).

The 'horticultural' model finds expression in centres where rehabilitation takes precedence, notwithstanding that for the congenitally impaired the term 'habilitation' may be more appropriate. The services offered can be divided into two distinct but frequently related areas of activity, namely, social rehabilitation and vocational/employment preparation. The former relates to the situation where the impaired individual may be taught to look after her/himself with respect, for example, to washing, bathing and social competence. The philosophy on which such programmes are based is summed up by the concept 'self-determination' (Henshall, 1985).

Elaborating on principles of common sense, Henshall argues that it is wise to avoid skin breakdown, becoming overweight and the weariness of living in a muddle. Social rehabilitation therefore involves an introduction to optimum hygiene routines, suitable eating habits and an orderly way of life. It addresses

> the function of a disabled person as it is carried out within the usual environment and lifestyle of the individual. It is concerned with very basic life skills without which everyday tasks become a burden to the disabled person. Independence in personal tasks, management of household chores and achieving mobility with ease are important to all (Hensall, 1985, p. 8).

Exponents of this approach acknowledge that personal independence in the normal sense is not possible for all impaired people. But it is claimed that this impasse can be overcome through mutual consultation between the impaired individual, her/his family (if s/he has one) and the rehabilitation personnel. Clearly here there is the potential for conflict over whose opinion should take precedence as to what is achievable. The danger for professionals to be over-paternalistic is a very real one.

The second type of rehabilitation concerns attempts to prepare for or return impaired individuals to employment. Day centres are seen as training centres preparing people for sheltered or open employment. There is evidence to show this does occur to a limited degree in adult training centres for the mentally impaired, notwithstanding that the data concerned is relatively old, collected before the recent employment crisis. But there is little to support the notion that rehabilitation occurs in centres for the physically impaired. The present employment situation prompted one service provider in a study of services for impaired young adults to state

> Give training for what? You cannot go on training until the client is 65 years old (Brimblecomb *et al.*, 1985, p. 86).

Nonetheless in the pursuit of this aim some units offer light industrial contract work, usually unskilled boring jobs, such as packing Christmas cards or rubber washers. Contract work for its own sake is deemed inappropriate since there is no satisfactory outcome in terms of either skill acquisition or financial reward. Day centre workers are only allowed to receive £15.00 per week. Any surplus is claimed by the agency running the operation. A few units have developed schemes where any profit is shared out amongst the users in kind so as not to encroach on their social security entitlement (Jordan, 1986). But such practices are seen as demeaning and exploitative (Tuckey and Tuckey, 1981). Arguably the most damning criticism levelled at such establishments is that the precedent afforded the work ethic overshadows equally important functions such as social rehabilitation (Oliver, 1983a).

The third model, 'enlightened guardian', is applied to centres which allow users to extend not only their social and cultural activities but also their vocational skills. The unit becomes a focal point for social and recreational activity as well as a kind of college of further education. In offering users the opportunity to play and/or to learn, these units combine both 'warehousing' and 'horticulturalism'. It is worth noting that although the Warnock Report on Education for Special

Needs (1978) had little to say on the subject of day centres, it did express concern about the general lack of educational input in these establishments and recommended both that there should be a specifically educational element in every centre and that the education department should be responsible for its provision. But these recommendations, like so many in the report, did not become universal practice. Moreover, since there is rarely any obligation placed on users with regard to rehabilitation in these units, it may be said that they have adopted a policy of what Warnock termed 'significant living without work'. Such a position tends to ignore the social, psychological and economic precedent our society places on work. Therefore, centres which adopt this philosophy are open to the accusation that they reinforce the perceived differences between the impaired and the non-impaired, since this provision is not generally available to the latter. In addition, these units are usually organized and run by the non-impaired who are themselves in work. Consequently, in the long term at least, it is likely that they also reinforce dependence.

As noted earlier, the idea that the impaired should remain passive recipients of services provided by others is being increasingly challenged. Hence the term 'disabled action' refers to those units where users participate fully in or control the organization and provision of services. One of the most celebrated and successful examples of this type of centre is the Primus Club in Stockport, where users have successfully controlled the budget and employed the staff for the past decade (Carter, 1981; Kent *et al.*, 1984). Since higher levels of user participation and control are now considered important by many people with impairments as well as some professionals in the caring industry, these units are often seen as the most appropriate. However, if they are exclusive to this section of the community, then like the others discussed they are socially divisive and do little to eliminate the deleterious historical divisions between the impaired and the non-impaired.[7]

It is important to remember that these illustrations are presented in ideal typical form. None of these options are mutually exclusive and some day units may incorporate some or all of the principal features identified here. But they do provide a useful means of broadly distinguishing different types of services.

Conclusion

It is clear that a cultural bias against individuals with physical and/or mental impairments was well established in Britain long before the transition to a modern industrial society began and that the low social status and pattern of local provision for such people was well entrenched before state intervention in this area. State involvement in social welfare was prompted by the economic, political and social upheavals of the seventeenth century.

At the outset the central authority pursued policies similar to those of today, namely, keeping the impaired within the confines of the family home whenever possible. As the pace of industrial development intensified and this number increased, the tendency towards segregating the more severely impaired into institutional settings was gradually extended to other indigent minorities. A number of structures, such as the asylum and the workhouse, were developed for this express purpose. By the end of the nineteenth century this practice was almost universal. Throughout this period, however, the moral dilemma posed by the harsh treatment of those viewed as overtly dependent, both in and outside institutions, prompted the central authority to initiate further categorization and segregated provision. But although this development had obvious positive effects, it made the division between the impaired and the rest of the community more pronounced.

Since the late 1950s there has been a concerted attempt by central government to reverse these policies. The motives for this policy change were/are similar to those which prompted their implementation a century earlier, notably economic stringency and an increase in the 'dependent' population. In an attempt to achieve this end a number of services, including day centres, were developed to prevent admission to residential institutions for so-called dependent groups. Although, as with previous policies, there is much disparity in provision at the local level, there has been an unprecendented expansion of these facilities.

From the perspective of the physically impaired, these developments are undoubtedly a step in the right direction. But day centres, like residential institutions, are open to a number of criticisms. Four main types of day centre were identified. These comprised the 'warehouse', the 'horticultural', the 'enlightened guardian' and the 'disabled action' models. All were found wanting since at worst they are said to induce apathy and passivity and to disable their users further, and at best, to perpetuate the 'traditional' divisions between the able and the non-able. In view of these considerations the emergence of day centres, like their precursors a hundred years earlier, can only be understood as a social and political response to the problems created by large numbers of people who, because of impairment, are excluded from the mainstream of economic and social activity. As a result they perpetuate discrimination and emphasize stigma.

Notes

1   The terms 'institution' and 'residential' are used here to refer to the same phenomenon, although as Jones and Fowles have pointed out the former is frequently used pejoratively and the latter non-pejoratively (Jones and Fowles, 1984).
2   Established in 1948, the Leonard Cheshire Foundation is the largest British charity providing residential accommodation for people with impairments (Miller and Gwynne, 1972).
3   In Britain residential care for people with physical impairments is mainly funded from three sources, voluntary agencies, local authority social services departments and area health authorities (Oliver, 1983a).
4   A government report on children with disabilities was scheduled to be published in April 1989. It was not available at the time of writing.
5   The distinction between care in the community and care by the community was made by Bayley in 1971. The former includes statutory institutional type services. The latter

denotes non-institutional provision and involves the receivers of care in the community itself (see Bulmer, 1987).

6   There is a growing awareness that this type of centre is no longer acceptable for other sections of the 'dependent' population, including the elderly (see, for example, Tester, 1989).

7   One notable attempt to avoid this problem was the 'community centre' approach favoured by Bob and Linda Tuckey at the Stonehouse in Corby. While concentrating on the needs of people with physical impairments, the centre adopted an open door policy to others in the community. Most users were under 45 years, and some were in their late teens and early twenties (Tuckey and Tuckey, 1981). At the end of five years there were about a hundred people using the centre in the course of a week, of whom only sixty were disabled. As the centre became more well known, problems resulted from what Carr terms 'squatters rights' (Carr, 1987), with different user groups claiming time and territory with little cross-fertilization. In consequence, non-impaired user status is now restricted to 25 per cent of the total membership and only to those 'who have an interest in Stonehouse' (Stonehouse Association Constitution, December 1985; Carr, 1987). Although user participation in running the centre is reported to be high (see Chapter Six) control of the centre's budget remains with Northamptonshire Social Services Department.

Chapter 3
Methodology

> 'Methodology' is a more or less systematic or organized way of acting. An account of one's methodology must therefore include a statement of one's intentions or aims. Aims, however, can only be defined in the context of some conception of the nature of the problem at hand, or of some 'theory'. Method, then embodies theory, and doing 'research' is not discovering new phenomenon but recovering what one had all along (Blum, 1970, p. 305).

When confronted with the obligatory chapter on research methods many social researchers seem to opt for a succinct but revealing autobiographical account of how and why their interest in the subject arose and how it affected their investigation (Bell and Newby, 1980). The following pages will broadly follow this tried and reliable formula. The initial aim is to outline the main reasons for my interest in disability generally and the interactions between the helper and the helped within the day centre environment in particular, as well as the considerations which prompted the conceptual approach. A further intention is to discuss the reasons for, and the choice of, the strategies employed in pursuit of those objectives. Thirdly, I will briefly chronicle how those strategies were put into practice in terms of setting up the study, the choice of location, samples, interview schedules and data collection. And finally, some of the principal methodological difficulties which occurred during the study will be examined.

Personal Biography

My initial interest in disability stems from personal experience. I was born with a hereditary eye disease and spent the first seven of my statutory school years in 'special' education, firstly in a residential institution for the blind and deaf and later in a school for the partially sighted. Indeed, had it not been for my mother, who persistently badgered the local education department with the request that 'I should go to an ordinary school like everybody else', it is highly likely that I would have remained there until leaving school, at which time, no doubt, I would have been directed toward 'sheltered' employment, like most of my junior school peers and my father before me. In the event I ended up with a relatively average education and an active social conscience. After several years in the hotel and catering industry I became interested in the problems associated with disability when I decided to become a teacher. At teacher training college I was disturbed by the remarkable lack of literature dealing with the meaning of disability. This was particularly alarming considering this was in 1981 — the International Year for Disabled People. I was subsequently advised by one of my tutors to look to sociology for explanations for this sorry state of affairs.

After studying many of the major works which constitute the bulk of undergraduate sociology courses I was still struck by the paucity of references concerning impairment and disability. Further research, however, revealed that the situation was not as bleak as it seemed. But like many of the authors studied, particularly those who were impaired themselves, I was unhappy with both the prevailing functionalist and interactionist approaches to this subject. The limitations of the sick role, the rigidity of its subsequent variations and the emphasis on individual responsibility for explaining the difficulties experienced by people with impairments were particular weaknesses associated with functionalism. The discovery of the work of the labelling theorists reaffirmed my belief that many of the problems associated with impairment were socially created, but offered little in terms of an explanation for the multiple economic and social disadvantages that many encounter. Hence I was drawn toward a more historically based, radical analysis currently referred to as 'social oppression theory'. Although I broadly accepted its central tenets, that impairment and disability are socially created and that much of traditional and present social policy can best be understood with reference to mechanisms of social regulation and control, I was less content with its analysis of the helper/helped relationship, particularly within the context of day centres for the younger physically impaired.

My interest in day centres again stems from personal experience. While at university I worked as a voluntary worker in three local day centres with a group of young adults with physical impairments. And although some of the general criticisms levelled at day centres (discussed in Chapter Two) were applicable to these services, others were not. For example, the centres were overtly segregative, all the users were impaired, the vast majority were elderly and many of the facilities offered were either inappropriate or inadequate for young people. However, censures regarding helper/helped interaction were less clear cut. At face value at least, the relations between the two were overtly positive. Moreover, it was my opinion that there was an empathy between many of the users and staff in the centres, and that the latter, rather than reinforce dependence actively sought to overcome it.

Moreover, since the formal mechanisms for user involvement in the running of the centres were relatively intact, although underused, I also had misgivings concerning the assertion that most day centres were essentially paternalistic (Oliver, 1983a), so far as the latter is taken to mean the benevolent philosophy of 'parens patrae' which disguises the fact that people are seen as immature, unworldly and incapable of making decisions concerning their own welfare or future (Kittrie, 1971). There had been little evidence of the extremes of this ideology in the centres. Although the behaviour of some of the users could be construed as childish or naive, there were other individuals in the units, who exhibited none of these characteristics. In fact there were crucial differences within the user group in which I was interested, those aged between 16 and 30 years, in terms of the degree of impairment and attitude toward dependence and toward the day centres generally. While some appeared relatively satisfied with the service, others were less enthusiastic.

In view of the recent heightened interest in the general areas of disability and social policy by both policy-makers and theorists, these considerations stimulated a number of important questions. For example, why, given the obvious limitations of this system and the lack of overt coercion in recruitment of members, did people use it? Why was there so little visible user participation in the running of the service and why, given that some of the less overtly disabled users were clearly dissatisfied with the centres, did they continue to attend? In my attempt to answer these questions I hoped to fulfil two specific aims: (a) to provide a comprehensive insight into the daily interactions between users and between users and staff, and thus contribute to the knowledge of those who formulate policy in this area and (b) to add to the theoretical debate concerning helper/helped relations.

Strategies

Since it is widely acknowledged (for example, Abberly, 1987; Hurst, 1984; Oliver, 1986) that interactionist methods are the most appropriate for studying the problems experienced by people with impairments, my choice of methodology appeared unproblematic. Like Goffman, Becker and countless other researchers before me, I would venture forth into 'the field' and take up the position of a participant observer, or to be more precise 'a complete participant' (Denzin, 1970). From the outset I intended to become a full time voluntary worker (VW) in the day centre system where I had previously worked. I felt secure in this choice of methodology as I was acutely aware of the major problems associated with this technique, but believed I was in a relatively strong position to overcome them.

According to a recent analysis by David Silverman (1985), there are several problems associated with this strategy. Firstly, the focus upon the present may preclude sensitivity to important events which occurred before entry onto the scene. Secondly, informants may be entirely unrepresentative of the other less open participants. Thirdly, the observer may change the situation just by her/his presence, so the decision as to what role to adopt will be fateful. Finally, the researcher may 'go native' identifying so closely with the participants that 'like a child' s/he cannot remember how s/he found out, or will be unable to articulate the principles underlying what s/he is doing.

With regard to the first difficulty, I had been involved with this day centre system and the young impaired, on and off for four years, prior to the decision to enter as a researcher, and so had some knowledge of the situation applying earlier. The second point seemed similarly irrelevant in my case, largely because the work I had already done in the day centres meant that I knew the vast majority of users in the age group I was interested in and all of the staff.

Secure in these assumptions, I felt my intrusion into the day centre system on a full-time basis would be almost negligible, as it was precisely the position I had been in on several occasions in the past, notably during the long summer vacations while at university. Moreover, the role of VW in my estimation is an ideal role for the researcher within this type of environment since VWs are generally seen in a positive light by both users and staff.

VWs are usually involved in social and/or didactic activities organized to provide psychological or social support for users. Consequently they are in a good position to 'talk' to both users and staff on a regular and fairly equal basis. They are not usually expected to perform physical tending tasks such as helping users with the toilet or bathing, although in practice I was often asked by both helpers and the helped to assist with the former due to the chronic shortage of male staff. The need for assistance with bathing does not often arise in relation to the younger impaired as most do not live alone and where necessary this function is performed by parents or guardians. With this in mind I was confident that my 'research stance', or the relationship the researcher has with her/his subjects and how it is linked to their attempts to grasp their own reality (West, 1979), was legitimate and defensible (from a 'researcher' point of view).

Although sympathetic to the central argument of the proposed thesis, my supervisors were less convinced. 'How will your account be anything other than your own interpretations?' 'How will you be able to validate your findings?' I was asked, and initially I must confess my confidence was severely dented by these blunt enquiries which pointed out the flaws in my chosen methodology. Following Goffman's study of a hospital for the mentally ill, I had originally planned to work in the centres for a year to accumulate the appropriate data. It was suggested, however, that I supplement this technique with a number of semi-structured interviews with a representative sample of users and staff. Although at first I was sceptical of this proposal, because of the positivist assumptions endemic to it (Silverman, 1985), on reflection it seemed like a good idea, since I was eager to make every effort to eliminate as much subjective bias as possible and keen to get on with it and 'tell it like it is'.

Setting up the Study

Once the choice of methods had been established, the next stage involved getting formal permission from the local authority's Social Services Department for entry into the day centre system on a semi-formal basis, semi-formal in the sense that I would no longer be simply a volunteer but also someone conducting field research. The recent volume of criticism directed at welfare agencies in general, and government departments in particular, left me uncertain about the prospect of getting official approval of the project. I was patently aware that a major part of my function as a sociologist would be that of critic, and that in all probability those in the Department would be aware of this too, or if not, I would have to tell them.

Because of my previous experience within the centres I was reasonably confident about the reception of my proposed intervention by users and staff, believing that it would evoke indifference at worst, but at best, enthusiasm. On a number of occasions during casual conversation, several individuals, both users and staff, stated that there was a relative lack of knowledge and understanding of the experience of disability, especially of life in day centres, on the part of both the general public and staff in other agencies. At the same time students in the centres were not uncommon since a local college of further education sometimes places people on community care courses in them to gain practical experience. In any event, given the general view that there were never enough staff, I felt that the chance of an extra experienced VW on a full-time basis for up to a year would be welcomed.

Before contacting the central offices of the Social Services Department I thought it important to discuss the proposed project with the people who were to provide the data, those who use and work in the centres. The reasons were twofold. Firstly, if anyone in the units had any objections to the project then I felt they should have an opportunity to say so. In the event of any serious misgivings I would have felt obligated to find other venues for the study, or revise it substantially. As it turned out everyone viewed the idea enthusiastically.

I then forwarded a letter outlining my proposals to the appropriate departmental office, including a copy of the research draft that I had submitted to the University and the Economic and Social Research Council (ESRC) in order to secure financial support for the project. A week or so later I received a formal letter asking me to contact the Residential and Day Care Officer (RDCO) in charge of the provision for the physically impaired, Mrs B. I rang her office immediately and was asked to report for interview a week later.

I had not met Mrs B before, and anticipated all sorts of constraints and demands would be placed upon my activities in order to prevent any possibility of the research showing the Department in a poor light. I went to the interview as soberly dressed as I knew how, keen to explain my ideas and defend the professional integrity of the intended enterprise. The interview lasted an hour and three-quarters and was far less traumatic than I had originally envisaged. Mrs B requested that I specify in writing the principal reasons for my study, indicate how it would be conducted and state my intentions with regards to the conclusion. This I did, re-emphasizing that a synopsis of the research and its findings would be submitted to the Department, albeit without the inclusion of any of the names of individuals, whether users or staff, who contributed to the study. This was particularly important since it was likely that the completed draft would include subjects' quotations and therefore it was crucial that respondents' confidentiality should be protected. Mrs B listened intently and when I had finished proceeded to give me a detailed appraisal of the current day centre services for the physically impaired provided by the Local Authority, and the increasing financial pressures restricting their expansion.

Mrs B then stipulated three preconditions which I had to accept if the research was to proceed. The first was that if I should change my research design or proposed methodology I should inform the Department straight away. Secondly, if I intended to use any form of printed questionnaires, postal surveys or other written material which respondents would be expected to sign, I should submit them for official scrutiny and await approval before proceeding further. Finally, I should allow Mrs B to formally introduce me to the users and staff in each centre where the study was to take place. The purpose of the last point was to ensure that everyone in the units was fully aware that compliance in any interviews or structured conversations would be strictly voluntary and to satisfy herself that no one had any objections to the investigation.

I agreed but had misgivings concerning the last point since I felt that a formal introduction to people I already knew might backfire. I was convinced that it would mean that I would be identified with the 'establishment' rather than as unattached observer. In the event, my fears were unfounded. After my 'presentation' by Mrs B to the people in the day centres, users and staff convinced me that the whole exercise was bureaucratic protocol and nothing more.

The Choice of Location

After my official introduction into the service I set about reaffirming my knowledge of the service to be studied. It was confirmed that in the city where the study was situated the group in which I was interested were served by one organization only which was referred to as the 'Contact group' and operated in three different centres on different days of the week. The centres were known as 'The Alf Morris', 'The Engineers' and 'The Dortmund Square' day centres.

Officially the Contact group existed to cater for the needs of those in the 16–25 age group while another two user groups, both named 'Insight', provided services for people aged between 25 and 45. Closer inspection of the registers revealed that there were thirty-six Contact users with an average age of 22.5 years, but three were in fact over 25. This is the primary reason why the age boundaries for inclusion in this study are 16 to 30 rather than 16 to 25. Only one of the two insight groups had users in the required age range. This unit had a membership of ten but only three were between 25 and 30. The average age of the remainder was 40. Moreover, since there was relatively little helper/helped interaction within the Insight framework, apart from when users needed help with physical tending, I felt my time in the centres would be better spent with Contact.[1]

The Sample

The criteria for inclusion of users in the study was fairly straightforward, namely, physically impaired regular day centre users within the designated age range. I decided to interview all those who qualified, making a total of thirty-six Contact members. This was deemed necessary because the number was a manageable one. However, as my knowledge of the limitations of 'representative samples' (Hughes, 1981) and because of the people in the group increased, it became clear this would not be possible. Two individuals eligible for inclusion, Michael and Alison,[2] were so severely impaired that coherent communication without the aid of a third party was impossible. Both had cerebral palsy and had hardly any recognizable vocal abilities. Indeed, I have never heard Michael utter a sound although I was assured he could.

Some individuals in the centres maintained they could talk with them both but I was never able to pass beyond asking questions requiring a yes/no response, which could be given by a nod of the head. Other physical activity was difficult for them both since they had little or no control over their limbs which invariably began to shake, sometimes violently, when they tried to concentrate or became excited. Consequently the use of two-dimensional communication devices, such as word boards, for example, was out of the question without help to steady their arms or legs. With reluctance I decided I would have to exclude them from the interviews. I explained to each individually my reasons for this decision and believe they both understood my predicament.

During the first six months of participant observation I discussed with both users and staff the idea of their being interviewed in a more formal setting. I had decided at the outset to conduct the interviews in the second half of the period devoted to empirical research. Although they had already been told of my intention by Mrs B, I felt this policy could help to alleviate problems during the actual interview period in case some individuals were apprehensive. As it turned out another user, Amy, decided not to take part in the interviews. She did not give a reason and although I broached the subject on several occasions she would not change her mind. In all, therefore, there were thirty-three Contact user interviews.[3]

It is important to remember that users' families also benefit from day centres. But while I have had several informal conversations with parents and siblings of some members, I only interviewed one individual's mother for this study, Mrs H. This is not because their impressions of the service are unimportant, but is solely due to the temporal constraints of the study. I endorse Carter's (1981) contention that further research in this area is sorely needed. As the following chapter shows, Mrs H's inclusion is necessary because she was partially, if not wholly, responsible for Contact's formation.

Choice of staff interviewees was less straightforward than for users. Clearly the accounts of all those permanently assigned to work within the Contact format took precedence. But because the group utilized the buildings and resources of three day centres and because users and staff were not rigidly confined to one particular area in two of those centres, those staff peripherally as well as those directly involved with Contact had to be included if anything like an accurate picture of the current provision was to be achieved. However, apart from the practical problems, it did not seem appropriate nor necessary to include all the workers from each centre, since it was clear that several had little contact with the younger users. This was particularly pertinent to the Engineers' day centre where the Contact group was consigned to one specific area of the building. Here they hardly ever interacted with others, users or staff, apart from the Officer in Charge (OIC) or Manageress, Mrs W, and an arts and crafts teacher named Hilary.

Table 3 Staff Respondents

Name	Functions	Unit	Other information
Jayne	SAO	Contact Group	—
Jackie	AO/SAO	—	—
Patrick	AO	—	—
Annie	CA(GS)	—	—
Peter	CA(GS)	—	—
Mary	CA(GS)	—	—
Tracy A	CA(GS)	—	—
Tracy B	VW/CA(GS)	—	—
Sean	VW/CA(GS)	—	—
Barbara	VW	—	—
Andrew	OIC	Alf Morris Centre	
Bob	AO	—	—
Rick	AO	—	—
Anrea	CA	—	—
Maria	CA	—	—
David	Tutor	—	Drama
Prudence	Tutor	—	Music and Drama
Margaret	Tutor	—	Literacy/Numeracy
Sandra	OIC	Dortmund Sq'r. Centre	
Denise	AO	—	—
Vera	CA	—	—
Sally	CA	—	—
Jimmy	CA	—	—
Janis	VW	—	—
Jessica	CO	—	Ex-Contact User
Mrs W	OIC	Engineers' Centre	
Hilary	Tutor	—	Arts and Crafts

All Units

Gef	Transport Manager
Jennifer	Specialist social worker for the younger physically impaired
Mrs B	RDCO

OIC	= Officer in Charge
SAO	= Senior Activity Organizer
AO	= Activity Organizer
CA	= Care Assistant
(GS)	= Government Sponsored Work Scheme
VW	= Voluntary Worker
CO	= Clerical Officer
RDCO	= Residential and Day Care Officer

Since the younger impaired were situated at the Alf Morris centre for three days of the week and because the level of user/staff interaction was relatively high at this unit, the majority of general staff interviewed came from here. Given these general considerations regarding inclusion of staff it soon became clear that my original target of twenty-four staff interviews would prove insufficient. In the event I talked to thirty staff in the semi-formal interview situation. Table 3 shows each staff member's name, their designated functions within the system, the centres in which they were based and any other information which explains their inclusion.

The Interview Schedules

During the first six months of participant observation the problem of interview schedules was never far from my mind. I did not wish to distort, constrain or 'impose violence' upon the statements of the contributors by the use of fixed-choice questions, but I was also aware of the advantages of this type of item, especially for people who demand 'hard evidence' to support an argument. It was my aim from the outset that this analysis should be accessible to everyone involved with the day centres, particularly policy-makers. It was important that the general meaning and phrasing of the questions used should be clear, concise and unambiguous in order that the respondents were not confused or put off by the language used. I support the view that meaning and meaning systems are best treated as sensitizing concepts which are

> a means of exposition which yields a meaningful picture, abetted by apt illustrations which enable one to grasp the reference in terms of one's own experience (Blumer, 1954, p. 9).

This is what I hoped to achieve for myself and for the reader. Consequently during the first two or three months in the centres I used the ample opportunities available to talk to people about their lives and their attitudes concerning current day centre provision. The ideas about what needed to be asked were gradually formed throughout this period.

It was ultimately concluded that a semi-standardized interview format would be the most appropriate for my purpose. This involves the interviewer asking specific questions, but being free to explore and probe as s/he sees fit (Hughes, 1981). The questions are essentially conversation openers and although many of the items may appear to require only a binary response, as the conversation progresses the respondent is given the opportunity to elaborate upon their position or change their mind if they feel so inclined. This type of approach also allows the interviewer freedom to phrase and re-phrase questions as necessary. In theory this strategy favours

> the creation of a situation which allows the respondent to define what is

significant to her/him in the area of questioning, how much time should be devoted to particular issues and so on (Voysey, 1975, p. 81).

This was the type of interaction I hoped to attain during the interviews. Such considerations are of particular importance when talking with people who through no fault of their own may have a limited vocabulary. By the time of interview, however, most respondents knew me sufficiently well not to let anything pass that they did not understand. On more than one occasion in both casual conversation and later in interview, I was told in no uncertain terms that 'You'll 'ave to say that again . . . , in English this time Colin so's I'll know what you're on about'.

Three interview schedules were finally constructed, one for each group of potential contributors, that is, (a) users; (b) direct service staff including VWs, care assistants (CAs) and teachers; (c) senior staff such as senior activity organizers (SAOs), activity organisers (AOs) and managers (OICs). Much of the initial inspiration of the item construction came from the questionnaires used by Carol Edwards and Jan Carter for the National Day Centre Survey conducted during the 1970s (Edwards and Carter, 1980). Item schemes for the auxiliary staff were conducted as appropriate on an ad hoc basis. The schedules used for the RDCO followed a similar pattern to that used for the senior personnel but were amended with questions relating to the relevant data already received, from both observation and the preliminary interpretations of the other interviews. Mrs B was formally interviewed as the empirical research drew to a close.

In broad terms all the interview schedules followed a relatively uniform pattern covering four principal areas. The choice of this formula was determined by a combination of the general hypothesis outlined earlier, plain necessity and the naive hope that comparison, quantification and finally conflation would be greatly simplified. The areas of common ground included biographical information, organization of the day centres, specifics of user participation and control in the units, and finally social considerations relating to the external environment and the future.

In many respects the first section speaks for itself. Respondents were asked about their background and specific items related to their family, education, employment experience prior to entry into the day centres and how they first became involved. At this point users were asked to talk about their impairments and the subsequent effects in terms of functional limitations. Throughout this study all references to user disablement are based solely upon users' interpretation of their abilities without recourse to official estimations unless otherwise stated.

The items relating to the centres began with questions concerning attitudes toward the service in general, staffing — levels, function and training, available facilities and activities, preferred activities and use of time spent in centres. The third section focused upon the mechanisms for redress of grievances within the system, internal organization, user involvement in policy making, attitudes toward user involvement, rules, sanctions and control. The final element of the interview schedule asked respondents to comment upon the day centres generally, the practice of mixing user groups, the possibility of heightened levels of integration with the able-bodied within the units, and how the service might be improved. Users were given the opportunity to give details of their recreational activities and social lives outside the centres, comment upon their subjective experience of societal attitudes and treatment of the impaired and their hopes and aspirations for the future.[4]

Data Collection

Information gathering during participant observation was by means of note-taking and the use of a hand-held dictaphone. With reference to the former, I would frequently disappear into the office or cloakroom as the necessity arose to frantically scribble down important data concerning relevant spontaneous conversations, accidents etc.. If I was particularly interested in someone's conversation I would ask them if I could use their comments for my research. Fortunately no one ever refused. At meetings, discussion groups or important events I would simply sit, as unobtrusively as possible, taking notes as necessary. At the outset this practice naturally aroused interest from both users and staff who wanted to know what I was writing about, although few people actually read what I had written. Indeed, at first my note-taking became something of a joke among some of the users. But the novelty soon wore off and my behaviour was tolerated.

Initially I intended to use a tape recorder but this proved impractical because of the poor acoustics of the rooms in which activities took place. The dictaphone also proved less successful than I had hoped for similar reasons. Although it was easy to carry about, fitting neatly into a jacket pocket, the microphone was so sensitive that it tended to pick up every sound in the room, and there is frequently a great deal of sound in a day centre for young people. Consequently I had to find somewhere relatively quiet before its use proved effective. At the end of each working day notes were rewritten and any taped comments written down. They were then filed under appropriate headings, for example, routines, activities, conflicts, etc., and a diary was kept documenting the sequence of the day's events as they unfolded.

Originally I had intended to hold the interviews in the respondents' homes as I believed that in their own environment they would be relaxed and more open in discussion. I decided against this approach for two reasons. Firstly, as my knowledge of the users grew it became apparent that a number of them were less likely to speak openly about their lives and their attitudes to the day centre service if there was any possibility of them being monitored by their parents. This suspicion was confirmed immediately before the period of interviewing began when I visited one individual's household. Because he was confined to a wheelchair, and due to the size of the house, his mobility was restricted almost exclusively to the living-room-cum-lounge. This meant he was in constant earshot of his mother. It proved impossible to hold a conversation without the mother's intervention. The second reason concerns transport. Since I do not drive, actually getting to and from the respondents' homes would have taken a great deal of time as many live outside the centre of the city in which the study took place.

Founded upon the belief that the views of the users should remain paramount, it seemed appropriate to interview this group of respondents first. But after six months in the centres it was inevitable that I would become aware of those who would have the most to say and those who would be shy. In order to circumvent any accusations of preferential treatment toward any specific individual, I decided that the simplest method of selection should be alphabetical order. This method was easily understood and was generally accepted. All interviews were prearranged at least one week in advance. In most instances the choice of date and time was left to the respondent.

When users were absent due to illness the next candidate on the list was asked if they would step in 'and get it over with'. They usually agreed. Apart from Amy, no one refused. All the user interviews were held upon day centre premises. For that with Mrs H, I went to her home. The longest user interview lasted one hour and fifty-five minutes and the shortest just over three-quarters of an hour, the mean being one hour and twenty minutes.

Apart from Jayne, the SAO for the Contact group, who left to undertake 'in-service' training half way through the study (January 1987) and was interviewed prior to her departure, all interviews of staff were conducted after completion of those with the users. The order of selection was largely determined by grade, those at the bottom of the staff hierarchy first and management last. Primacy was accorded Contact workers, then staff from Alf Morris, then Dortmund Square, and finally Hilary and Mrs W from the Engineers' centre. Discussions with the auxiliary personnel were undertaken as the interview period drew to a close and the last semi-formal conversation held was between myself and the RDCO, Mrs B. The reasoning behind this strategy was that if points considered sensitive were raised in discussion with those in positions of power pressure might be brought to bear upon those lower down in the structure. In retrospect this was perhaps over-cautious, but at the planning stage it seemed a sensible precaution to take.

As with user interviews, the time and venue for the staff contributions were arranged in advance, normally a week to ten days, in order that the interviewing process would not clash with the general routines of the centres. Most of the interviews were conducted during working hours, although all the CAs assigned to the Contact group and those who worked at the Alf Morris centre were interviewed when their shift had finished. The sites for these discussions were the same as those used for the users, except for two, Janis, a VW, and Denise, an AO, both of whom were based at Dortmund Square. Janis only worked on Thursdays, when the young impaired were at this centre, and felt that our conversation would be less intrusive on time spent with the users if it was conducted on another day. Consequently the discussion was held in the back room of her shop one Wednesday morning. At the time of her interview, Denise had just begun an in-service training course. Our conversation took place in her home on one of her 'study' days. The duration of staff interviews varied between one hour and five minutes for one of the VWs, to just over two and three-quarter hours for the SAO for the Contact group. The mean for the thirty discussions was two hours.

On average the length of time spent in conversation with staff was longer than that with the users. This was not because the schedules for the former were any longer but simply reflects the fact that many of these respondents, particularly those at the higher levels of the day centre hierarchy, were more thoughtful and loquacious in their responses to the questions, often using examples to illustrate statements or re-emphasizing points which they felt were particularly important. There was no noticeable difference between the amount of time in conversation with some of the younger, less experienced staff than there was with the users.

All the interviews were tape recorded. The quality of the recordings was enhanced by the fact that the interviews were held in quiet surroundings with only myself and the respondent present. The tape recorder never let me down. The only difficulty experienced was due to my reluctance to spend money on new batteries resulting in the playback quality of one conversation being particularly faint.

Although some of the users had problems with their speech this was not really a cause for concern. By the time the interviews came round I had become sensitized to likely difficulties of some individuals and felt confident enough to mention if I had trouble understanding what they were saying. In addition, I had few of the problems of self-presentation which plague many researchers. When the interviews began everyone knew exactly who I was and why I was there.

At the start of each interview I told the respondent that any information received during the subsequent discussion would be treated in the strictest confidence and gave a pledge that any quotes used in the finished product would preserve her/his anonymity. At the end, subjects were asked to refrain from discussing our conversation with others in the centres in the interests of validity. I believe the majority respected this request. All the respondents were asked if they would like to hear the playback of the recorded interview, but only two of the users wished to do so. Both lost interest after the first ten minutes or so. Everyone was given the opportunity to view the written interview transcript once complete. One CA, Annie, who was leaving the service, requested to do so but after reading it carefully she returned it without comment.

Each interview was transcribed in full in longhand, catalogued according to the date and indexed by page and line where it was felt statements were of particular importance. This technique proved extremely time-consuming and resulted in a mountain of material which defies quantification. This method may seem a trifle ponderous and indeed unnecessary but may be explained in the context of researcher insecurity. The interview transcripts were subsequently read, and re-read and coded in relation to specific areas of interest and the sequence of events that occurred throughout the year. Quantification and comparison were then completed and a preliminary synopsis of both user and staff interviews, of approximately 30,000 words, was produced to synthesize the salient tenets of the central argument into a more manageable form.

Where respondents' comments are used in the text every effort has been made to reproduce the exact colour and texture of the language used as faithfully as possible, with reference to dialect etc. The abbreviations used to depict it in print, when appropriate, are analogous to those used by Geoffrey Pearson who recently conducted an ethnographic study of heroin misuse in the same part of the country (Pearson, 1987). Each respondent was told of this intention and only one user offered any reservations. His concern was not about how the statements were reproduced but rather what was reproduced. He told me,

> 'I don't care 'ow you put it . . . , as long as you don't mek' us sound thick.'* — Billy

As they appear in the analysis statements made during interview are marked * and those made in conversation during participant observation + .[5]

I endorse the point made by Max Bloor (1983) that contributors should be given the opportunity to pass comment on the investigator's findings. With this in mind, the preliminary conclusions of the study have been discussed at length with several of the respondents. Moreover, one year after the empirical research had concluded I returned to the centres on a number of occasions to assess any changes which had occurred during this period and discuss those changes with those who took part. A brief commentary on those visits appears in Chapter Eight.

Difficulties Encountered during Data Collection

Apart from Michael and Alison, one other user in the Contact group, a young man named Charles who was severely paralysed in a motorcycle accident, had no means of verbal communication. As he could only control, with any accuracy, the little finger on his right hand, communication with him was only possible through the use of a small hand-held card containing the letters of the alphabet. In response to conversation he would spell out his reply using his little finger. The card was held by the person communicating with him. If he wished to 'say' something he would attract attention by smiling and nodding his head. Conversation by this method was not really a problem although a little slow. My discussion with Charles was one of the longest of the user interviews.

A principal worry with regard to the user interviews concerned discussion of the knowledge individuals had of their respective impairments, and their aetiology. In cases where it is known that impairments are caused by a progressively degenerative disease which may result in a relatively short life span and when the condition is at a visibly advanced stage, this is an area of considerable delicacy. This was the situation with one of the respondents, Gavin, who had muscular dystrophy (a genetically transmitted degenerative illness causing progressively severe impairments and premature death, often at a relatively early age). Before his interview I was extremely apprehensive about posing items relating to Gavin's knowledge of his impairments or his illness, as I had never heard him discuss these subjects in general conversation. After careful consultation with the senior staff, who were in regular contact with his mother, it became clear that no one in the units had any real idea of how much he actually did know, or indeed wanted to know about his condition. I have to admit that during the interview I deliberately avoided raising these issues, other than to ask if he knew the name of the disease, which he did. Gavin died three months after the empirical analysis was completed. He was nineteen.

A similar problem occurred with another user, Billy, who suffered from Friedrich's ataxia (a progressive inherited disease of the central nervous system affecting the spinal column, coordination and occasionally the eyes). During the interview Billy refused to discuss his condition and was evidently agitated by its mention, saying that he did not like to talk about it with anyone. I quickly changed the subject, but it became apparent later that this behaviour was largely attributable to ignorance. Some days after the interview he explained apologetically that he had only recently been told of the seriousness of the illness, by which he meant being made aware that a cure was unlikely. He only knew how the disease had affected him to date, which was visible to all, but little else.

Difficulties encountered in staff interviews were relatively minor. One girl, Andrea, developed a 'headache' immediately before the scheduled discussion. But a date was fixed for the following day and the ensuing conversation progressed without a hitch. One of the OICs postponed our meeting three times, due, she said, to the pressure of work. Because I was aware that her unit had in fact the highest level of staff and the lowest user attendance figures this explanation seemed somewhat hollow. I approached her re-emphasizing that her compliance in the investigation was voluntary. She apologized and reassured me she wished to take part. A fourth date was fixed for the interview. At this meeting she maintained that she could only spare me half an hour. In all her contribution took three separate interview sessions to complete.

During two of the other staff interviews, Mrs W, the OIC at the Engineers' day centre, and Jackie, the AO for the Contact group, the conversation was interrupted a number of times, six for the former and four for the latter. The discussion with Mrs W was held in her office and our conversation was punctuated by the telephone and by staff using the telephone or making enquiries about activities or other matters pertinent to the days' events. A similar situation arose in my discussion with Jackie, although instead of staff seeking her attention it was the users. After the fourth interruption it was mutually agreed that in order to avoid further hindrance the interview should be abandoned until the users had gone home later that day. This we did and our conversation proceeded without incident.

Conclusion

From the above discussion it may appear that the completion of this study was relatively trouble-free. This was not due to any particular skill on my part, but rather a number of factors which included constant support and much needed advice from both my supervisors, the perceived importance, by all those taking part, of the subject under investigation, the willingness of all the individuals who used and worked in the day centres to contribute to the study, and the choice of methods used, which were undoubtedly ideally suited for this purpose. By drawing upon the information provided by these individuals and the employment of these methodologies, the following chapters will develop fully the argument outlined in Chapter One.

Notes

1 It later transpired that the policy of non-involvement by staff in the affairs of the Insight groups was a deliberate strategy by management intended to stimulate higher levels of user autonomy and self-determination within the centres.
2 To ensure confidentiality all names used in this study have been changed.
3 A detailed discussion of the social characteristics of the user sample appears in Chapter Five.
4 Copies of the three principal interview schedules used in the study are provided in the Appendix.
5 Dates when the interviews were conducted are given in the Appendix.

Chapter 4
A Day Centre System for the Younger Physically Impaired — The Contact Group

I suggested in Chapter Two that the development of day centres for the physically disabled can be seen as a social and political response to the perceived needs of individuals who, because of impairment, are excluded from the 'work based distributive system' (Stone, 1985). Although there has been some expansion of these services in recent years there is no coherent national policy on their development, or on the role they should perform. Hence there is some variation in the services now available. To simplify analysis I divided day centres for the younger user into four ideal types. While each type had some positive features, all were open to some criticism. My primary objectives in this chapter are (a) to locate the day centre system studied within these models, (b) to provide a broad description of the main features of this service, and (c) to identify some of its main strengths and weaknesses. It is divided into three distinct but related parts. The first concerns the theoretical aspects of helper/helped relations. Secondly, I document the development of the provision studied. The third section looks at the staff, their organization, training, roles and principal aims with regard to services for the younger user. The data show that although the services as a whole resemble the 'warehouse' model, provision specifically for the younger user, namely, the Contact group, was more in keeping with the 'enlightened guardian' construct. This is explained with reference to a number of factors including the recent and relatively ad hoc nature of Contact's development, the environmental limitations in which it operates, the professional and social characteristics of the Contact personnel and their relations with the younger users.[1]

The Helper/Helped Relationship

Help, assistance and care may be provided either informally by kin, neighbours, friends, self-help groups and mutual aid organizations, or formally by statutory, voluntary and private (for profit) sources. Although an over-simplification, informal care may be understood as involving relations of *gemeinschaft* or community, and formal help, relations of *gesellschaft* as characteristic of modern society. While the giving of informal care may be explained with reference to tradition, duty, and reciprocity, etc. (Bulmer, 1987), explanations for the provision of help and aid in a formal setting are more difficult.

Since caregiving in either a formal or informal setting is normally seen as a largely altruistic activity, I shall begin with the concept 'altruism', which is commonly defined as 'the regard for others as a principle of action' (Bulmer, 1987). There are two principal forms of altruistic behaviour, firstly, that which is situational and relatively infrequent and secondly, that which is a regular activity. The occasional gift to charity and a regular commitment to voluntary work provide contrasting examples. It has been suggested by Thomas (1982) that altruism may be the result of personal feelings of inadequacy and inferiority. An occasional charitable act may be an attempt to soothe a damaged ego in a 'warm glow of momentary superiority'. Other writers have pointed out that altruism may have a basis in religious or moral beliefs which emphasize usefulness and a concern for others (Krebs, 1970). Whichever is valid, the focus on altruism challenges psychological theories of human action which emphasize the significance of struggle, domination and self-enhancement as the prime motivator of conduct.

Although the individual act of giving may be explained with reference to moral, religious, social, psychological, legal or aesthetic principles (Titmus, 1970), explanations become more complex when altruism occurs within the context of a job and is institutionalized in a formal environment. Individuals who work in the caring industry have been referred to as 'paid altruists' (Thomas, 1982). They are people employed to take on tasks which society regards in an ambivalent way. This is reflected in the discrepancy between publicly expressed esteem and low prestige. In all formal welfare systems there is a division between 'clean' and 'dirty' work and those who do the dirtiest work, both unpleasant and arduous, are the least rewarded, financially and socially. It has been noted that to do this work is to become involved in the ambivalent notions surrounding it.

> It is part of the confusion of values to question the motives of those who take on such tasks and to invent moral categories — unworldly, saintly, over-compensating, finding gratification in being superior — to explain a willingness to find a role in association with the stigmatized (Thomas, 1982, p. 71).

Explanations are further complicated when it is remembered that the perceptions of helpers may be shaped by the environment in which they work. Goffman (1961) noted in his analysis of the mental hospital how the moral career, or the successive changes in individual self-perception of staff as well as inmates, were influenced by the demands of the institution. While patients' beliefs about self were transformed by the process of mortification and regimentation, staff were subject to the counter equivalent of 'professional indoctrination'. This included rites of passage and the learning of new language codes appropriate to the staff role.[2] In addition, paid helpers are suspect because in many occupations financial reward is the obvious motive and 'people work' is usually poorly paid. Consequently those who do it are sometimes asked to justify their motives. It is likely, however, that no single explanation for this type of activity is appropriate or adequate. As Thomas says,

> 'Compassion for hire' takes many forms, it may be a vocation, a job, or a vehicle for the satisfaction of psychological needs (Thomas, 1982, p. 74).

Evaluation of the helper role is made more complex when viewed from the perspective of those being helped. It is generally accepted that in certain cases the receiving of aid and assistance is quite legitimate. This is true, for example, of children, the sick and the elderly. Beyond this, society expects and increasingly demands that adults take care of themselves. Hence those who require long-term aid through disablement have a significant part of their adult status undermined. And although the appropriate status for an individual with an impairment is said to be 'one who is helped' rather than a 'helped person' (Thomas, 1982), a formulation which emphasizes individuality above dependence, constantly needing help may reverse this position. Helpers can quickly lose sight of the fact that people with disabilities are individuals first and disabled second. In turn the assistance they regularly give may transform the self-perceptions of the person with an impairment to the degree that the helped person status is internalized and accepted (Thomas, 1982). In recent years, however, an increasing number of people with disabilities have become aware of this situation. Consequently the internal dynamic of the helper/helped relationship is not only shaped by the values and attitudes of society generally, but also by those of the parties concerned.

In their analysis of attitudes surrounding people with disabilities, Dartington, Miller and Gwynne (1981) maintain that the relationship of the disabled to the able-bodied as interdependent is only theoretically possible. Relations which involve a conceptualization of the helped person as having a dependent status avoid uncertainty while those postulating interdependence demand negotiation. Building on their own empirical research they claim that our society sanctifies the exceptional and rewards the conformist and that the pressures to keep the disabled in infantile dependence are pervasive. At the societal level, for example, this pressure implies a furtherance of the traditional social order in helping to perpetuate humanitarian values in an overtly materialistic world and keeps large groups of workers in employment. At the interactional level it fulfils some of the psychological needs of some of those workers.

Real integration, or the irrelevance of difference, is seldom achieved. Even the minority of 'super-cripples' who transend the barriers to integration and attain 'honorary normal' status are never considered ordinary or unexceptional. 'Honorary normal' is undoubtedly extraordinary. Dartington, Miller and Gwynne (1981) point to the economic, social and political advantages for people with impairments of identifying with the disabled label but suggest that this can lead to a loss of individuality. Those who work with the disabled, on the other hand, experience difficulties because they have to relate to both the individual and the 'undifferentiated member of an (assumed) group or category'. A generalized attitude toward a specific category of people, disabled or black, for example, applied indiscriminately to individuals in that category is a major feature of prejudice. The problem of individuality is therefore a principal concern for both the helper and the helped. Identity can only be retained through constant negotiation.

Dartington *et al.* claim that transactions are always problematic since they invariably involve a degree of inequality. This relates to physical and/or mental capability and of superior and inferior, with respective associations of guilt and envy. Hence negotiations can evoke strong and anomalous emotions in both parties. While the range of feelings which may be brought to this interaction are infinite, Dartington *et al.* maintain that generally both the helped and the helpers agree on a reciprocally acceptable 'construct' of interaction which permits certain types of behaviour but prohibits others. Notwithstanding that the general attitudes surrounding disablement have changed in recent years, Dartington *et al.* suggest that most constructs reflecting the inequality of power between the disabled and the able-bodied have been historically imposed on the former by the latter, and that people with impairments are socialized into accepting and believing the constructs that the able-bodied have assigned. Founded on empirical evidence, they identify four basic constructs, or ideal types, of interaction which they term (a) 'less than whole person', (b) 'really normal', (c) 'enlightened guardian', and (d) 'disabled action'. Each of these constructs corresponds to one of the four models of care discussed in Chapter Two. 'Less than whole' relates to the 'warehouse' model, 'really normal' is associated with the 'horticultural' variant and 'enlightened guardian' and 'disabled action' to those with corresponding names. It is notable that these constructs tend to undervalue the fact that the paid helper is dependent upon the helped for her/his livelihood. Types (a), (b) and (c) represent images of the impaired primarily from the perspective of the able-bodied, although (b), 'really normal', may also reflect the views of the impaired. Disabled action, on the other hand, is a perception of the disabled presented by the disabled, in response to an oppressive society dominated by able-bodied norms and attitudes. In diagramatical form these constructs are presented in Table 4.

'Less than whole person' represents the 'traditional', almost universally accepted, view of disability. Until fairly recently it has been the only construct available for interactions between the impaired and the non-impaired. At best, it usually involves assumptions of mutual obligation by both parties, and, at worst, persecution and rejection of the impaired. It also warrants an acquiescence by the disabled of their 'inferiority'. Dartington *et al.* point to an alternative view of impairment rooted in some technically less advanced societies where the ability to overcome disability is seen as a form of supernatural power, invoked to explain the process of 'sanctification' bestowed on the minority of disabled individuals who overcome their limitations. Helen Keller is a good example. The rarity of these 'heroic' figures is used as a justification for the application of the 'less than whole' label to the rest of the population with disabilities.

Table 4   Types of Interaction Involving the Impaired and the Non-impaired and Corresponding
Models of Care

Type of interaction	Role of the impaired during interaction	Role of the non-impaired during interaction	Model of care and function
Less than whole	Dependent	Dominant	Warehouse (care)
Really normal	Equal	Equal	Horticultural, (self development and independence)
Enlightened guardian (less than whole, really normal)	Ambiguous	Ambiguous	Enlightened guardian, (realistic adjustment)
Disabled action	Autonomous	Defined by disabled	Disabled Action, (independence, political activity)

Source: adapted from Dartington, Miller and Gwynne, 1981

'Less than whole' is a construct which emphasizes difference and negates sameness. It finds expression in the 'warehouse model' of care generally associated with segregated institutions where there is a definite cleavage between helpers and the helped. Any physical dependence on others is translated into total dependency. It allows the able-bodied helper to project onto the helped their own psychological inadequacies.

> With their own superiority safely established the carers are free to care (Dartington, Miller and Gwynne, 1981, p. 127).

Dartington *et al.* contend that very often the disabled, providing they accept this view, are infantilized or made into 'objects'. It has been observed in this regard that 'cabbages' make the best 'patients'.

Failure by the impaired individual to accept this position can sometimes lead to the application of sanctions by helpers which are unwarranted. Jones (1975) noted in an analysis of life in a residential hospital that there was a tendency among some nurses to treat their patients as though they were their children, with the right of reward and punishment and with an expectation that the inmate should be grateful. The 'less than whole' construct exemplifies and perpetuates the patterns of a stable society in which roles and statuses are fixed and not negotiable. As I noted in Chapter Two this model is applicable to those day centres where the emphasis is on 'care' and little else, where there is a clear division between staff and user and where control is firmly in the hands of the former.

The liberal response to this totalitarian approach, termed the 'really normal construct', emerged during the late 1960s and 1970s and was championed by articulate representatives of the impaired community as well as some professionals[3] from the caring industry. This paradigm rejects the 'less than whole' construct and its heroic variant and finds expression in the 'horticultural' mode of care. Professional energy is devoted to the denial of difference and dependence, and the aim is individual autonomy.

> The goal is independence which may be seen as attainable through treatment, prosthetics, slave labour or even will power. By implication independence is regarded as the normal state of the able-bodied and once the disabled have attained it, the problematic boundary will vanish (Dartington *et al.*, 1981, p. 129).

It has been suggested that there are a number of problems with this position. Firstly, it has been shown that the efforts of professional experts to re/habilitate people with impairments can often have the converse effect. One of the most well known examples of this argument is Robert Scott's (1970) study of 'blindness workers' in America. Secondly, since coping or adapting[4] to disablement may be seen as heroic by the non-impaired, Dartington, Miller and Gwyne (1981) note that this might have the effect of making the able-bodied feel inadequate thus inhibiting normal interaction. Thirdly, since emphasis is placed on subjective autonomy by participants in this type of interaction, the psychological consequences for those who cannot achieve it may often be harmful. Finally, given the extensive environmental, economic and social barriers to integration which confront people with disabilities (see Chapter Seven), the 'really normal' construct might be considered unrealistic.

Because of these shortcomings, Miller and Gwynne (1972) proposed in an earlier analysis a model of care which would accommodate both the dependent and the less dependent. It is known as 'enlightened guardian' and has become increasingly important since its inception. In political terms it is said to occupy the centrist position of the social democrat and incorporates elements of both 'less than whole person' and 'really normal'.

> It corresponds perhaps to the relationship between parents and adolescent offspring. It moves away from the infantilization of the less than whole person but clings to the notion of responsibility. It acknowledges the drives toward autonomy and independence, but at the same time asks of disabled people that they should be realistic about their aims and aspirations (Dartington, *et al.*, 1981, p. 130).

Inherent in this model is the idea of adjustment to a reality. But as Dartington *et al.* later pointed out, adjustment and reality are elusive concepts, especially when people with impairments are expected to adjust to a reality defined by the able-bodied.

Dartington *et al.* note that because adjustment is implicit in the 'less than whole' model, 'enlightened guardianship' has coercive and authoritarian overtones. Moreover, because it holds a central position in an otherwise polarized world, interactions are ambiguous, often problematic and have an unpredictable and oscillating character. In addition, since, in conjunction with the 'less than whole' paradigm, 'enlightened guardianship' is a model generally advocated by the non-impaired, it has been severely criticized by a number of disabled writers. Hunt (1981), for example, attacked Miller and Gywnne for exploiting the disabled in order to further their own career as experts in the management of disability. Oliver (1987b) has added that these authors, and the research which prompted this model's development, have contributed little, if anything to improving the lives of people with impairments.

In Chapter Two I likened this construct to day centres adopting a philosophy of 'significant living without work', which has been proposed by the able-bodied for the disabled and clearly means adjustment to a reality defined by the former. Providing services for both the dependent and the autonomous, these units combine 'warehousing' (explicitly social activities and pastimes) and 'horticulturalism', (vocational and educative pursuits). These activities are generally organized and controlled by non-impaired helpers.

Dartington *et al.* contend that the 'really normal' construct, although implying that the non-impaired are the primary reference group for the disabled, is a model which has been favoured by many individuals with impairments in protest against the imposition of the 'less than whole' variant. These writers see it as the first of a two-stage process leading to what they term 'disabled action'. They argue that a minority group seeking recognition passes through two distinct phases. The first incorporates a 'desire to please' and the second an assertion of identity. The analogy of 'Uncle Tomism' and 'black power' are examples of this process. Hence, 'really normal' is the first stage in the shift to 'disabled action'. The latter is exemplified by the following statement.

> I am a whole human being and as such have the same legitimate rights as all others, whether disabled or not. It is society that is handicapping me by depriving me of these rights (Dartington, Miller and Gwynne, 1981, p. 131).

'Disabled action' therefore opposes each of the other three constructs. In terms of welfare provision, including day centres, it would imply effective control by the disabled of resources and services. (This subject is discussed in more detail in Chapter Six). To locate the service studied within this theoretical framework, the next section looks at its evolution and the environments in which it operates.

The Development of the Day Service Studied and the Centres in which it Operates.

In this section I shall outline the history of the service, with particular emphasis on provision for the younger user, and provide a brief description of the day centres used. The data show that although the system studied evolved during the general expansion of state welfare between the 1950s and the 1970s, services explicitly for disabled adolescents did not emerge until the 1980s. Because the latter was developed largely in response to consumer demand, and was therefore ad hoc and unstructured, it broke new ground in terms of service delivery. For example, in contrast to other provision available, it offered a five-day service, and was peripatetic, moving between three centres throughout a given week. In addition, although the centres used for the service had been extensively adapted for people with impairments in terms of access etc., they still embodied many of the negative features discussed in Chapter Two. They were segregative in appearance and admission policies, there was a majority of elderly users in each, and the facilities were barely adequate for the number of people who used them.

The study was carried out in a large industrial and commercial metropolis situated in the heart of northern England. It had a population of 710,000 in January 1987 and unemployment stood at 37,767 (11.2 per cent of the workforce). According to the local authority, only 14,219 individuals were registered as disabled at that time. Of these, 4,365 were visually impaired, 1,476 hearing impaired and 3,398 were designated 'handicapped persons, general classes'. This last category included people with congenital malformations, organic neuroses, psychoses, disorders of the respiratory system and heart, arthritis, and injuries of the spine and limbs. Only 315 — 115 males and 155 females — fell within the age group of this research.[5]

The criterion for inclusion in the department's list was that the disability had to be verified by a doctor and that it be 'substantial and permanent'. Registration was not a necessary prerequisite for access to services and/or concessions provided by the Council, but individuals seeking aid were encouraged to have their name included. It is likely, however, that these figures were an underestimate. Due to a number of economic, political and social factors, many people choose not to register. One estimate is that most local authorities' registers are as much as 30 per cent or more inaccurate (Warren, 1979). Although legislative measures like the Disabled Persons (Employment) Act 1944 and the National Assistance Act 1948 required that registers be kept for those in receipt of services, how these lists are compiled and maintained, and the criteria used for inclusion, vary from area to area (Oliver, 1983a).

Day services for the physically impaired began in 1954 when, in response to the needs made apparent by the register, the Authority's Welfare Services Department opened two centres in local churches for one day a week. Each unit accommodated only fifty users a day. Fairly quickly these services were over-subscribed and with an initial outlay of £13,000, the Department acquired, refurbished and opened an old Victorian school building in 1956 as the Dortmund Square Day Centre. As this unit opened, the others closed. It catered for a hundred users a day and most only attended once a week. From the outset the role of the centre was essentially social, offering trips, outings and later group holidays. As the service developed, craft-based pastimes such as basketry and toy-making were introduced. Consumer demand outstripped provision and the Department opened the Alf Morris day centre in the summer of 1964. This new unit had facilities for what were termed 'vocational/diversionary' pursuits, such as woodwork, sewing and later pottery. In response to pressure from younger users, a fortnightly evening social club was opened in 1965 for those under 40. In the same year an Adult Training Centre, or ATC, sponsored by the Spastics Society, began operations with a capacity for forty physically and mentally impaired adults.

Eight years later, in line with the general growth of services after the publication of the Seebohm Report in 1968, the renamed Social Services Department opened a purpose-built day centre specifically for the physically impaired named the Engineers' Day Centre. After some initial experimentation as to what services should be offered it quickly settled down to the same pattern as its predecessors. In 1980 the Department realized that the day centre users were ageing. Most of the people who began using the service in the 1950s and 1960s were still regular attenders and the majority of the new entrants were 55 plus. The needs of the younger physically impaired were not being met.

The Authority was alerted to the needs of the disabled adolescent by the efforts of a lone parent of a boy confined to a wheelchair who left special school in the summer of 1980. Alarmed by the paucity of post-school provision for individuals like her son and the apparent lack of interest by the social services and the careers service, Mrs H confided,

> 'He was just left and I saw nobody an' it just got on me nerves. Just thinkin' that . . . , you know, 'e was just gonna sit there all day . . . . I was really down, I was on me own [Mrs H is divorced] an' I didn't know what to do'.*

In desperation she wrote to her local MP who as an ex-Cabinet Minister. This was a strategy she had resorted to once before in order to get the Council to fund the necessary alterations to her home to accommodate her son Norman's needs.[6] Shortly afterwards she received a letter asking her to contact the director of the local social services. This she did, and was told that plans for facilities for people like her son were being formulated.

A group was subsequently set up specifically for the young disabled adult aged between 16 and 25. The new service constituted a break with tradition since hitherto eligibility for user group membership had been determined by one explicit criterion, namely, disability. Access to this new facility in contrast was determined by both disability and age.

After two or three weeks, Mrs H was contacted by telephone by Jayne, the newly appointed Senior Activity Organizer (SAO) for the Young Disabled Person's Group. At that time the group had neither a name, a day centre, nor even members other than Norman. After the introduction Mrs H says she knew Jayne had little or no idea of what was expected of her or where to start.

> 'She [Jayne] said to me "like you it's new to me". She didn't know whether it was gonna work out at the time or not. She didn't know 'ow to set it off. She was just thrown into it. I don't think at first she knew what to do.' * — Mrs H.

This was confirmed by Jayne herself and Mrs B, the Residential and Day Care Officer (RDCO). Jayne stated that in 1980-81 her main functions included approaching individuals who where eligible for the new service and locating them within the Department's three day centres. She was originally only given funding for twelve people but after six months this proved inadequate.

The practice of organizing day centre users into user groups or clubs was established shortly after day centres came into being in the 1950s and 1960s. This policy had advantages for both staff and users and is common to day services generally (Jones *et al.*, 1983). Besides making administrative and organizational tasks much simpler, user group membership is reputed to promote a positive social atmosphere and provide the appropriate environment for the development of mutual support networks.

In April 1981 Wednesdays at Dortmund Square were set aside specifically for the younger users. Pressure for the service to be extended to the rest of the week came from users and their families and the group began visiting the other centres on the remaining weekdays, in conjunction with other user groups. Wednesday remained the only day when they had a unit to themselves. As in most day services (Carter, 1988) these units were normally closed at weekends. This policy meant that Jayne and any subsequent staff assigned the group would be peripetetic, unlike other day centre workers who were based in one location only. As noted earlier, during the study period there were thirty-six people on the group's register and, in contrast to the majority of other day centre users. most used the service three times a week or more. Only six attended twice while ten of the group visited the centres every weekday.

After working with the younger users for three months on a voluntary basis, Jackie was appointed the group's permanent Activity Organizer (AO) in 1982. In the following year the group adopted the name Contact. As most people used day services only once or twice a week, each centre had five separate user groups known by the day when they met, for example, the Alf Morris Monday group. Contact was the first group in this system to adopt a specific name. The idea is said to have emerged from both users and staff and the name was chosen for its explicitly social connotations.[7] Twelve months later Dortmund Square was closed for a year for extensive renovation and the group moved to Alf Morris on Wednesdays. The service changed little until after the study period (see Chapter Eight) apart from the introduction of explicitly educational activities and the addition of more staff. When the local authority began employing workers through government-sponsored employment schemes in 1985, Andrea was appointed Contact's official Care Assistant (CA). After her twelve-month contract expired and she took a permanent post at Alf Morris, she was replaced by Annie and Pete. In June 1986 Contact's complement was increased to five when Mary was employed on the same basis. Hitherto the tasks normally performed by CAs were done by Jayne or Jackie, or when necessary by workers from the host centre.

The evidence suggests that the expansion and development of this day centre system has been stimulated and influenced to a large extent by consumer demand. The original service was expanded because the facilities were inadequate and over-subscribed. User stimulation highlighted the need for separate social activities for the younger impaired in the mid 1960s. But specific provision for this user group was not forthcoming until the 1980s. Whether or not the Local Authority was formulating plans for the introduction of this service at that time is difficult to ascertain, but the data suggest that it finally came into being because of external pressure initiated by the lone parent of a disabled youth. Moreover, since its inception the evolution of this provision has been decidedly ad hoc and unstructured, and much influenced by users. As a result several established policies within the system were changed. Firstly, eligibility for membership of the new user group was dependent on two specific criteria rather than one, namely, impairment and age. Secondly, a five-day service was demanded and subsequently provided. Thirdly, the group had its own permanent staff. Fourthly, the group adopted a name which conveyed a particular meaning. And finally, the new service was not based in one day centre but in three.

The three centres used by the group were all larger than the average day centre which accommodates forty-eight users (Carter, 1981). But they differed from one another in terms of age and architecture. The Alf Morris centre was the largest with a capacity for 120 users. It was used by Contact on Mondays, Wednesdays and Fridays. Situated about three miles from the centre of the town in a relatively deprived urban area, it comprised three separate buildings, each with its own kitchen and toilets, joined together by one single corridor (see Figure 1). The complex did not stand alone but was an adjunct to the much older social services offices used by the authority's social workers, (known locally as 'The Blind Welfare' because they once housed welfare services for the blind), a large sheltered workshop for the physically impaired, and the central garage for the city's social services transport division.

The front of the Alf Morris centre is separated from the road by narrow unkempt gardens and wrought iron railings. Across this road stands a separate sheltered workshop for the physically and mentally handicapped which opened in December 1986. The centre's three entrances were easily visible as there was a large white sign at each advertising the building's name, function and sponsors.

The largest of the main buildings, known as 'the bottom', housed a number of craft areas, a large hall, which was almost empty, and the office used by Contact staff. The middle structure included a large hall with a stage at one end, in front of which stood a full-size grand piano. It was furnished with plastic-topped dining tables, each surrounded by an assortment of office-type chairs. This was the centre's main dining area throughout the research period. The smaller rooms adjacent to the hall were all the size of a large domestic lounge, and contained softer lounge-type chairs and coffee tables. They were used for discussion groups and small classes. The remainder of the building accommodated more craft areas, the sick room, the general office — which housed the clerical staff and the Officer in Charge (OIC) — and the two rooms used by the Contact group.

The larger of these rooms measured 12 by 6 metres and the smaller 6 by 7. At the far end of the larger room was a fire escape leading to the grass verge. This was generally open in the summer so users could sit out in the sun. Both rooms were

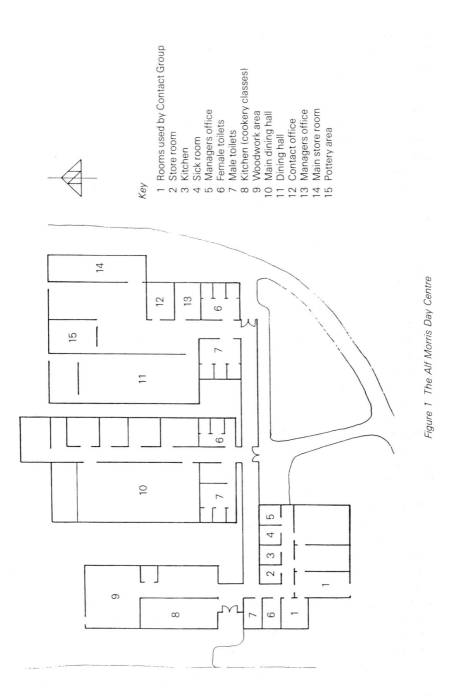

Key

1 Rooms used by Contact Group
2 Store room
3 Kitchen
4 Sick room
5 Managers office
6 Female toilets
7 Male toilets
8 Kitchen (cookery classes)
9 Woodwork area
10 Main dining hall
11 Dining hall
12 Contact office
13 Managers office
14 Main store room
15 Pottery area

Figure 1 The Alf Morris Day Centre

skirted on two walls by cupboards similar to those found in domestic kitchens. Other furnishings included several office chairs, two or three lounge chairs and a free-standing set of shelves containing a plethora of literature pertaining to disability. This included pamphlets about welfare benefits, organizations for the disabled and self-help groups. In the centre of the large room four tables were usually pushed together and surrounded by chairs. A quarter-size snooker table stood in front of the fire doors. And to the right of the door there was usually a tea trolley containing coffee and tea making facilities for users to make their own drinks. The smaller room contained a pool table, three or four lounge chairs, a small coffee table, a metal cupboard containing games and equipment, a fish tank with tropical fish, and a dozen or so small potted plants. When the rooms were being used by Contact there was usually a television, a record player and a computer in evidence. The walls, as in the rest of the complex, were painted in pale pastel shades and covered in posters, paintings and photographs. Although there was an official notice board outside the OIC's office, anything of interest to the Contact users was stuck to the wall immediately above the drinks trolley. As in the rest of the centre there were no carpets on the floor. It was covered with heavily cushioned vinyl material. There were no stairs in the centre and all facilities such as toilets, doors and so on, were specially adapted for people with impairments.

It was evident, however, that the entire structure was in need of redecoration and repair. Although the walls and woodwork were painted in light colours, their hue had diminished with time and continuous wear and tear. They appeared drab and dingy. The roof leaked in several places when it rained. Throughout the study buckets had to be placed in the centre of the main corridor just outside the Contact areas and in the middle of the large room itself to catch rainwater. In the male lavatory adjacent to the Contact rooms one of the two toilet seats was detached from the bowl from August to November. Two of the four fluorescent tubes which lit the smaller Contact room were out of action for the whole of the study. And the piano was unplayable because it needed tuning. This sorry state of affairs was attributed by all respondents to the authority's lack of funds.

The Engineers' day centre was used by Contact on Tuesdays. Only twelve years old in 1986, it was situated in the middle of a municipal housing development built around the turn of the 1960s about three miles from the centre of the city. It was easily distinguishable from its surroundings because it was the only structure which was one storey high and stood in its own grounds approximately thirty metres from the adjoining roads. There was a large car park in front where one or two of the social services' minibuses were usually parked. (These vehicles were painted bright red with the local authority logo etched out in white on the sides and back and were unpopular with many users because of their stigmatizing appearance). There was also a large sign over the main entrance similar to that at Alf Morris. The furnishings and fittings were in almost immaculate condition and there was a general sense of order which was lacking in the other two units used. There were no visible recreational facilities such as snooker tables, for example, and there was little on the walls in terms of posters or photographs. The area used by Contact was slightly smaller than the two rooms at

Figure 2 The Engineers' Day Centre

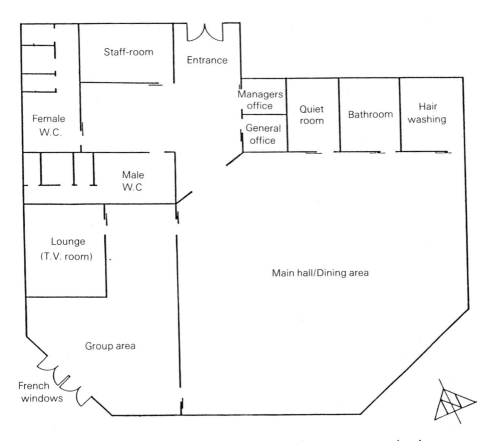

Alf Morris. But the french windows opened onto a large concrete patio where users could sit or play ball games when the weather allowed (see Figure 2). The room was furnished with a number of dining tables, which doubled as workbenches, and several chairs. Lunches were normally served in the hall. Adjacent to this area was a fully carpeted lounge-type room measuring 6 by 7 metres which housed several comfortable chairs, a coffee table and a large television. It was rarely used by Contact but was frequently used by other user groups for discussions and classes.

Located close to the centre of the town in a run-down residential sector of the inner suburbs, the Dortmund Square day centre also stood out from its neighbours because of its well-maintained exterior. There was also the obligatory sign next to the front door, and there were usually one or two social services' minibuses parked outside. To the west of the structure was a small car park which was once a playground. Entry was through the double doors at the front. The doors leading to the car park were seldom open. (See Figure 3). Although once regarded as a 100-place unit, Dortmund Square only catered for sixty users a day in 1986-87. The hall was filled with twelve dining tables, each surrounded by five or six chairs, and a quarter-size snooker table. In front of the stage were a number of lounge chairs, a coffee table and an old radiogram. At the opposite end was a small table holding a computer and monitor, and a dartboard was pinned to the wall next to it. In the library there were eight lounge chairs, a coffee table, a television, and a bookcase which held less than twenty books. The walls of the hall were adorned with artefacts similar to those at Alf Morris. And the floor was covered in the same vinyl material apart from the area in front of the stage which was carpeted. All the fittings had been adapted for the disabled. Dortmund Square was the only centre where the younger users did not have an area specifically for their own use.

Figure 3 The Dortmund Square Day Centre

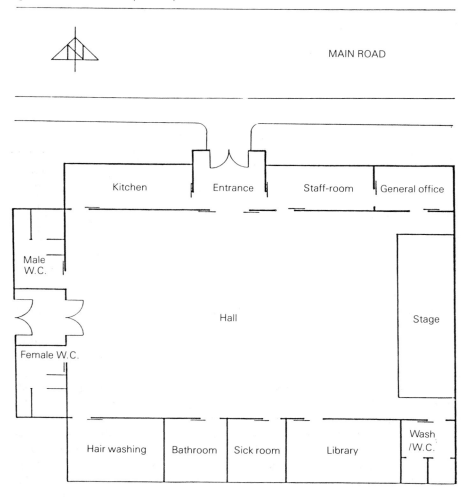

All three centres were used exclusively by the physically impaired albeit but the majority of other users were significantly older than the Contact group. Table 5 shows the average number of other users during the period of formal participation.

Table 5 Average day centre attendance: 1 July 1986 to 1 January 1987 (not including the Contact Group)

Day	Centre	Capacity	Other users				Total
			Over 30 years		Over 60 years		
			Male	Female	Male	Female	
Mon	Alf Morris	120	24	10	26	19	79
Tue	Engineers'	100	11	9	21	10	51
Wed	Alf Morris	120	22	13	35	25	95
Thu	Dortmund Sq	60	6	4	11	6	27
Fri	Alf Morris	120	16	15	39	18	88

Note: these figures do not include individuals who were expected but did not attend due to illness.

Source: data provided by the OIC of each unit

Table 6 Average attendance for the Contact Group: 1 July 1986 to 1 January 1987

Day	Centre	Numbers on register			Actual attendance			Other users
		Male	Female	Total	Male	Female	Total	
Mon	Alf Morris	16	17	33	13	15	28	79
Tue	Engineers'	13	12	25	8	9	17	51
Wed	Alf Morris	17	17	34	15	15	30	95
Thu	Dortmund Sq	14	15	29	12	13	25	27
Fri	Alf Morris	10	9	19	8	7	15	88

Source: official Contact register for 1986–87[8]

Table 6 shows the average attendance figures for the Contact group for the same period.

In all three centres priority was given to the elderly. The areas allocated to Contact at both Alf Morris and the Engineers' were disproportionate to the group's size and the space available. At Dortmund Square specific tables were 'unofficially' reserved for elderly users. This was generally accepted by all concerned. Contact members would normally congregate at one end of the building while other users sat at the other.

In the interests of safety the younger impaired were not allowed to use the kitchens in any of the centres. This did not apply, however, to other user groups. At both the Engineers' and Dortmund Square, there were constraints on the level of noise allowed because of the close proximity of the elderly. I never saw a radio or tape recorder at the former and while the younger users did play the radiogram at the latter, it was kept low. Even at Alf Morris the youngsters were occasionally asked to keep 'the volume down' if older users complained or Alf Morris staff felt that the noise coming out of the Contact area would upset them. These restrictions stimulated much resentment from some elements within the Contact group which was made worse by the fact that many of the principal activities in the centres were organized for the elderly. At Alf Morris for example, the main dining hall was frequently used for 'old-time' dancing but never a disco. At both the Engineers' and Dortmund Square centres 'Bingo' or 'Oi' (a similar game involving playing cards) was played religiously every Tuesday and Thursday afternoon between 2.00 and 2.30. One of the few organized entertainments at the latter during 1986 was a recital by two retired light opera singers, whose choice of material was Gilbert and Sullivan. Such activities were not appreciated by most of the Contact members, underpinning the view that the needs of the younger day centre user are incompatible with those of the elderly.

This section has shown how the three day centres used by the Contact group were segregative in terms of location, appearance and admission policies. While it may be argued that this is unavoidable to some degree since any structure which is adapted for people with disabilities will stand out from its neighbours and because limited resources prevent local authorities siting day centres in more appropriate neighbourhoods, differences were accentuated by stigmatizing signs and symbols such as social services' minibuses. It also shows how provision was generally organized around the needs of the elderly who were given priority with regard to facilities and activities. Besides underpinning the assertion that the development of services for the younger user were unstructured, the data identifies some of the difficulties encountered in centres serving both young and old.

The Staff and their General Aims with regard to the Younger Day Centre User

This section focuses on the organization, training and roles of the day centre personnel, as well as their general aims in relation to the younger user. It is divided into four separate but related parts. The first, covering the organization of staff, suggests that the occupational structure is organized for services consonant with traditional notions of 'care' and 'warehousing' but that the more formal aspects of that organization, apparent in the system generally, are not visible in the Contact framework. The second part covers staff training and reports that the majority of senior personnel held professional qualifications. This contrasts with the findings of earlier research in this field (CCETSW, 1974; Carter, 1981; Kent *et al.*, 1984) but is in keeping with recent trends in the personal social services and residential institutions in particular (Goodall, 1988). Training was noticeable by its absence in other sectors of the workforce, notably among CAs, but this was less problematic in the Contact format than in other day centre units. The third section suggests that senior staff roles in Contact were more complex than their equivalent in other user groups and that the role of CAs in relation to the younger user was essentially social. Finally, I examine the general aims of staff regarding this user group, which encompass the provision of social and, where possible, re/habilitative activity within an unfettered atmosphere. I argue that this is compatible with the 'enlightened guardian' model discussed above.

Because, strictly speaking, day centres do not have goals or aims, albeit individuals within them do, and because goals in this situation are impossible to measure and may be indistinguishable from means (Carter, 1981), the notion of aims is problematic. In any case little official documentation on goals in relation to the younger user exists. However, the RDCO, Mrs B, suggested that,

'because we're lumped with the elderly I suspect the policy that would come out of higher management would be that it's [the aim of the service] to provide social and environmental amenities for people during the day and give relief to relatives.' *

This aim was reflected by the division of labour in the centres which included no acknowledged re/habilitation professionals. The official staff/user ratio for each unit was one to ten and higher than the national average.[9] But senior staff suggested that it was nearer one to eight.

Although Tables 7, 8, 9 and 10 suggest that the staff/user ratio is lower than one to eight, the hours worked by part-time senior staff varied considerably and all part-time CAs, both permanent and those employed on government schemes, worked alternate shifts — 9.00 a.m. to 1.30 p.m., or 10.30 a.m. to 4.00 p.m., with half an hour for lunch — amounting to twenty-five hours per week. The data does not include maintenance staff, cleaners and caretakers who are not normally

Table 7 Staff working at the Alf Morris Day Centre: 1 July 1986 to 1 July 1987

Job Title		Full-time Female	Male	Part-time Female	Male
Officer in Charge	OIC	1	1	—	—
Clerical Officer	CO (GS)	—	—	1	1
Senior Activity Officer	SAO	1	1	—	—
Activity Organizer	AO	2	1	2	—
Care Assistant	CA	—	1	9	1
Care Assistant	CA (GS)	—	—	1	1
		Total 24 permanent staff			
Voluntary Workers	VW	—	—	1	—

Key
(GS) = Workers sponsored by Government Employment Schemes

Source: data supplied by OIC

'Cabbage Syndrome' The Social Construction of Dependence

Table 8 Staff working at the Engineers' Day Centre: 1 July 1986 to 1 July 1987

Job Title		Full-time Female	Male	Part-time Female	Male
Officer in Charge	OIC	1	—	—	—
Clerical Officer	CO	—	—	1	—
Senior Activity Officer	SAO	1	—	—	—
Activity Organizer	AO	—	1	—	—
Care Assistant	CA	—	—	3	3
Care Assistant	CA (GS)	—	—	1	1
		Total 12 permanent staff			
Voluntary Workers	VW	Not known			

Key
(GS) = Workers sponsored by Government Employment Schemes

Source: data supplied by OIC

Table 9 Staff working at the Dortmund Square Day Centre: 1 July 1986 to 1 July 1987

Job Title		Full-time Female	Male	Part-time Female	Male
Officer in Charge	OIC	1	—	—	—
Clerical Officer	CO	1	—	—	—
Senior Activity Officer	SAO	1	—	—	—
Activity Organizer	AO	1	—	—	—
Care Assistant	CA	—	1	4	1
Care Assistant	CA (GS)	—	—	1	—
		Total 11 permanent staff			
Voluntary Workers	VW	—	—	1	—

Key
(GS) = Workers sponsored by Government Employment Schemes

Source: data supplied by OIC

Table 10 Staff working with the Contact Group: 1 July 1986 to 1 January 1987

Job Title		Full-time Female	Male	Part-time Female	Male
Senior Activity Organizer	SAO	1	—	—	—
Activity Organizer	AO	1	—	—	—
Care Assistant	CA (GS)	—	—	2	1
		Total 5 permanent staff			
Voluntary Workers	VW	—	—	2	1

Key
(GS) = Workers sponsored by Government Employment Schemes

Source: data supplied by SAO (10).

present when users are in the centres. Nor do they include teachers employed on a contract basis. These tables underpin Carter's (1981) findings that more women than men work in day centres and the general view that women make up the bulk of the labour force in the caring industry.

In terms of official occupational demarcation, responsibility for all day services for the physically impaired, as well as residential care, rested with the RDCO, Mrs B. She was accountable to the chief executive of the Local Authority and responsible for the organization, administration and running of the centres. This included finance, staffing, development and user welfare. OICs bore the responsibility for the internal workings of each centre and were accountable to the RDCO. Their duties included administration (which according to the three OICs interviewed took up at least 40 per cent of their time) staffing (recruitment, 'on the job' training and deployment in conjunction with the RDCO) and the general organization and coordination of internal resources and facilities. They liaised with users' families and other agencies, such as social workers, and took responsibility for users' welfare while they were in the centres. Within the units COs carried out the routine paperwork.

The SAO's primary function concerned the development, organization and delivery of services and activities for a given user group. This included the deployment and supervision of subordinate workers. They were expected to assume the duties of the OIC when necessary, if the latter was ill or on holiday for example. The AO was directly accountable to the SAO and had a similar function but was more involved with the actual activities at user level. As with the SAO, they had a supervisory role in relation to CAs and VWs. Whether employed by the Social Services Department or sponsored by government employment schemes, CAs were at the foot of the staff hierarchy. Their primary tasks included physical tending where appropriate, which involved helping users with the toilet, bathing or eating, and psychological support through conversation, participating in activities and general social interaction. In contrast to all other categories of permanent workers who worked in the system, CAs spent almost their entire working day with users. VWs also fulfilled an essentially social function, although in specific cases they adopted a didactic role if helping users master new skills such as computing. Officially they were not expected to cater to any of the users' physical needs.

While there were no uniforms or formal badges of authority worn in the centres there were clear divisions between those with authority and those without. The two female OICs interviewed had decidedly 'cultured' accents which the Contact users and several of the younger staff interpreted as 'posh' or 'stuck up'. And although most of the staff were referred to by their first name this did not apply to Mrs W, the OIC at the Engineers', or Mrs F, her opposite number at Alf Morris, and one or two of the older AOs. There was also a significant age gap between most of the senior staff and the CAs. The recent policy of introducing CAs into the system via employment schemes had apparently transformed both the staff/user ratio and age distribution of staff generally. While most of the senior staff were in the middle age group, Mrs W being the exception at 62, the average age was 36. This was in accord with Carter's (1981) findings. CAs on the other hand were much younger. Only three of those interviewed were over 25, and their mean age was just 21 years. Two of the four VWs were in this age group, and the other two were 30. Of the four teachers who took part in the study, only Hilary from the Engineers' was middle-aged. The others were under 30.

In two of the units formal policy was mediated through a combination of staff meetings and direct supervisory control. At Alf Morris there were different meetings for each level of staff. The OIC discussed each day's activities with SAOs and AOs between 8.30 and 9.00 a.m. before the users arrived. The SAOs and AOs then met with the CAs and VWs who were assigned their particular section at 10.15. Although supervisory staff felt that there was some two-way communication between them and OICs, it was generally agreed that the meetings between them and CAs involved little more than a dissemination of information from supervisor to subordinate. At no time during this study were meetings held where all staff were present. At Dortmund Square, however, staff meetings took place immediately after lunch at 1.00 and did include all the workforce. But junior staff said that there was little scope for them to put their ideas forward and that policy was determined by management. Mrs W at the Engineers' considered staff meetings unnecessary because she felt she was always in close contact with 'her people'. While her authority was legitimized by her position in the staff hierarchy she also had an unmistakable authority that comes with age and years of practised professionalism. She had the demeanour of a hospital matron, a reputation for unrivalled efficiency and fairness and was held in high esteem by all the Engineers' workers and the centre's elderly users. This view, however, was not shared by several of the Contact members.

In all three day centres, a staff rota system was operated which applied to all workers except those AOs who had a particular skill or were in charge of a specific user group. For example, Bob and Rick at Alf Morris were exempt from the rota, the former because he was a qualified woodwork teacher and in charge of the carpentry shop, and the latter because he was responsible for the Insight group. This policy was rationalized by management on the basis of giving them more flexibility in terms of staff deployment, it enabled workers to acquire new skills and it maintained the necessary social distance between helpers and the helped. This last point is generally considered desirable in most institutions where long-term care is provided in order to preserve staff's fairness and impartiality when dealing with users and to minimize undue stress and anxiety for both parties through excessive personal involvement (Miller and Gwynne, 1972).

The divisions between different staff levels and between staff and users also extended to tea breaks and mealtimes. In all the centres OICs usually had their breaks in their office while other workers had designated recreational areas where they could go for a cup of tea, eat their lunch or socialize with colleagues away from users.

None of these formal arrangements, however, were evident within the Contact framework. Because the group was peripatetic, there no facilities specifically allocated for Contact staff's use. Even the office at Alf Morris used by

Jayne and Jackie was shared with other personnel. All workers were on first-name terms both with each other and with users. Neither Jayne nor Jackie was considered 'posh' or 'stuck up' by other workers or by the younger users. And although they were both in their mid-thirties the age gap between them and the younger staff as well as some of the Contact members seemed minimal. Both women wore relatively fashionable clothers and had little difficulty discussing topics of mutual interest with CAs and users. Jayne attributed this to their considerable experience 'working with the youngsters'.*

Another factor unique to the Contact workforce was that none was included in any of the formal staff meetings held in the centres. Any data regarding them or the younger users were given direct to Jayne by Mrs B, the RDCO, or one of the OICs as appropriate. It was then passed on to whomever it concerned. Staff discussions about group policy were held between 8.30 and 9.00 a.m., before the users arrived or whenever the situation warranted it, usually in the same room as the users. Staff rotation did not apply to the Contact workforce. And since staff and users had free access to tea and coffee throughout the day and smoking was not prohibited, tea breaks were regarded as unnecessary. In addition, they ate their lunch in the same areas as the Contact members.

Carter (1981) has shown that the type of staff generally employed in day services are often well suited to the 'caring' role.[11] However, with the growing emphasis on rehabilitation rather than 'warehousing', particularly for the younger user, one source has suggested that there is an urgent need for the recruitment of therapists and other 'professionals in rehabilitation' to work in day centres (Kent *et al.*, 1984). The evidence shows that while there was an absence of such recognized rehabilitative professionals as occupational therapists working in this system, those employed in senior posts were professionally trained. This level of training was not evident in other sections of the workforce, especially those at the foot of the staff hierarchy.

Apart from Mrs W, a CA at Dortmund Square named Vera, and Hilary, the arts and crafts tutor at the Engineers', all those who worked with Contact during the study period had been employed from the time of, or since the group's inception. Only one of the senior staff interviewed had transferred from what could be termed a 'blue collar' occupation, in contrast to the pattern found by Carter (1981) in the 1970s whereby nearly a quarter of day centre personnel had transferred from blue collar or manual trades. The exception among those studied was Patrick, who joined the service in April 1986. He had formerly worked in the office of a road haulage firm. Though he had no prior experience of work with the disabled, he decided he wanted to do something 'worthwile' after being made redundant, having been sensitized to the difficulties of impairment by his mentally handicapped niece. The remainder were all experienced in this or related fields and/or were professionally qualified.

Mrs B, the RDCO, was a state registered nurse (SRN) and had a successful career in the health service before joining the Social Services Department in 1982. Of the three OICs interviewed, Mrs W had worked in the civil service as an administrator before her appointment as manageress of the Engineers' in 1974.

Her husband was impaired and she had been heavily involved in voluntary work for disabled ex-servicemen since 1945. Andrew at Alf Morris was employed in boys' clubs and residential homes for the mentally handicapped before he joined day services in 1985. He held the Certificate in Social Services (CSS) and was a study supervisor for in-service students on this course.[12] Sandra at Dortmund Square had a degree in Home Economics and before joining Dortmund Square in 1985 had been involved in charity work for the church.

Those workers in the the middle tiers of the day centre hierarchy were equally well qualified. Bob, the AO at Alf Morris, was a trained teacher. Denise, who held a similar post at Dortmund Square, had been a physical education instructor and had worked as an auxilliary nurse in hospitals for the mentally ill. Both began working in day services in 1981 and both held the CSS. The remaining AO interviewed, Rick, had a degree in Fine Art and before his employment at Alf Morris in 1986 had worked in residential institutions for the physically impaired. Jayne was a qualified youth worker and had been employed in this capacity until 1978, when she took a job in the local Physically Impaired and Able-bodied (PHAB) club. Her associate in Contact, Jackie, was an SRN and held the Certificate of Qualification in Social Work (CQSW). Before joining day services she had held posts in both professions. The four teachers interviewed were all experts in their respective fields but had no specialist training for work with the physically impaired. Apart from Hilary, who started work at the Engineers' shortly after it opened, the other three had all been employed on a part-time basis since 1985 specifically for work with the younger users. All these individuals perceived working in the caring industry as more than simply a job. It was their chosen occupation, in other words, a vocation.

The background and motivation of the CAs were very different from those of their senior colleagues. Of the nine CAs interviewed, only the three who worked at Dortmund Square had not joined the service through government employment schemes. Before his employment with social services in 1984, Jimmy had worked for six months in an old people's home. One of his two colleagues, Vera, had worked at Dortmund Square since 1962. She became a CA after being made redundant from her job as office cleaner for the local authority. Her associate, Sally, had no prior experience of work in this or related fields, other than nursing an invalid relative at home. She joined the Dortmund Square staff in 1983.

Of those who entered the service via employment schemes, only Annie had any acknowledged marketable skills. She had a degree in the History of Art. The remainder had little work experience at all other than temporary and part-time unskilled jobs in the service sector. None appeared to feel the need to justify their choice of work. They each said their main reason for taking the job was to get off the dole. None of them had any previous knowledge of disability and confessed that if it had not been for the current employment situation, they would never have considered working with people with impairments. It is not surprising therefore that their introduction into an environment where the majority of people were impaired was traumatic.

Initial encounters between the able-bodied and the physically impaired are frequently uneasy, especially if the former have little experience of the latter. This is due to the value our society places on physical wholeness and our tendency to formulate opinions of others on relatively superficial information such as eye contact and physical appearance (see Goffman, 1968). Segregating the disabled from the able-bodied in institutions such as special schools, compounds this problem further, since neither group is equipped with the necessary skills to overcome its unease. Due to their experience and training senior staff had few difficulties in this particular area, but this was not the case for the young CAs. The situation was not helped by the lack of preparation they received before entering the units. Their initial training consisted merely of a verbal description of their duties at the formal interview for the job and a brief look around the centre where they were to work. All the CAs said this process gave them no idea of what to expect.

None of these workers was prepared for the variation in impairments, the different behaviour patterns and different values and norms which existed in the day centres. Some spoke of the acute embarrassment they felt when they first saw individuals without clothes whose limbs were a different shape to theirs and of their compulsion to stare. Others were shocked by the apparent normality of epileptic-type seizures and how other users and some staff virtually ignored them. One male CA said he had never seen anybody have a 'fit' before, but on his first day there were two. Another girl found it hard to get over being asked by a complete stranger to take her to the toilet. Others commented on feeling sick when they first fed someone who could not swallow properly and ate with their mouth open. As Annie put it just before she left,

'Most people think disability's just about wheelchairs . . . , it's not.'*

How these workers coped with these experiences varied from individual to individual, but some never managed successfully. All the staff could recall CAs who had left the service after only a few days because they could not cope with the work.

The trauma of these experiences might have been avoided with careful induction and training. The only real training they received was the 'on the job' variety and six afternoon classes, each one week apart. Since the latter were only run at specific times of the year, most CAs worked in the centres for some time before they went to them. For example, Annie and Pete joined the service in April 1986 and their training course did not begin until the middle of June.[13]

Ironically, because these workers were at a psychological disadvantage when they started in the centres, initial interactions between them and users were conducted on a relatively equal footing. This was evident on the two occasions when new CAs began working in the centre and conversations were initiated by users. This is consistent with Thomas's (1982) observation that young people with disabilities are adept at helping the able-bodied through the 'awkwardness barrier' during social interaction. Once the period of adjustment was over, all the CAs adopted what Dartington, Miller and Gwynne (1981) term a 'really normal' position in their attitude toward users.

'It's a bit of a shock at first, but you soon get used to it, an' then it's like they're not handicapped. You don't realize they're handicapped. It's just at first it's a bit of a shock.'* — Tracey A

Once they had adopted this view many became sympathetic to the difficulties and injustices experienced by the users outside the centres.

'There's a lot more that they [Contact members] could do than come to a day centre that's full of old people. They're on'y 'ere 'cos people outside won't give 'em a chance. There's a lot o'people in 'ere who'd be OK outside if people'd just give 'em a chance.' * — Pete

It is common for able-bodied people who are in close contact with the impaired to take this or a similar view. In his analysis of interactions between the stigmatized and the normal, Goffman (1968) referred to such individuals as 'the wise'. It is important that any barriers between staff and users are quickly broken down because in Contact the biggest part of the CAs' role was social.

Some researchers have argued that the constant movement of staff in institutional settings is responsible for many of the problems associated with helper/helped relations (Menzies, 1960; Strauss *et al.*, 1964). It has been suggested that where there are established staff and stable relations between staff members, flexible patterns of work and informal specialization can develop (Alaszewski, 1986). The following data suggest to some degree that this had occured within the Contact group.

From the users' perspective, the roles of SAO and AO were the same. The only difference according to Jayne and Jackie related to overall responsibility, which rarely concerned users, and paperwork, which in practice the two women shared equally. Although in the centres generally the responsibilities of the two roles were clearly specified, several of the senior staff felt their respective job descriptions were grossly inadequate when considered in relation to the system's limitation, in terms of 'on site' professional support, back-up services generally, and the complex and varied needs of the younger users.[14]

Because of these considerations, senior Contact staff had adopted an explicitly flexible approach.

'You've just got to do what's necessary at the time. We've never worked any other way. I know there's pressure on for everyone to do their bit, the care assistant does the caring, the activity organizer does the activities and the management does the managing. But I don't think in this type of work you can have that because the youngsters don't care whether you're a manager or a care assistant for starters. I mean the point is, if their needs are there then I don't think it matters who you are.'* — Jayne

Because of this flexibility the roles of SAO and AO within the context of the Contact group had innumerable sub-roles which were largely dependent on the perceptions of others, both users and other professionals. Apart from the designated functions, which entailed the development, coordination and organization of user activity and the supervision of subordinate staff, the six most notable sub-roles included resource worker, social worker, advocate, counsellor, nurse, careers advisor and CA. A more apt description of the senior staff role(s) within Contact would be 'in-house key worker(s)'. This term was used by Glendinning (1986) to refer to a designated resource worker situated in a local authority department whose task was to provide information, advice, practical help and support to families caring for a severely handicapped child. In respect to the present study, however, it refers to senior day centre staff who provide a similar service not just for day centre users, but also their families.

With regard to the SAO's and AO's official duties, data gleaned from formal interviews suggested that much of the impetus for user activities came from the users themselves. The main problem for staff was trying to accommodate their ideas within the limited resources available.[15] Supervision of junior staff was carried out during the normal course of the day's events with the minimum of fuss. The only visible conflict between senior Contact personnel and the group's CAs throughout this study concerned Pete's lateness. And although this problem was never fully resolved it was not considered serious enough to be referred to a higher authority by either of the two women.[16]

Frequently users, their families and other professionals drew on the expertise of senior Contact staff on matters relating to users' needs. For example, one girl asked Jackie where she could by rubber shoes for her crutches. Another user's family asked Jayne's advice on firms specializing in wheelchair repairs. Jackie was also involved in the acquisition of grants for a special typewriter for a girl with limited hand movements at the suggestion of the girl's doctor. These types of incident occured because a number of users and their families had had little or no contact with social workers and seeking help from them was said to be a long drawn out process. Consequently they looked to day centre staff in times of crisis. This pattern accords with the claim of one source that social workers regard working with the handicapped and elderly as less rewarding than social work in other areas (Rees, 1978).

Elderly users' kin would normally deal with the OIC when the situation warranted it, rather than the SAO/AO of her/his user group. But partly because of the youth of the Contact members and the fact that the group was peripatetic, there was a higher level of involvement between some users' families and senior Contact personnel. Certain users also sought staff's help when dealing with other professionals. One individual who lived in a residential home asked Jackie to help her seek new accommodation because she was unhappy where she was living. A male user whose disabled girlfriend was pregnant asked the SAO for help with maternity grants. She also acted as their advocate at a case conference concerning their eligibility for parenthood. Counselling facilities are increasingly considered an imperative for institutions dealing with young people with disabilities (Henshall, 1985), but since there was none available in this system counselling was an integral component in the senior staff's repertoire of roles.

Counselling sessions took one of two forms, involving either spontaneous confidential discussions when the situation warranted it, or a prearrranged series of private conversations. There were several examples of the former during this study. Usually the topics covered were general depression or difficulties with parents, and regular meetings were set up if the problems were persistent. One example of this occurred when one of the male users was experiencing acute anxiety over the insidious deterioration of his health due to his incurable disease. He had difficulty discussing the subject with his parents. Neither type of counselling was initiated without mutual agreement between user and staff.

Over two-thirds of the user respondents said they would discuss personal matters with one or other of the senior staff. This is consistent with the findings of such commentators as Anderson and Clarke (1982) who note that young people with disabilities typically discuss their feelings and difficulties with day centre staff. It is generally considered desirable to have sexual counselling facilities in institutions for young people with disabilities (Anderson and Clarke, 1982; Meredith Davis, 1982; Henshall, 1985) but in the centres studied this was a 'no-go area' in consequence, or so it was said, of the attitudes of social services higher management rather than day centre staff.

Despite the variety and seriousness of many of the users' impairments, there were no specialist medical staff in any of the units. According to official policy, at least one staff member should have qualifications in first aid, but the identity of this individual was not common knowledge among users nor many of the staff. Consequently junior staff and users looked to those in authority when problems arose. And since adolescents with impairments, like their able-bodied peers, are prone to 'messing about' and/or knocking each other around, accidents were not uncommon. On top of this several of the Contact group regularly experienced epileptic-type seizures. In one week in November (3–7 November 1986) I counted seven and this was not unusual. Usually when this or other medical problems emerged Jayne or Jackie would be sought out to act as nurse. Jackie was a qualified SRN but this was not a prerequisite for the job, nor was it common knowledge in the centres.

While all the senior staff acknowledged that because of their relative disadvantages and society's treatment of people with disability generally some form of institutional support may be necessary for some of the Contact users for the rest of their lives, Jayne and Jackie took the view that that support need not necessarily take the form of a day centre. They appeared to take every opportunity to encourage users to seek opportunities elswhere, providing literature relating to voluntary work, paid employment and training schemes, and giving careers advice and assistance where appropriate. This had benefited a number of Contact members in the past, but during the study period only one male user was introduced to sheltered employment through their efforts. In addition, one girl who left the group to work in a local sports centre claimed that conversations with Contact's senior staff had been the motivating force which made her get off her 'backside' to look for a job. And while she found the job herself, Jackie helped her fill in the application form and stood as her reference. But if not always leading to placements, informal conversations about work, education and re/habilitation were often held between helper and helped around the main tables in the contact areas at Alf Morris, particularly when new information concerning this subject became available. Eight of the users interviewed recalled specific conversations with staff about this issue.

Because the younger user group was regarded as a separate entity in the centres, Contact personnel were expected to cope without assistance in the event of staff shortages. Although Contact had a relatively low helper/helped ratio, there were specific periods in every day when one or two of the CAs were missing due to the shift system they worked. Staff shortages occurred between 8.30 and 10.30 a.m. and between 2.00 and 4.00 p.m., notwithstanding the fact that users began arriving at 9.00 a.m. and did not leave until approximately 3.45 p.m. Moreover, apart from illness, all staff had four weeks holiday a year and both for this reason and because helpers accompanied users on outings or regular activities outside the centres, staff shortages were common. For example, every Monday, four of the group went swimming and Jackie and Pete went with them. Consequently either Jayne or Jackie could be called on to help with physical tending, tasks normally performed by CAs.

Physical tending tasks, bathing, toileting and helping with meals were less demanding and less frequent in Contact than in other user groups in the system. Because those users who needed help in bathing were bathed by their parents, Contact staff did not have to help in this regard. Although ten of the group needed assistance with the toilet some were reluctant to ask for help because of the social taboos attached to this activity.

'For some of them the fear of embarassment is worse than constipation.'* — Jackie

And while five group members needed help eating, one never ate in the centres, another only used the service in the long summer holidays when he was not at residential college and a third only needed a minimum of assistance. The main tasks for senior Contact staff as well as the group's CAs were therefore essentially social.

For adolescents with impairments, particularly those who have been segregated in special schools, social interaction with able-bodied peers is now considered essential in the process of rehabilitation since it helps develop the social skills and emotional maturity necessary for the transition to adulthood (see, for example, Anderson and Clarke, 1982; Kent *et al.*, 1984; Cantrell *et al.*, 1985; Brimblecomb *et al.*, 1985). Most of the CAs working in the day centres were ideally suited to this task as they were in the same age group as the younger users, from similar socio-economic backgrounds and shared the same interests and values. In the Contact group, CAs were expected to initiate, encourage and participate in user activities as appropriate. This usually took one of three basic forms: one-to-one work, formal group activity, and spontaneous interaction.

One-to-one work was generally frowned on in the centres because of fear of being accused of favouritism, but was sometimes accepted as a necessity in some cases by senior Contact staff. It normally involved a member of staff and those users who, because of the severity of their impairments, or because of their temperament, were unable to initiate social interaction on their own and were ignored by other members of the group. These interactions could involve board games such as chess or draughts or discreet conversation. Formal group activities meant CAs involvement in organized activities such as quizzes, board games, group tournaments and competitions. Spontaneous interaction refers to any social activity which is not formally structured or organized by staff. It could be initiated by individual staff or users and could include almost anything from chatting to listening to music or playing pool. VWs also participated in these activities.

In the circumstances it was inevitable that the level of sociability between these staff members and users was high and that relationships developed which could be considered 'unprofessional'. For example, some of these workers occasionally went to the pub with users outside working hours. Two of the female CAs sometimes visited the PHAB club used by the majority of the Contact group on Friday evenings. When their year of employment in the centres finished[17] and Annie, Pete and Mary left the group, a number of the Contact members were clearly upset. While this emotional involvement may be considered problematic by some observers, in view of the perceived need for this type of interaction and the fact that any interpersonal relations, social or otherwise, runs this risk, such developments can only be seen in a positive light.

While CAs may be criticized for their lack of experience and training, this was not considered a major problem within the Contact framework. Both senior staff and users alike were more interested in their social skills than their technical knowledge. They could not be accused of adopting a patronizing attitude due to professional expertise, unlike others within the day centre hierarchy and the caring industry generally.

It was plain from the empirical data that, despite the limitations of the system, the Contact staff were providing more than simply social and environmental amenities associated with 'warehousing'. All staff interviewed acknowledged that there were crucial social and attitudinal differences between members within the Contact group and that some were more dependent than others. There was also a general consensus that the group's needs were fundamentally different from those of the elderly. Kent *et al.* (1984) suggest that the basis for this difference lies in the fact that while the elderly have established and developed their individuality during the course of their lives, the young have not and need the opportunity to do so. The following statement exemplifies the staff view regarding this subject:

'The youngsters haven't had the experience of life that the old folk have had. A lot of them have led very cushioned lives. They need space, they need to rebel, they need to try things out. The older groups have experienced so much in life, they come here [day centre] for the social aspect. They're quite happy to come, chat and doddle around — not all of them — but most of them are. The youngsters, they need something else.' * — Jayne

All the staff respondents felt that the social environment was important if only because some of the younger users and their families saw this as the principal reason for day centre attendance. They were also aware that others were looking for something more.

'Some of the youngsters and their families see it as a social centre and just somewhere to go. Unfortunately social services is seen as the last option. It's the end of the road. Now, there are some who are quite happy with that, but others aren't.' * — Jayne

Each senior worker maintained that facilities for rehabilitation should be an essential part of day centre provision for younger users, albeit reservations were expressed by some over the term rehabilitation.

'Rehabilitation has to be built in. You work with issues like rehabilitation and independence in a social setting. There's never been anything written down about rehabilitation. And you can come up with all sorts of problems if you talk about rehabilitation. Rehabilitation is associated with the medical model and we don't have the facilities. But we've had inroads into further education, which helps with the rehabilitation process. It's not an official line. I'd say the way it's evolved, it's moving more and more toward independence training.' * — Jackie

The RDCO, Mrs B, was quite clear which way she hoped the service would develop.

'I'd like to get to the stage where any disabled person, regardless of age, that comes into a day centre, would hope that ultimately his potential or ability, will be rehabilitated to the state where they no longer need us.' * — Mrs B

With regard to the younger staff, most were unsure of what the official aims of the service were and some said that they had never been told. They were agreed when asked whether they thought they were social or rehabilitative, however, that they were probably, or should be, both.

Based on interview data, staff's aims with regard to services for the younger day centre user can be summarized as follows: (a) to provide the practical services and support necessary for young people with disabilities during the day and therefore a respite for relatives and/or their principal carer(s), (b) to provide a social atmosphere where younger day centre users can socialize with peers, (c) to provide information and advice for users and their families, and (d) to provide social/recreational/diversionary/vocational[18] and, in the non-medical sense, re/habilitative facilities appropriate for young people with physical disabilities. It is important to note that these aims are not listed in any specific order of merit or importance.

In terms of group policy this meant that in the areas allocated to the younger users, all services and facilities were provided in as unconstrained an atmosphere as possible. Contact members were encouraged to look after themselves. For example, transport was available but only if users wanted it. Unlike the policy in other user groups Contact members could help themselves to drinks whenever they felt like it. Helpers only assisted those who could not look after themselves (or fetched boiling water when necessary because the younger users were not allowed in the kitchens). There was none of the ceremony or ritual attached to mealtimes as reported in other institutional settings (see, for example, Alaszewski, 1986). Users could order a meal if they wanted one and sit down for lunch at the same time as other user groups or eat as and when they felt like it. Social services' lunches were unpopular among most Contact members although in 1986 a two-course meal cost only 50 pence. This was because the choice of menu was restricted and repetitive and the quality of the food was regarded as poor. The meals were cooked elsewhere and brought to the centres in pre-heated containers. Consequently their quality had deteriorated by the time they arrived. Usually about half the group ate sandwiches brought from home or bought from the local shops and consumed them in the Contact areas with staff. User participation in all activities was voluntary and controls were kept to a minimum. It was, however, clear that user involvement in the organization and delivery of services was minimal. These issues are dealt with in more detail in Chapter Six.

The staff regimes within the three day centres were officially organized to provide social and environmental facilities for people with impairments as well as a respite for relatives. I likened this to the 'warehouse' model of care. The division of labour in the service generally was traditionally structured with clearly defined staff roles and a relatively formal chain of command. As a result there were clear social and professional cleavages between different staff levels and between staff and users. However, because provision for younger users was peripatetic and had a permanent staff, few of these divisions were visible in the Contact group.

I then reported that senior personnel were adequately qualified both in terms of previous experience and professional qualifications. But this was not the case for the CAs, most of whom had no prior experience of, or training for, work with people with impairments. The data suggest that entry into the service was traumatic for CAs but that this experience was less difficult within the Contact framework. This may be attributed to a number of factors including the similarities in age and socio-economic background between them and the younger users and the fact that many young people with impairments are skilled at helping the able-bodied through the awkwardness barrier. An empathy between these workers and the users developed fairly quickly and had positive results.

Analysis of staff roles illustrated how the stability, informality and attitudes of the Contact workforce led to a flexible pattern of work and informal specialization which was both appropriate and beneficial to the needs of the younger users, particularly in view of the limited facilities available to this user group both inside and outside the centres. Senior staff provided information, advice, practical help and support for users and their families while the principal role of the younger staff was largely social. I suggested that although social relations between CAs and users might in some aspects be considered unprofessional, they should be viewed in a positive light because of the latter's perceived need for this type of interaction and its implicit rehabilitative function. Staff were aware of the disparities within the Contact user body, of the fact that their needs were different from those of the elderly and that the Contact service needed to provide for both the dependent and the less dependent. This was reflected in their general aims regarding provision for the younger user which incorporated both a social and rehabilitative dimension, or, a combination of 'warehousing' and 'horticulturalism'. As there was little evidence of user involvement in the organization and delivery of these facilities I suggest that this approach is compatible with 'enlightened guardianship'.

Conclusions

In this chapter I have documented the evolution of the specific day services studied, described the environments in which the service operates, and outlined the organization, training and principal roles of staff involved with the younger day centre users. The development of this day centre system occurred at the same time as the expansion of welfare provision generally but its development was fairly ad hoc and unstructured. It was also evident that consumer initiative played a large part in that development, particularly as regards provision for the younger user. The service generally had evolved along 'traditional' lines. Although the three day centres used were suitably adapted for people with physical impairments, they were segregative in terms of appearance and admission policies. The principal user groups served were the elderly impaired and the services and facilities provided were organized accordingly. These included care and support and social and recreational activities commensurate with the phrase 'tea and Bingo'. The needs of the younger users were swamped by those of the elderly.

Partly in response to the task in hand and the nature of the clientele, provision for the younger user evolved along different lines. It was not based in one specific centre but three, had a permanent staff and a clear sense of identity which resulted in the adoption of the name Contact. As a result the level of helper/helped interaction within the Contact boundary was relatively higher than in other user groups. It is notable that all the senior staff involved with the younger users were well qualified, both in terms of experience and professional qualifications, particularly the two women permanently involved with the younger users. However, this was not the case with the young CAs whose contribution to the service was considerable.

This chapter clearly illustrates that the facilities available to the younger user within the Contact format included social and rehabilitative activity, broadly in keeping with 'enlightened guardianship'. But while it is likely that a number of factors contributed to the adoption of this policy, including the inclinations of Contact members, their families and the staff, it is clear that there was little directive toward this end from outside the centres, either from within the Social Services Department, or from other agencies reputedly in the business of rehabilitation. This may be one of the reasons why the facilities for user self-development or 'independence training' within the service have not developed further. Another may derive from the users themselves. They are discussed in the following chapter.

Notes

1 The users and user interaction are dealt with in Chapters Five and Six.
2 For a comprehensive discussion of professionals and professionalization see Wilding (1982).
3 Throughout this study the term 'professional' is used to include those who work in the acknowledged professions such as doctors and lawyers, and in the 'aspiring professions' such as social workers, teachers, etc. (Wilding, 1982).
4 In deference to Matteson (1972, reported in Anderson and Clarke, 1982) the terms 'coping', 'adapting' and 'effective functioning' are interchangeable,
5 These figures are reproduced from an official document circulated to the Equal Opportunities (Disabled) Subcommittee by the Local Authority on 19 December 1986.
6 Initially the Council had been loath to finance the construction of a downstairs toilet and bedroom because Mrs H was an owner-occupier and not a council tenant.
7 This strategy was later adopted by management when the two Insight units were formed in 1986.
8 These data may not include those persons who did not use the transport facility and 'dropped in' after the register has been taken. In addition, some users avoided registering because the register contained a record of amenity fund subscriptions and users were not asked to contribute for days when they were absent. All day centre users were asked to contribute to an amenity fund to supplement resources. In 1986 this amounted to 50p per week, but in January 1987 it increased to 65p.
9 As noted in Chapter Two, in 1981 Carter (1981) found that the average staff/user ratio in day centres was one to eight.
10 On 1st January 1987, after Jayne was replaced by Jackie, Patrick became Contact's full time AO. In April of that year when Annie and Peter left the group, Sean, the male VW included in Table 10 was appointed Contact's male CA. In June, when Mary left, Tracy B, one of the two female VWs took her place. The VWs were not replaced during the study.
11 The types of staff currently employed in day centres have been described as best suited

to the caring role (Carter, 1981; Kent *et al.*, 1984) presumably because the majority are female, middle-aged and not professionally trained.

12 His associate at Alf Morris, Mrs F, was unavailable for interview for much of the study period due to illness. She was, however, similarly qualified.

13 In her formal interview on 22 June 1987 Mrs B, the RDCO, said that staff training was currently under review.

14 This view accords with findings of recent studies whose authors have drawn attention to a general need for such facilities in day centres for the younger physically impaired (Meredith Davies, 1982; Kent *et al.*, 1984; Jordan, 1986; Owens, 1987).

15 This subject is discussed in detail in Chapter Six.

16 Relations between supervisor and subordinate were less convivial in other areas of the day centres. Some senior staff and occasionally elderly users criticized the young CAs for their perceived lack of aptitude, discipline and training. This may, however, be partially attributable to the considerable age gap between them.

17 In 1986–87 government-sponsored work schemes such as the Community Programme only lasted for twelve months. In many cases when government sponsorship finished so did the job.

18 These terms were used interchangeably by different day centre staff.

Chapter 5
The Contact Users

From the evidence presented in the last chapter it is clear that the Contact group developed in response to the needs of disadvantaged young people with physical impairments. Implicit in that discussion was the suggestion that there were significant differences among the Contact users in terms of abilities, dependence and attitudes. In this chapter I shall outline the extent and variation of their disadvantage, describe how they were introduced into the day centres and identify the principal divisions within the user body. The evidence demonstrates that for most of the Contact members, over two-thirds of whom were congenitally impaired, subjective disadvantage resulting from physiological causes such as limited mobility had been compounded by other factors including the nature of their education, lack of employment and relative social isolation. The data show that although all the user respondents were aware that day centre attendance was voluntary, many felt that they were offered little else when their education ceased. Although there was some homogeneity among this user group in terms of previous experience and general disadvantage, there were also discernible subdivisions within the group determined largely by degree of impairment and perceived dependence. These include two factions or cliques with contrasting attitudes toward disability, dependence and the day centres. These differences are explained with reference to the degree of impairment and differential socialization.

The chapter is divided into four inter-related parts. Since the majority of Contact members were congenitally impaired, the first part provides an overview of the likely consequences of a childhood with an impairment. The second looks at the users' social characteristics and relative disadvantages and provides an insight into their biographies. The third documents their introduction into the system and the fourth examines user interactions within the context of the Contact group.

Impairment and Childhood

As we have seen in previous chapters, in contemporary Britain, as in most modern industrial societies, there is still a considerable cultural bias against people with impairments. This is manifest in institutionalized exclusion from mainstream economic and social activity and stereotypical perceptions of the disabled as at best 'superhuman' and at worst, but still most commonly, 'less than whole'. These essentially negative perceptions are transmitted through language. For example, people with impairments are often referred to as 'in-valids' or invalids (Hurst, 1984). But more broadly such perspectives are embedded in the very fabric of social encounters. The negative stereotype which the disabled endure is reinforced by the generalized ideal of physical perfection and competence that is presented in mass culture through the media and conventional recreational literature (Abberly, 1987). As a result, living with disability is generally associated with a life of poverty, social isolation and stigmatization or 'second-class citizenship' (Sieglar and Osmond, 1974). Consequently,

> to become disabled is to be given a new identity, to receive a passport indicating membership of a separate tribe. To be born handicapped is to have this identity assigned from the moment of discovery and diagnosis. Both involve a social learning process in which the nuances and meanings of the identity are assimilated (Thomas, 1982, p. 38).

This social learning process was discussed in detail by Goffman in *Stigma* (1968). His analysis of the 'moral career', or changes in self-perception, of individuals with a socially stigmatized status, suggests that the acquisition of the devalued identity which usually accompanies impairment involves, initially at least, a two-stage learning process. The first relates to learning the beliefs and values of normal society and the general idea of what it would be like to be viewed abnormally. The second begins when the individual learns that s/he is viewed in this way and discovers the consequences of this perception. The timing and interplay of these two stages are crucial, Goffman claims, for future development of the individual's ability to adapt to her/his circumstances.

He suggests that this learning process, applied to persons with impairments, can be conceptualized in four ways. The first concerns the congenitally impaired and involves individuals being socialized into accepting their disadvantaged circumstances even while they are learning and incorporating the standards against which they fall short. The second also relates to those impaired from birth but involves individuals being shielded from the full extent of societal perceptions of the disabled by institutions such as the family until they enter the wider community either at school, or later during adolescence when looking for work. The third variant refers to individuals impaired later in life and concerns the re-evaluation of self after the ascription of the disabled identity. Goffman's fourth model is less applicable to people with disabilities and concerns individuals socialized into an alien culture, who are confronted with the problem of self-reappraisal after learning that their adopted norms and values are not viewed as appropriate by those around them. Implicit in this analysis is the suggestion that the first pattern identified is the least psychologically problematic, if only because unlike the others it is a gradual process rather than a new experience.

While Goffman's analysis may be criticized because it is incumbent upon profoundly negative perceptions of impairment which ignore the material basis of society's oppression of people with disabilities (Finkelstein, 1980) and therefore precludes the experience of disability or adjustment as normal, it does provide a theoretical framework for understanding the different processes by which many people with impairments come to terms with a disadvantaged status. It is particularly useful in relation to childhood impairment and socialization.

Briefly, individuals learn the social norms and cultural expectations, or shared standards of behaviour, of society through the process of socialization. Primary socialization relates to the experience of childhood. It is generally regarded as the most important, and usually takes place within the family. Other important agencies of socialization include peer groups, the education system, occupational groupings and the work experience. Through interaction with 'significant others', which may include parents, siblings, peers or teachers, the child learns the meanings of 'significant symbols', or language and communication, and the role(s) s/he will be expected to perform, both as a child and adult. Socialization is not confined to childhood but continues throughout life.

Perceptions of self are therefore derived through social interaction. An individual comes to know who s/he is and how s/he is perceived through her/his interactions with others. We assemble a concept of self based on how we imagine others see us. Our sense of identity is therefore constructed on the basis of others' definitions. Consequently, how a child with a congenital impairment adapts to societal perceptions of disability will, initially at least, be greatly influenced by interactions within the family.

The birth of a child is usually regarded as a joyous occasion but the arrival of an infant with a disability is generally considered a difficult time for families. Parents are said to experience a mixture of emotions including shock, guilt, shame and helplessness, accompanied by feelings of frustration and rejection for the child (Selfe and Stow, 1981). Some are said to over-compensate, which can in turn lead to other problems. For example, Meredith Davies (1982) points out that there may be a complete change in the lifestyle of the mother who, determined to love and care for her offspring, partly neglects other family members which can lead to marital difficulties. A contrasting view is that of Roith (1974) who has argued that the birth of a disabled child does not necessarily promote adverse reactions in parents. Although this debate remains largely unresolved, a major cause of family stress is likely to be the financial and practical problems of caring for the impaired child or children.

Disability in a child has a fundamental impact on the family budget. On the one hand, family incomes tend to be lower because the mothers of disabled children have fewer opportunities than mothers of non-impaired children to take paid work outside the home. On the other hand, extra expenses are needed for a wide variety of items including, most commonly, heating, transport and clothing (Baldwin, 1985). These problems are exacerbated further when families are situated at the foot of the class structure.

There is considerable evidence showing that the mortality and morbidity of the manual working classes is poorer than that of other sections of society (Black

Report, 1981; Townsend *et al.*, 1987) but little showing the relationship between social class and impairment in children. One source, however, commenting on the fact that in a sample of 279 families with an impaired adolescent selected from the Family Fund's register,[1] only 32 per cent were headed by a non-manual worker (as against 40 per cent for the general population) stated,

> The social class distribution may reflect a bias towards the manual classes applying to the family fund. It may also reflect a bias to manual social classes in the prevalence of severe disabilities in children. In all about three out of four of the young people in this sample lived in a disadvantaged home background where this included unemployed, low waged, elderly chronically sick or lone parents (Hirst, 1987, p. 64).

Whatever the cause, there is evidence that impairment in children does have an adverse effect on family life, often resulting in family breakdown. For example, a study of families with a child with spina bifida found a marked increase in family problems. Only one in four were free from difficulties and relationships within the marriage tended to deteriorate over time. The divorce rate was twice that of the control group (Tew and Lawrence, 1974, reported in Meredith Davies, 1982). There is also ample evidence showing that these families face additional financial and social problems, particularly where the lone parent is a woman (Finer Report, 1974).

Because few families are equipped to cope with the emotional, financial and practical problems accompanying the birth of a child with an impairment, parents normally come into contact with a wide range of professional experts including doctors, health visitors, psychologists, educationalists and social workers. Consequently, professionals have a significant impact on both the family and the child's future. There are a number of views regarding the effects of professional intervention. Voysey (1975), for example, shows that parental attitudes and definitions are greatly influenced by their interactions with professionals or 'significant others'.

Another writer, however, suggested that parental perceptions of their child's disability were shaped by a number of other factors, including previous experience, social class, race and ethnicity (Darling, 1979). Booth (1978) maintained that parents adapted to the problems associated with their child's impairment in distinctly individualistic ways which struck a balance between professional definitions and their own life experiences. He concludes that parental appraisals of their child's disability are generally more influential than clinical perceptions and definitions. Whichever view is taken, the level of professional involvement in families where childhood impairment is present is likely to be far higher than that in families where is is not. This situation not only sensitizes the family and the impaired child to the functions and power of professionals, but it also helps to separate them from the rest of the community.

In addition, families where impairment is present are sometimes subject to what has been termed a 'courtesy stigma' (Bierenbaum, 1970). This refers to the situation where the negative attitudes surrounding disability are extended to the rest of the family. When this occurs the prejudice and ignorance which surrounds disability is projected onto other family members, particularly when they are out with the impaired child. This tends to confine social activities within the home and restrict social contacts to a limited number of close and considerate friends (Thomas, 1982), causing adverse reactions in parents which may directly or indirectly effect the developing child. A common cause for concern among professionals is parental over-protectiveness, where parents refuse to allow children with impairments to take risks and grow up normally (Meredith Davies, 1982). On the other hand, it has been suggested that attachment and dependence cannot be measured, even in families where impairment is not present, and that it is far more difficult with disabled children to say which aspects of parental behaviour are unnecessary (Anderson and Clarke, 1982). Moreover, since many disabled children are separated from the family at a very early age, in hospitals or in residential schools for example, their primary socialization is very likely to be markedly different from that of their non-impaired contemporaries.

Besides being generally associated with parental deprivation and separation, childhood hospitalization also entails the learning of new roles and new relationships. Hospital admission necessitates that the child is thrust into what Parsons (1951) referred to as the 'sick role' and 'patient role' which are the precursors to the dependent or 'impaired role'. They are synonymous with freedom from normative role obligations, dependence and deference to professional authority. Davis' (1963) analysis of the hospital experience of children with polio outlines this process. He identifies the moral implications of what he terms the quintessence of protestant ideology, 'not whining for home' and the 'slow patient and regular pursuit of long-term goals' in order to get well.

For all children school is a particularly significant phase in development. For the child with disabilities it can be the start of a life-long process of stigmatization, or the beginning of normalization. For Goffman it is especially significant since interactions in formal education can ram home generalized perceptions of her/his devalued status for the stigmatized individual.

> Public [normal state] school entrance is often reported as the occasion of
> stigma learning, the experience sometimes coming very precipitiously on
> the first day of school with taunts, teasing, ostracism and fights.
> Interestingly the more the child is handicapped the more likely he is to
> be sent to a special school for persons of his kind, and the more abruptly
> he will have to face the view which the public at large takes of him
> (Goffman, 1968, pp. 47–78).

The term special school refers to institutions for children termed 'handicapped, exceptional or in special need' (Barton and Tomlinson, 1984). While teasing and bullying are often discussed with reference to the placement of children with impairments in normal schools, it has been reported that similar behaviour also occurs in segregated establishments (Anderson and Clarke, 1982).

Whether or not children with special needs should be placed in separate schools is a contentious issue, and one with respect to which parents are particularly vulnerable to the advice of professionals, notably educational psychologists (Tomlinson, 1981, 1982). It is frequently argued that due to the lack of practical skills, difficulties caused by physical abnormalities, the disruption caused by hospitalization, and poor facilities in normal schools, children with impairments are better suited in establishments where teachers are specially trained, and class sizes are smaller. Alternatively such institutions can be criticized on the grounds that they reinforce difference by segregating the impaired from the non-impaired. Moreover, because many of these schools are residential they compound this problem by removing the child from the family and the local community, and severing any community ties and any peer group contacts which may have been made (Oliver, 1983a).

There is evidence, however, to suggest that, largely due to a felt need to be with like-situated individuals, some children prefer this type of establishment (Hurst, 1984). It has also been suggested that in some cases children placed in these schools are able to achieve higher levels of independence than would be possible if they remained in the protective environment of the family. Additionally, it has been noted that some parents have difficulty maintaining that independence when the child returns home (Brimblecomb *et al.*, 1985). Conversely, others view these schools less positively.

One study of the experience of impaired pupils in residential schools claimed that they went through several distinct phases. These included 'disorientation' due to the severence of domestic ties and 'depression' as a result of their new-found status given their placement with peers with similar conditions who had not been cured. This was followed by a period of 'pre-adolescent revolt', before moving into a state of 'acceptance' (Minde, 1972). In addition, since many of these establishments bear some, if not all, of the main features of a 'total institution', there is always the danger of 'institutionalization', where the resident begins to prefer life inside, rather than outside the institution (Goffman, 1961). There are also data showing that many special schools do not provide either an adequate education or the skills necessary for adulthood.

All modern education systems, including special schools, purport to fulfil at least two explicit functions: (a) socializing individuals into the norms and values of society, and (b) providing them with the necessary training to find work in accordance with societal needs. In a modern technologically advanced society educational achievement is essential for all young people. For those whose employment opportunities are limited as a result of physical impairment, it is crucial (Hurst, 1984). Yet one commentator has argued that many special schools do not provide even the barest rudimentary knowledge which constitutes a normal primary school curriculum (Tomlinson, 1982), condemning these students to a lifetime characterized by 'dependence and powerlessness' (Barton and Tomlinson, 1984).

There is plenty of empirical evidence to support these claims. For example, an analysis of spina bifida children reported that over a third were considered retarded in reading skills and a large proportion were deficient in maths abilities, although they had no acknowledged mental defect (NFER, 1973). The government-sponsored report on special educational needs stated that

> The evidence presented to us reflects a widespread belief that many special schools underestimate their pupils' abilities. This view was expressed in relation to all levels of ability and disability (Warnock, 1978).

The serious implications of this situation and the ensuing disadvantage caused for individuals with impairments have been reiterated by many writers in the past decade. In a recent review of research about disabled young adults' preparation for and movement into work, which covered research dealing with both normal and special education, Parker stated:

> adequate school leavers' programmes for those with special needs still seem to be the exception rather than the rule. The opinions of both young people and their parents indicate a considerable gap in preparation for life beyond school. Young people with disabilities, especially when they are physical, are less likely to be placed in work experience schemes than other pupils (Parker, 1984, p. 71).

Although there has been some expansion in further and higher education for students with special needs in recent years, the proportion of physically disabled students remains small in comparison to the numbers of disabled people in the population as a whole (Hurst, 1984; Stowell, 1987). One of the main obstacles relates to environmental factors and problems of access and support. While many colleges can and do accommodate students with learning difficulties and mental handicaps, a recent national survey conducted for the Department of Employment by the National Bureau for Handicapped Students (renamed 'SKILL' or the National Bureau for Students with Disabilities in 1988), found that three in five colleges 'might' have to deny a place to students with physical handicaps because of access difficulties or the absence of the 'necessary support' (Stowell, 1987). There is a dearth of analyses of the experience of further education from the perspective of people with physical impairments (Hurst, 1984).

Although it is often said that further education enhances social and work skills and improves the likelihood of employment, this is not the case with regard to teenagers with impairments (Kuh et al., 1988). There is a substantial and growing body of evidence showing that unemployment is disproportionately high among this section of the population (Brimblecomb et al., 1985; Cantrell et al., 1985; Hirst, 1984, 1987; Kuh et al., 1988). People are categorized through work, or paid employment, in terms of class, status and influence. Apart from income, work provides a sense of identity and self-esteem, opportunities for social contacts outside the family home, skill development and creativity, as well as a sense of obligation, time and control (Fagin and Little, 1984). It is particularly important for young adults, as work is generally regarded as the major factor which determines the successful transition from childhood to adulthood. For example, a recent Department of Education and Science study of the views of young people found that employment was seen as defining adulthood and unemployment was the most significant area of concern.

> Employment was the most important symbol signalling entrance into the adult world and was therefore a goal all were striving towards. Unemployment robbed the individual from successfully crossing the boundary between adolescence and adulthood and forced him/her back into a role of dependence on the adult world (DES, 1983, quoted in Kuh *et al.*, 1988, pp. 4–5).

In addition to the general hostility of some employers towards employing people with impairments, it has been suggested that some bosses feel that disabled people are only capable of performing limited tasks. In times of recession when there is a surfeit of labour these problems are made worse (Hurst, 1984). For individuals excluded from the world of work due to physical impairment, the economic, social and psychological implications are clear. Sheltered workshops are sometimes proposed as an acceptable alternative, but since by definition these establishments are segregative, they restrict social interaction with the able-bodied and consequently do little to eliminate a disabled identity.

The teenage years are generally associated with the concept 'adolescence'. While there is no general agreement regarding the duration of the adolescent period, it denotes a psychological process which begins with the individual's awareness of her/his pubescent physical changes and extends to a 'reasonable resolution' of her/his social identity. For most this is said to occur between the ages of 11 and 21 (Anderson and Clarke, 1982). Although there is little systematic data to support this view, some writers see this period as a process of identity formation which involves an emotional separation and detachment from parents (Erikson, 1968). To live independently from parents is commonly perceived as the second most important goal for young people (Hirst, 1987), following the acquisition of paid employment. It is a period in which individuals are said to acquire and/or be ascribed new roles. But the acquisition of new roles is frequently problematic and sometimes associated with psychological maladjustment and conflict, notably with parents. While it is a period regarded as difficult for most children, several studies have shown that adolescence is especially difficult for people with physical impairments.

For many young people with impairments adolescence signifies a growing sense of difference between themselves and their able-bodied peers. In the post-school years many teenagers become critically aware of the future and the limits which their disabilities and society impose upon their performance of a full complement of adult roles (Thomas, 1982). This can cause severe psychological problems which one source referred to as the 'slough of despond' (Brimblecomb *et al.*, 1985). One of the most influential studies concerned with these issues compared the post-school experiences of teenagers with congenital impairments to those of the non-impaired, and found that adolescence with disability was synonymous with four main characteristics. These were: (a) a high incidence of dissatisfaction concerning their social lives, particularly during the post-school years, (b) the feeling that they had little control over their lives and knew little about their 'handicaps' or the services available, (c) a poverty of choice available to those unable to find open employment, and (d) an ill-preparedness for the realities of life as adults (Anderson and Clarke, 1982). Their general lack of preparation for the adult world reflected the fact that they had been socialized into a life of social and economic dependence which would be unacceptable for other sections of the population. It is not surprising that those individuals disabled in adolescence are reluctant to accept this devalued and dependent position.

The evidence clearly suggests that the experience of childhood for those with impairments is very likely to be different to that of the able-bodied, that any subjective disadvantage resulting from impairment is frequently exacerbated by other economic and social factors, and that as a result they face a future of extreme economic and social disadvantage, dependent on both their families and/or the state. The following section shows that many, if not all, of the considerations discussed above were applicable to most Contact users.

The Main Social Characteristics of the Contact Users prior to their Introduction into the Day Centres

In this section I shall examine the data gleaned from both user interviews and, where appropriate, official day centre records regarding the users' life experiences before they began using the day centre service. It is divided into five separate parts covering (a) age distribution and social class, (b) impairments, (c) education, (d) work experience, and (e) accommodation. The evidence shows that besides physical impairments, the majority of this user group were seriously disadvantaged in terms of education and work experience and were dependent on their families for domestic arrangements. Consequently they were unable to attain the necessary economic and social independence normally associated with adulthood.

(a) Age Distribution and Social Class

Of the thirty-six Contact users fourteen were female. One of the group, Wendy, was from an Afro-Carribean background. One male named Mark was also black, but left shortly after the study started because he was found a place in a residential institution outside Contact's catchment area. The average age of the Contact members was 22.5 years. Eight of the group were 25 or over, the oldest being 30. Eight were under 20. The youngest was 17. In respect of the Registrar General's occupational classification (OCPS, 1980) only four of the sample were originally from homes where the head of the household was a non-manual worker. At the time of interview, apart from Wendy and Clive who had been living in local authority homes since the ages of five and seven respectively, fifteen respondents lived in households that were characterized by unemployment, elderly, chronically sick or lone parents. Of the three not interviewed, Amy and Alison were from one-parent families and Michael lived in a foster home. This pattern is particularly significant considering the mounting evidence of the financial burden endured by families caring for children with impairments.

(b) Impairments

Including Amy, Alison and Michael, twenty-five of the thirty-six Contact members were congenitally impaired. Fourteen were born with cerebral palsy and seven with spina bifida and hydrocephalus. Spina bifida describes a number of congenital malformations of the spine which sometimes causes paralysis. It is often accompanied by hydrocephalus which refers to excessive fluid around the brain. Cerebral palsy and spina bifida are the two most common causes of impairment in children in modern Britian (Anderson and Clarke, 1982).

Of the remainder congenitally impaired, one girl, called Molly, was born with curvature of the spine and another, Sheila, had dystrophic dwarfism. She was barely 122 centimetres tall. Karen, a rubella victim, had no overt physical impairment but her activities were inhibited by respiratory and heart problems. Two males had contracted hereditary degenerative diseases. Gavin had muscular dystrophy and had been unable to walk since he was 10, and Billy's Friedrich's ataxia become overt in his 16th year. Two other males became impaired due to severe cerebral haemorrhages. Matthew's was caused by meningitis which he contracted at 8. It left him a partial hemiplegic. Bruce's paraplegia was the result of a brain haemorrhage caused by a benign brain tumour when he was 5. Including Amy, four of the Contact members were prone to epileptic-type seizures. These included Bruce, Andy, a 27-year-old with cerebral palsy and Angela, who had spina bifida. Nancy was born with hydrocephalus. Roger, the eldest in the group, contracted a neurological disorder of unknown origin with similar symptoms to muscular sclerosis at the age of 25. He was easily tired, extremely weak and walked with a permanent stoop. Five males, John, Charles, Spike, Philip and Robert, were impaired as a result of road traffic accidents.

Other than Robert, who would be termed functionally blind although retaining approximately 4 or 5 per cent of what he could see before his accident when his eyesight was considered normal, a number of the group had noticable eye problems. Several wore thicker than normal spectacles and held books or objects of interest unusually close to their faces when looking at them. Three users, Billy, John and Norman, said they were supposed to wear glasses for reading but chose not to, and five others had pronounced squints. Margaret, Gavin, Nancy, Millie and Curt would be regarded as grossly overweight, a common problem among teenagers with mobility problems (Anderson and Clarke, 1982).

Although Nancy had no problems with walking, she, along with the other four, who were all reliant on wheelchairs, had been on permanent diets for as long as they could remember.

Although the criterion for group membership was officially physical impairment, one user, Richard, had no such recorded condition. He was said to have experienced 'behavioural difficulties' as an infant. He had joined the group

Table 11   Age and Principal Impairments of the Contact Users

| Name | Age | Age at onset of Impairment | Cause of Impairment | Extent of Impairment | | |
				Lower Limbs	Upper Limbs	Others
Margaret	23	birth	SB/HC	both	—	—
Tony	18	birth	CP	both	both	—
Joyce	25	birth	CP	both	both	—
Billy	17	15.5	FA	both	—	—
Andy	27	birth	CP	one	one	epilepsy
John	20	17	RTA	both	both	—
Sheila	20	birth	DD	both	—	—
Jamie	24	birth	CP	one	one	—
Sally	19	birth	SB/HC	both	—	—
Karen	18	birth	Rubella	—	—	respiration/heart
Molly	25	birth	SC	—	—	—
Matthew	24	8	Meningitis	one	one	—
Paul	18	birth	CP	one	one	—
Gavin	19	birth	MD	both	both	—
Norman	22	birth	CP	both	—	—
Barry	18	birth	CP	one	one	—
James	22	birth	SB/HC	both	—	—
Henry	20	birth	CP	one	one	—
Marilyn	25	birth	CP	one	one	—
Bruce	20	5	BT	both	one	epilepsy
Nancy	20	birth	HC	—	—	—
Angela	21	birth	SB/HC	both	—	epilepsy
Millie	21	birth	SB/HC	both	—	—
Richard	20	unknown	Behavioural	—	—	—
Wendy	18	birth	CP	one	—	—
Curt	21	birth	SB/HC	both	one	—
Roger	30	25	NDUO	—	—	—
Elizabeth	23	birth	CP	one	—	—
Charles	27	17	RTA	both	both	speech
Spike	21	18	RTA	one	—	coordination
Philip	28	24	RTA	one	one	—
Robert	26	20	RTA	—	—	eyesight
Clive	21	birth	SB/HC	both	—	—

Key
SB	= Spina Bifida		MD	= Muscular Dystrophy
CP	= Cerebral Palsy		BT	= Brain Tumour
RTA	= Road traffic accident		HC	= Hydrocephalus
DD	= Dystrophic Dwarfism		FA	= Freidrich's Ataxia
NDUO	= Neurological disorder of unknown origin		SC	= Spinal curvature
			—	= no impairment

Source: user interviews and official day centre records

in 1982 on a probationary basis, largely because he had attended the same school as most of the other group members. Apart from a spell in Spain, where his mother went to work in a bar, he has been with the group ever since.

It was clear from the formal interviews that while a minority knew a great deal about their conditions, Joyce, Jamie and Marilyn being notable examples, the majority knew relatively little. Eleven did not know the name or the cause of their impairments. In addition, all the group had spent lengthy periods in hospitals, many before they went to school. Several could recall first meeting other Contact members while in hospital, This applied not only to the congenitally impaired. Matthew, for example, was at one stage in the same ward as Charles and Spike.

In terms of mobility, sixteen of the group were solely dependent on wheelchairs. Three could not walk without crutches and Sheila, who had a double prosthesis for her legs, used a walking frame when indoors. These four all used wheelchairs when outside the centres or the family home. At least five of the remainder were receiving mobility allowance, which at the time of this study was a state benefit paid to individuals who were deemed by a doctor to be unable to walk more than 200 yards due to physical impairment (see Disability Alliance, 1986/7), because of their unsteady gait. Only Richard and Robert walked normally, although Robert seldom moved about without a guide. Five had restricted use of both upper limbs and a further ten had limited use of one arm or hand. Joyce, Billy, Karen, Marilyn and Spike all had mild speech impairments. Although these defects did not apparently impede verbal communication they were a source of embarrassment since they all 'slurred' their words, which they felt made them sound 'thick' or 'stupid'. Ten Contact members were incontinent and a further three needed help with toileting.

(c) Education

Twenty-six of the respondents had attended special schools of one kind or another at some stage during their pre-16 school years. Nine had received some of their education in residential schools, seven of these between the ages of 5 and 11. Sheila had spent all but one of her school years in this type of institution. Moreover, five of the group had attended the same boarding school and twenty-two had been to the same day school, which I shall call the Christy Brown School.

Christy Brown is described in official documents as 'an LEA school catering for the special needs of physically handicapped pupils between the ages of 2 and 16' (Huchinson, 1987). It is non-residential with a capacity for 120 children. The staff includes teachers, special unit teachers for communication aids and special needs, nursery nurses, nurses, care attendants and physiotherapists. The school provides facilities for education and 'personal and social development'. All pupils have transport provided by the school and the school day starts at 9.30 a.m. and finishes at 3.30 p.m.

Of those who attended residential schools only Clive maintained he was happy to have left home because his parents were in the process of separating at the time. All the others in this group said they had not wanted to go, but with hindsight believed it had been beneficial in terms of improving self-determination and personal independence. Seven of the sample had attended both special and normal schools. One of them, John, had been assigned to a school for children with learning difficulties when he was eleven, six years before the accident which caused his paraplegia. Only seven members of Contact had attended ordinary state comprehensives for their entire school lives. Of these, two had manifested impairments before their sixteenth birthday.

Sixteen of those who had been to special schools said they were dissatisfied with their education. Fourteen had difficulty with the three Rs, and ten reported problems when handling money. All blamed their schooling for this state of affairs. Some felt their teachers had concentrated far too much on their physical problems and not enough on their formal education. Of the seven who had attended both special and normal schools, Karen, Nancy, Richard and Wendy, all ambulatory and marginally physically impaired when compared with others in Contact, had profoundly unpleasant memories of time spent in ordinary schools. They each said they were targets for bullying by non-impaired children and were much happier after they returned to the special school. All had been introduced to a normal school environment before the age of 8 and none stayed longer than a year. Andy and James both went into an ordinary comprehensive when they were 14. Andy was non-commital about the experience, but James was relatively positive about it, although he admitted he missed his former classmates.

The highest achievers were those who had gone to ordinary state or segregated boarding schools. Robert had seven GCE O level passes and Charles, Philip and Roger each had four. Billy and Matthew got one CSE apiece. Spike maintained he had had little interest in school and said that after the age of eleven he had done his best 'to avoid the place'.* Andy got one GCE and one CSE and James passed CSE maths. Of those who had been in residential institutions at some point, Sheila had attained three CSEs, Marilyn two and Joyce one.

None of the Contact group had any experience of higher education but nineteen had been on some form of post-16 provision. Excluding Roger, Charles, Philip and Robert who had been to college in conjunction with their employment before their disablement, sixteen users had been on vocational education and independence-type courses for the physically impaired. Andy and Jamie had attended residential colleges for one and two years respectively, and Tony was actually on one of these courses at the time of the study. He only used Contact during the vacations. Robert had been on a three-month independence training programme for the visually impaired at a college in Torquay in 1984, three years after his first accident and one year after his second when he was knocked down by a car.

The majority had been on the same independence-type course, albeit not all at the same time. It was a one or two year scheme depending on perceived need. Six had taken the two-year option and seven the one. Although this course was situated in an able-bodied college it was clear from the numerous informal discussions with ex-students that there had been little interaction between them

Table 12 Education and the Contact Users

Name	Type of school			Further Education		
	Normal	Special	Qualifications received	Normal	Special	Qualifications received
Margaret	—	12 yrs	—	—	2 yrs	—
Tony	—	12 yrs R	—	—	1.5 yrs R	C&G
Joyce	—	12 yrs R	1 CSE	2 yrs	2 yrs	6 GCE
Billy	12 yrs	—	1 CSE	—	—	—
Andy	2 yrs	10 yrs	1 CSE	2 yrs*	1 yr R	1 GCE
John	6 yrs	6 yrs	—	—	—	—
Sheila	—	12 yrs R	3 CSE	—	2 yrs	—
Jamie	—	12 yrs R	—	—	2 yrs R	—
Sally	—	12 yrs	—	—	—	—
Karen	1 yr	11 yrs	—	—	—	—
Molly	—	12 yrs	—	—	2 yrs	2 CSE
Matthew	12 yrs	—	1 CSE	—	—	—
Paul	—	12 yrs	—	—	1 yr	—
Gavin	—	12 yrs	—	—	—	—
Norman	—	12 yrs	—	—	—	—
Barry	—	12 yrs R	—	—	1 yr	—
James	2 yrs	10 yrs	1 CSE	1.5 yrs	1 yr	C&G
Henry	—	12 yrs	—	—	—	—
Marilyn	—	12 yrs R	2 CSE	—	—	—
Bruce	—	12 yrs	—	—	—	—
Nancy	1 yr	11 yrs	—	—	—	—
Angela	—	12 yrs	—	—	1 yr	—
Millie	—	12 yrs	—	—	1 yr	—
Richard	1 yr	11 yrs	—	—	2 yrs	—
Wendy	1 yr	11 yrs	—	—	1 yr	—
Curt	—	12 yrs	—	—	—	—
Roger	12 yrs	—	4 GCE	—	—	—
Elizabeth	—	12 yrs	—	—	2 yrs	—
Charles	12 yrs	—	4 GCE	1 yr*	—	—
Spike	12 yrs	—	—	—	—	—
Philip	12 yrs	—	4 GCE	2 yrs*	—	—
Robert	12 yrs	—	7 GCE	4 yrs*	3 mts R	BTEC
Clive	—	12 yrs R	—	—	1 yr	—

Key
yr/s = years   CSE = Certificate of Secondary Education
mts = months   GCE = General Certificate of Education
* = part-time   R = residential
C&G = City & Guilds
BTEC = British Technical Education Council
       Award

Source: user interviews

and the non-impaired, either in the classroom or the common room. The reasons for this were unclear.

Three respondents had been on courses for the non-impaired. Joyce had studied full-time for two years for GCE O levels and received six passes. Andy successfully completed a two-year part-time GCE maths course and James had been on an eighteen-month computer training scheme. All three viewed these experiences positively because they had enjoyed the social aspects of college life.

But they were clearly disappointed that their efforts had not led anywhere, particularly with regard to finding employment.

(d) Work Experience

Only seven of the thirty-six Contact users had any experience of paid employment other than government supported work or training programmes. Charles, Roger, Spike, Philip and Robert were not impaired when in work. None of them have

Table 13 Work Experience and the Contact Users

Name	ATC Duration	YOP Duration	Open Employment Description	Duration
Margaret	1 month	—	—	—
Tony	—	—	—	—
Joyce	—	—	—	—
Billy	—	—	—	—
Andy	10 weeks	—	labourer	6 months (PT)
John	—	10 months	—	—
Sheila	—	—	—	—
Jamie	10 weeks	—	—	—
Sally	—	—	—	—
Karen	—	—	—	—
Molly	—	12 months	—	—
Matthew	—	12 months	—	—
Paul	—	—	—	—
Gavin	—	—	—	—
Norman	1 week	—	—	—
Barry	—	—	—	—
James	—	—	—	—
Henry	2 weeks	—	—	—
Marilyn	—	—	shop work	6 months
Bruce	—	—	—	—
Nancy	—	12 months	—	—
Angela	—	—	—	—
Millie	—	—	—	—
Richard	—	—	—	—
Wendy	—	—	—	—
Curt	—	—	—	—
Roger	—	—	various	9 years
Elizabeth	—	—	—	—
Charles	—	—	engineer	1.5 years
Spike	—	—	soldier	1 year
Philip	—	—	various	6 years
Robert	—	—	surveyer	4 years
Clive	—	—	—	—

Key
ATC   = Adult Training Centre
YOP   = Youth Opportunity Programme
PT   = part-time working

Source: user interviews

worked since the onset of their impairments. Of the twenty-eight labelled 'disabled' at 16, only two had any experience of a proper job. Andy got himself some part time work in a local garage 'just 'elpin' out'.* But he had to give it up when his back was injured after being hit by a car on his way to work. He had been knocked down twice in his life, once when he was 10 and again in 1984 at the age of 24. When Marilyn left school her careers officer got her a job in a local branch of a well-known British-owned department store. She was sacked after three days on the grounds that she constituted a fire risk. Her father then secured her a post in a local supermarket filling shelves. She was dismissed after six months after a management change, because her work was considered too slow.

Four of the group had been on government work schemes which at this juncture were referred to as the 'Youth Opportunities Programme'. John, who was not impaired at the time, moved straight from school on to one of these schemes. His attendance was cut short after ten months by his accident. Matthew went on a similar programme to learn the upholstery trade. Molly and Nancy worked in the kitchens of old people's homes to gain an insight into the catering industry. Although these three all said that they enjoyed the work and encountered no difficulties doing it, when the government support finished so did the jobs. They had not worked since.

It is important to note that Andy, Marilyn, Molly and Nancy were moderately impaired compared to others in Contact. They were all ambulatory and although Andy, Matthew and Marilyn each had restricted use of one arm, they each felt this did not pose a major problem. Five of the group had been directed toward the Adult Training Centre (ATC) run by the Spastics Society before their involvement with Contact. None of them viewed the experience positively in terms of skill acquisition or personal development. They all maintained that the high percentage of people with mental handicaps in this establishment had been the single most important reason for leaving. The stark absence of work experience among the majority of Contact members is particularly alarming considering the importance our society places on gainful employment and the long-term economic, social and psychological implications for the individual due to the lack of it.

(e) Accommodation

Only three of the Contact users had set up homes of their own. Two others were living in long-stay residential institutions and the remainder were living with one or both of their parents or guardians. Two of the adventitiously impaired members of this group had moved out of the family home before the onset of their impairment, but had to move back in after they became disabled.

Philip had been married for two years before his accident and was living with his wife and daughter. Jamie and Andy were the only two congenitally impaired Contact users who had managed to become independent from their respective parents, albeit both were from one-parent families. The former shared a council flat with his disabled girlfriend Alice and their baby daughter, prior to which he had lived with his father. Alice was a partial hemiplegic which was caused by a stroke when she was 25. Before her preganancy in 1986 she had been a regular day centre user. Andy was the only Contact member who lived alone. He had a small bedsit about half a mile away from his mother's home which he visited almost daily.

Although Wendy lived in a children's home with able-bodied peers, she was deeply unhappy there. She felt the other children were always making fun of her

Table 14 Accommodation and the Contact Users

Name	User's home	Others living in home	Current occupation of male head of household
Margaret	PH	M/F	builder
Tony	PH	M	—
Joyce	PH	M/F	overhead cable jointer
Billy	PH	M/F/2S	unemployed
Andy	OH	—	unemployed
John	PH	M/F	factory worker
Sheila	PH	M/2S	—
Jamie	OH	G/D	unemployed
Sally	PH	M/F/2S	telephone engineer
Karen	PH	M/F/1S	lay preacher
Molly	PH	M/1S	—
Matthew	PH	M/F	motor mechanic
Paul	PH	M/F/1S	auditor/cashier
Gavin	PH	M	—
Norman	PH	M	—
Barry	PH	M/F/A	retired
James	PH	M/F	salesman
Henry	PH	M/F	lorry driver
Marilyn	PH	M/F	builder
Bruce	PH	F	gasfitter
Nancy	PH	F	cook
Angela	PH	M/F	motor mechanic
Millie	PH	M	—
Richard	PH	M/1S	—
Wendy	RH	unknown	—
Curt	PH	M/F	unemployed
Roger	PH	M/SF	engineer
Elizabeth	PH	M/F/1S	council worker
Charles	PH	M/F	retired
Spike	PH	M/SF	unemployed
Philip	OH	W/D	unemployed
Robert	PH	M/F/2S	toolmaker
Clive	RH	unknown	—

Key
PH = parental home   SF = stepfather
OH = own home   S = siblings
RH = residential home   G = girlfriend
M = mother   D = daughter
F = father   A = aunt
                            W = wife

Source: user interviews

and desperately wanted to move somewhere else. Clive was situated in a residential institution for the physically impaired run by the local authority and had been since he left college. While he was used to life in segregated institutions and had few happy memories of life with his parents, he disliked his present circumstances since he had no privacy and little independence. Of the remainder, Bruce and Nancy lived with their respective fathers and seven others with their mothers. Although they had both left home before their impairment, Roger and Spike were living with their mothers and stepfathers. The former had initially left because he could not get on with his mother after his father had died and did not like her choice of boyfriend, the man who later became his stepfather. Both Spike's mother and stepfather were disabled. She had multiple sclerosis and he rheumatoid arthritis. Both were regular attenders at the Alf Morris centre. Seven of the sample lived in households where there were siblings present.

For the majority, therefore, some degree of dependence on parents was inevitable. With regard to the problem of parental over-protectiveness, fifteen users complained that they were 'mollycoddled' by one or both of the principal family members. Nancy, for example, said that as she grew older her father's attitude towards her seemed to be becoming more restrictive. Joyce felt she was 'smothered' by both her parents. Nine respondents expressed an awareness of regular conflict within the family home, either between themselves and one or, where appropriate, both parents which they felt was the result of their impairment. In most cases this was related to their need for independence and parental reluctance to give it.

I have focused on the main social characteristics of the Contact users and have shown the majority to have been disadvantaged both with regard to open employment and residential independence of parents, the two most important prerequisites for entry into the adult world. Most of the Contact users were from the manual working classes and were brought up in environments characterized by some form of parental or economic deprivation. Although there was some variation in the level and cause of impairment, the majority were congenitally impaired and mobility was a major problem for most. Consistent with the findings of other studies in this field, there was a lack of knowledge among respondents about their impairments. Although all definitions are problematic, I believe that the majority would be regarded as moderately to severely impaired by the general public.

Most of the group had spent much, if not all, of their childhood in segregated environments, in hospitals, special schools and in some cases residential institutions. Many had attended the same hospitals and schools. They expressed a high degree of dissatisfaction about their education, particularly in terms of their academic achievements, which adds weight to some of the criticisms levelled at special schools. Those who had attended residential schools viewed the experience positively in terms of independence skills. Although over half of those impaired at 16 had been on some form of vocational/independence training in further education and a minority had gone on to courses for the non-impaired, these experiences did little to help them find a job.

The experience of paid employment for those disabled at 16 was extremely limited. This was in stark contrast to that of the five adventitiously impaired who had never been out of work prior to the onset of their disability. It is significant that none had worked since. As a result all were economically dependent on the state. In addition, the data show that most of the group were dependent on their families for accommodation and that there was a high degree of dissatisfaction among many concerning their domestic arrangements.

In short, the majority of these young people entered the post-education phase with few opportunities to develop control over and responsibility for their own lives. They had literally been socialized into a life of economic and social disadvantage and child-like dependence. The remainder were thrust into this disadvantaged position after the onset of their impairment. It is clear that all were particularly dependent for the quality of their future lives on the services provided for them. The following section examines how they were channelled into the day centres and how they have adapted to this situation within the context of the Contact group.

How the Contact Users were Introduced to Day Services

Since day centre attendance is not compulsory and is frequently regarded as the least desirable option available to young people with physical impairments, it is important to establish how and why the individuals in the Contact group first became involved with the service. The data in this section show that the majority entered the system for explicitly social reasons, either to maintain long-standing peer group relations or to escape the debilitating social isolation encountered when their education finished. It is also apparent that some were directed toward the system to assist in their rehabilitation. The evidence in this section underpins the poverty of economic and social opportunities available to these young people after formal education, shows how little control they had over their lives during this period and highlights how influential professionals are with regard to shaping their future.

Throughout the study, eligibility for a day centre place for the younger physically impaired, as for other potential day centre users, was dependent on a recognized physical impairment and a referral by an acknowledged professional such as a doctor, social worker or careers officer. If an individual contacted one of the centres with a view to becoming a user, they were directed to their nearest social services offices where someone would furnish them with the necessary document. All senior staff maintained that refusal was almost non-existent.

Unlike other day centre users, however, the introduction to the idea of day centre use for the younger impaired who had been through some form of special education, could be either a collective or an individual experience. The Christy Brown school and the local college of further education which ran courses for students with special needs periodically organized visits to the Contact group for students who the school or college staff felt would have difficulty finding alternatives. The visits were initiated by careers officers at the school and college and organized through consultation with Contact staff. At least nine of the users vividly recalled being made aware of Contact through this method.

The practice began shortly after Jayne had forged links with these two institutions in 1981–82, when she was getting the group started. Recent amendments to the Youth Training Programme, however, such as the introduction of the YTS2 scheme in April 1986 (Cooper, 1986), have meant that these visits have been less frequent in recent years and that the level of impairment of those recommended for referral has become noticably more severe.

One of these visits took place on 14 May 1987 as my involvement with the centres was drawing to a close. One Wednesday morning at the Alf Morris centre, Jackie, who was at this time the senior activity organizer (SAO) for Contact, casually announced that in the afternoon the group was to be visited by a party from the local college of further education. No special arrangements were made, no extra tidying up was done and none of the users or staff seemed unduly concerned about the event. When I asked Jackie why no special preparations were made, she told me she did not wish to give any false impressions of the group which might detract from the relaxed social atmosphere which normally prevailed. At about 1.45 p.m. the party arrived. It consisted of Graham, the careers officer at the college, a home economics tutor and four students, three boys and a girl. Two of the boys were wheelchair-bound and had muscular dystrophy. The other youth walked using arm crutches but had a severe speech impairment. He had been seriously injured in a motorcycle crash. The girl needed no assistance walking but had an unsteady gait due to cerebral palsy. She was also an epileptic.

Upon arrival the party were casually introduced to everyone by Jackie, although it was clear that for many no introduction was necessary, since no sooner had they arrived than the newcomers began to renew acquaintances with those Contact members who had recently attended the college, and/or were introduced to others they did not know by those they did. Gradually they dispersed into a number of subgroups where the general conversation revolved around recent developments at the college and life in the day centres. As far as I could tell, none of the users were derogatory in their references to the Contact group or the Alf Morris centre. The college staff proceeded to chat with some of their ex-students and the centre personnel. Once the interaction was well under way, Jackie and Graham adjourned to the Contact office where the relevant information about the prospective users was discussed. After about fifteen minutes they returned and Contact staff served tea and biscuits to the visitors in the larger of the two rooms. This was the only concession to formality which occurred during the entire afternoon. At 3.00 p.m. Graham decided it was time to leave. Goodbyes were exchanged and the party left. The visit was viewed by everyone in the Contact group as a largely social event, but they were aware of its purpose since many had been through a similar experience themselves.

Individual introductions generally followed a similar pattern but the candidates would be brought to one of the centres by the professional making the referral. These visits could also include members of the individual's family or, if s/he lived in a residential home, one of the institution's staff. This occurred twice while I was with Contact. On 2 July 1986 Paul was brought to Alf Morris by Graham from the college mentioned above, and a similar sequence of events took place, apart from the tea and biscuits. According to senior Contact staff, however, it was more usual for those making the referral to contact the SAO, who would then either visit the potential user and her/his family at home and subsequently arrange a visit to the centres, or, if this was not deemed appropriate or necessary, they would be invited to have a look round. This happened on 3 November 1986 when Jayne brought Clive and the manager of the residential home where he lived to Alf Morris. Both Paul and Clive knew other Contact users before their visits and both joined the group one week later.

At some stage during these proceedings a discussion between the SAO and the users concerning the facilities offered, proposed attendance and transport arrangements would take place. Although not always possible, these discussions were seen as crucial by senior Contact staff for three reasons. Firstly, the data on many of the referrals is considered grossly inadequate in relation to the degree of impairment, abilities, and the level of disadvantage experienced. Initially some referrals contain as few as thirty words, including only the individuals' name, address, date of birth, GP's name and address, and primary disability. And according to Andrew, the officer in charge (OIC) at Alf Morris, the latter 'may only be three letters — CVA (cerebral vascular accident or stroke)'.* There is often little reference to the extent of the individual's impairment, secondary impairments, previous experiences, emotional state, or family background. Arguing that too much information could influence their attitudes and subsequent interactions with users some staff easily defended the paucity of data on referrals. They felt staff/user relations should be constructed on first-hand experience and not on data received from external sources.

A second reason for an initial discussion with prospective users is to ascertain how their needs could be accommodated within the service on offer. For example, some people might require a five-day service, others less. Thirdly, for some prospective Contact users, either because of their youth or degree of impairment, the initial decision to attend day centres is not always theirs. Consequently their expectations of the service, and sometimes those of their families, may not correspond to the facilities and services provided.

These considerations were underpinned when related to the users' accounts of their preliminary involvement with the day centre system. While some appear to have begun using the service without much objection, others entered the system with varying degrees of reluctance. At least three maintained they were given little opportunity to do anything else. Two of the group joined Contact before they left school, simply because there was no one at home to look after them during the long summer holidays. They appeared to be relatively happy with this situation and had given no serious thought to the alternatives. Both were confined to wheelchairs and had been educated in special schools throughout their lives. Four others started with the group as soon as they left formal education.

Although they were all aware that the day centre option was voluntary, they viewed it with an air of fatalistic optimism. Sally for example stated,

> 'We cem round from school an' I knew a few of 'em 'ere, Margaret an' Norman an' them. An' it looked alright, nobody seemed to be tellin' 'em what to do or owt. So I couldn't see any point in goin' to college so I cem traight 'ere.'*

Although familiar with the day centre service through school or college, many of the group initially rejected the idea of attendance in the hope that they would find something else. Over two-thirds had previously held distinctly negative views of the day centre option, a view shared by many similarly disadvantaged young people (Jowett, 1982; Kent *et al.*, 1984). However, after protracted periods of inactivity, which ranged from a matter of weeks to almost a year in one case, they each decided that it was better than nothing and contacted either Jayne or their social worker. In all, nine joined Contact via this method. A typical example was Sheila who had been made aware of the group by the careers officer at college, but had not bothered to have a look round because she anticipated finding a job.

> 'I wasn't very interested when she [the careers officer] was on about it at college. I thought I'd get something better . . . . But it didn't work out like that. As soon as I left college I was quite stuck. So after about eight weeks I thought I'd better do something about this 'cos I was gettin' really fed up. So I rang Jayne and asked her if I could come and have a look round. And . . . , I started a week later.'* — Sheila

Several of the users interviewed felt that, at the outset at least, they had little choice whether or not they should begin using the service. Four said that the decision to take up this option had been made by their parents in an effort to find something to do and get them out of the house. Nancy, for example, stated,

> 'Me dad just said "a kind o' social worker's been". He says to me "I've got you in like a day centre where it'll get you out an' about to meet friends". So I says, "Is that so?" So 'e says "Ye'h it is, it's down M----- Road as far as I know, an' I can't tell you any more". So I says, "Well what do they do there?" An' 'e says "you can do anything there". That's 'ow I first got to know about this place. The followin' mornin', taxi cem to pick me up.'*

One member of the group, Jamie, maintains he was coerced into going to the centres by his probation officer on the basis that it would help 'straighten' him out after his second criminal conviction. Others were advised to use the service on medical grounds. Three respondents clearly recalled their doctors and physiotherapists recommending day centre attendance as part of their rehabilitation after the onset of their respective impairments. However, one individual suffering from a degenerative hereditary disease, was presented with little alternative during his final year at school.

> 'Well me social worker cem to our 'ouse right. Well first of all in March [1985], before I left school . . . , when I was 16, this woman cem, an 'ealth an' safety worker or som't like that, a fattish woman wi' blonde 'air, she drove round in a BMW right. She told me I didn't need to try to get a job right. 'Cos I 'adn't t' fix machinery or owt like that, 'cos o' me safety. Like at Remploy or on a YTS scheme OK. In August Karen [specialist social worker for the physically disabled at that time] cem, an' she said she was gonna' tek me down the YTS. She told me if I didn't like it then I could come to a day centre. We went down this YTS place right, an' I didn't like it.'* — Billy

Up to this point Billy had led a relatively normal life, despite the fact that he had been diagnosed as having Freidrich's ataxia. He had attended a normal comprehensive school, knew little of his disease — neither its name nor its degenerative nature — and had experienced few visible symptoms other than an occasional loss of balance.

While Jamie and those directed into the system on medical grounds felt they had little real choice as to whether they should begin using the service, at least they had some inkling of why they were there. This was not the case for Wendy and Paul. Both said they were directed into the system after one year of further education by college staff, without any alternative being offered and with no explanation.[2] Paul stated,

> 'Graham, careers tutor at college, 'e cem up to me an 'e says "I think I've got somethin' for you", meanin' 'e's got some kind 'o place right, on a YTS or somat. An' I got all excited an everythin'. So I says "Where is it?" An 'e says "It's Alf Morris day centre". An' me face dropped . . . . Like we'd been round it at school an' I didn't think much of it then . . . . An' 'e just says, "When do you want to start"? An' I didn't know what to say . . . . So I just says, "Monday?" I 'ad a week off from college, an' that were it.'*

These placements were surprising since neither Paul nor Wendy suffered from a degenerative illness. They were both relatively moderately impaired when compared to others who had remained on the course for two years, but both had difficulty with basic literacy and numeracy skills. According to Jayne, they were referred to Contact simply because college staff felt that neither would benefit from another year in further education and there was nowhere else for them to go.

Despite the fact that all the users were aware that their continued attendance was voluntary, many felt they were presented with little alternative once their education ceased. Although conscious of the unemployment situation generally, they felt that the specialist careers services were at fault. In particular, they had been presented with inadequate information regarding other options and claimed they received no practical help in finding a job. This seems to be a common complaint among most young people with special needs who do not, on the whole, find contact with careers services very helpful (Parker, 1984). It is not surprising therefore that a substantial number were deeply unhappy about their present situation.

Three main reasons emerge as to why the majority of users sampled began using day centres. Firstly, some saw the centres as an opportunity to maintain long-established peer group contacts. This is an important consideration for all adolescents (Brake, 1980), but particularly so for individuals like those who, due to their restricted physical mobility as well as educational and social disadvantage had few social contacts outside school and were almost certainly aware that making new ones would be difficult. This is a common concern for many young people with physical impairments (Anderson and Clarke, 1982). Secondly, others, acutely conscious of the stigma attached to day centres and those who used them, viewed attendance as the only alternative to the debilitating psychological effects of the social isolation they encountered in the post-education year. Thirdly, some, mainly the adventitiously impaired, believed they were channelled into the system to aid their rehabilitation.

While this evidence clearly demonstrates the influence of professionals with regard to shaping the futures of young people with impairments, it also underlines the extreme lack of economic and social opportunities available to these individuals once formal education concludes. Moreover, although some criticism may be levelled at professionals for introducing people to the day centre environment at such a relatively young age (particularly since many are likely to be susceptible to professional guidance, if only because of their previous experiences, and day centre attendance is normally seen, by both the general public and many day centre users, as the last option) any censures against these workers must be set within the context of restricted opportunities.

User Interactions within the Context of the Contact Group

There were four main user subdivisions within Contact which were differentiated by the degree of impairment and perceived dependence. Among these subdivisions were two friendship groupings, cliques or subcultures. The term subculture is used here to refer to the

> accumulated meanings and means of expression through which groups in subordinate structural positions have attempted to negotiate or oppose the dominant meaning system. They therefore provide a pool of available symbolic resources which particular individuals or groups can draw on in their attempt to make sense of their own specific situation and construct a viable identity (Murdock, 1974, quoted in Brake, 1980, p. 63).

One of these friendship groupings was characterized by its members' homogeneity in terms of physical impairments, long-established relations and affective interactions, and the other is distinguished mainly by its members' autonomy. These two cliques were characterized by opposing perceptions of dependence and day centre attendance, a disparity explained with reference to the degree of impairment experienced by the principal clique members and by their socialization. The remaining two subdivisions were less cohesive and exhibited less internal homogeneity. For neither would be designation 'subculture' seem appropriate yet they were distinguishable from one another and from those two subdivisions which coalesced as cliques. None of the various subdivisions was determined by gender, although sex-related behaviour was clearly evident in each of the groups observed.

The four subdivisions will be discussed sequentially with reference to the generally perceived level of physical impairment, the more severely physically impaired coming first. Although it is accepted that all organizations, regardless of size, will have an informal hierarchy (Hargreaves, 1975) the order of presentation is not intended to imply anything about status position in any such hierarchy. While some of the members of the fourth grouping identified were accorded the highest regard by many users, and to some degree by the staff, because of their relative autonomy outside the day centres, this did not apply to all. The question of informal hierarchy is further complicated by the severity and nature of impairment. For example, individuals from both the first and third subdivisions were universally held in high esteem, but excluded from a great deal of informal social activity because of their physical limitations.

In focusing on informal interactions within Contact, it is important to emphasize that user behaviour was variously constrained by environmental features characterizing the three day centres. Intra-group cleavages were almost impossible to detect, for example, at the Engineers' centre where users' movements and interactions were controlled by both the environment and the type of activities provided. The following evidence, unless otherwise stated, is for this reason taken from the observed interactions at the Alf Morris and Dortmund Square units.

The first subdivision, subgroup A, included five users who were the most severely physically, and in one case psychologically, impaired people in the Contact group. They were Alison and Michael (two of the users I was unable to interview), Tony, Charles and Robert. Unlike many 'blind' people, Robert had no confidence whatsoever and would seldom move without assistance from staff after arriving at the centres. He attributed this to the psychological impact of losing his sight. Because of their impairments, all five were generally 'parked' on their arrival at the central tables in the main room at Alf Morris, or at a convenient table at Dortmund Square, where they remained for most of the day unless they had a social services' lunch which had to be taken in the dining hall. They were normally excluded from most informal user activity which tended to go on around them. Although interaction with other users did occur, this was usually only when little else was going on, or with one of the others who had only weak subgroup

Table 15 Observed subdivision among Contact Users during Participant observation

Name	Age when started using Contact (years)	Length of attendance (1.1.87) (years)	Weekly attendance (days)	Use of transport	Subgroup location
Margaret	18	5	5	yes	B
Tony	16	2	5	—	A
Joyce	18	3*	3	—	D
Billy	16	1.5	5	—	D
Andy	21	6*	3	no	D
John	19	1	3	yes	C
Sheila	19	0.5	5	yes	C
Jamie	18	6*	3	no	D
Sally	16	3	5	yes	B
Karen	17	1	3	—	C
Molly	19	6*	2	no	D
Matthew	21	3	4	yes	D
Paul	18	0.5	3	—	C
Gavin	16	3	5	—	C
Norman	16	6	5	—	B
Barry	17	1.5	3	—	C
James	20	1.5*	3	—	B
Henry	18	2	3	—	C
Marilyn	19	5	3	—	D
Bruce	17	3	3	—	C
Nancy	18	2	3	—	C
Angela	16	5	5	—	B
Millie	16	5	5	—	B
Richard	17	3*	3	—	C
Wendy	17	1	3	—	C
Curt	16	5	3	—	B
Roger	25	5	3	—	D
Elizabeth	18	5	5	—	C
Charles	24	3	3	—	A
Spike	18	2	3	no	D
Philip	18	4	2	—	D
Robert	23	3	3	yes	A
Clive	20	0.5	2	—	C

Key
* = attendance broken for more than one month when user left Contact to pursue other activities.

Source: user interviews, Contact register and field notes

affiliations, such as Richard or Amy, both of whom were reputed to suffer from 'behavioural' difficulties and were accorded low status by the rest of the group.

These five people were frequently the primary focus of attention for staff both with respect to physical tending and social activity. All apart from Robert needed help with the toilet, although Charles was one of those people who never used it while in the centres. All five were viewed with varying degrees of sympathy by the rest of the users and were considered a high priority for staff/user interaction by all Contact personnel, although like the users some of the care assistants (CAs) appeared to forget them if they were involved in other activities. None of the three interviewed displayed any coherent perception of the centres or of the other users. Charles viewed his attendance and his interactions with the rest of the group as essential for his 'complete recovery'.* He felt empathy with the other users because as far as he was concerned they were in the 'same boat' as him. Tony, the youngest of the five, saw the centres as a 'doss place' where people only came to 'mess about'.* He had no particular friends in the group but still enjoyed coming. Robert, in contrast, was compelled to use the system by his parents and admitted he would stay at home if given the opportunity. He had no friends in the centres other than Sean, the VW who replaced Pete as the group's male CA.

The second subdivision, subgroup B, were easily the most visible and the most cliquish in terms of close personal relationships. The social bonds between members were based on homogeneity, in terms of both appearance and attitude, longevity, regular interaction and emotional involvement. It was also a relatively small association. It has been shown that personal relations between primary group members are likely to be stronger the smaller the groups are, the longer established they are, the more frequently members interact and the more homogeneous they are (Bulmer, 1987). All of these considerations were applicable to subgroup B. Everyone in it was born with spina bifida and hydrocephalus, although it is unlikely they were aware of this fact since they knew little of their conditions. They were all confined to wheelchairs and had been all their lives. All were doubly incontinent although not all sought assistance. In addition, apart from Curt, they were all relatively small in stature. They had all known each other since primary school and, with the exception of James, had attended Christy Brown school for their entire pre-16 education. James had also attended this school but left at 14 when his parents insisted he go to a local compehensive. None of the seven group members, Margaret, Sally, Norman, Angela, Millie, Curt and James, had been separated from their parents for more than two weeks[3] and none of them had ever had a job. The oldest of the group was 23 and the youngest 19.

They were easily distinguishable from the rest of Contact because they were rarely apart. Invariably they would sit together chatting or listening to music on one of their own portable radios or tape machines, usually away from the rest of the group. At Alf Morris this would be outside the main rooms used by the group, either in the cookery room or one of the side rooms if they were vacant, or outside if the weather permitted. At the Engineers' and Dortmund Square, James and Curt were conspicuous by their absence since neither liked the atmosphere or the activities at these units. Sometimes at Alf Morris, Norman or James would join in formal group activities, if staff were involved. In this case the girls would adjourn to the large waiting area inside or immediately outside the ladies' loo.

Although they all wore reasonably smart clothes, none was overtly fashionable. Part of the reason for this lies in the fact that people with impairments often have difficulty finding clothes which fit. It was apparent that their wardrobes were chosen for their utility, and by their parents. Their interests were similar to those of working-class youth generally, revolving around leisure, peer groups and, to a lesser degree, style (Brake, 1980). Their relative lack of enthusiasm for the latter is likely to be due to the fact that they were unable to wear overtly stylish clothes. Their conversation was generally lightweight, covering day centre gossip, the previous night's TV programmes, mainstream pop music, the type of music they listened to, and their personal relationships.

The only lasting personal relationship in Contact was within this subgroup. Norman and Angela had been engaged for over two years, although neither appeared to take the relationship seriously in the conventional sense. When asked if they intended to marry Angela would shrug and simply say she had no idea and it was up to Norman. For his part, he said he was not interested in marriage because he intended to stay with his 'mam'. Apart from their liaisons at the day centres, which usually meant Norman leaning on Angela and feigning sleep, their only other contact was at the Physically Handicapped and Able-Bodied (PHAB) club or when they went out with their families, who were neighbours, had known each other since their offspring's childhood and also frequented the same social club on Saturday nights.

Other relationships within this group were extremely transient, often lasting no more than a day. For example, one day Millie would declare with complete confidence and sincerity that she was 'going out' with one of the others in the group or that she had a new boyfriend. The next day the romance would be off with little apparent regret. Personal relationships were discussed with an air of naivety appropriate to much younger individuals. They were generally interpreted as an indication of childishness by several of the other users and the majority of staff. Often the CAs were discussed in this light, but no attempt at contact or approach was ever made. As one female CA put it,

'It's just like little kids, it's just like they're playin' at bein' grown up. I don't think any of them have had a proper boyfriend . . . , or girlfriend. It's all in their minds, it's just somethin' to talk about'.* — Maria

The staff generally viewed this group as relatively immature for their years. This is often said of young people with impairments. Anderson and Clarke (1982), for example, point out that 'handicapped youngsters' are more likely to be functioning in terms of social and emotional maturity at a level two or three years below that of their peers, particularly if they have been educated in special schools. While social interaction between staff and this group of users did occur it was usually on a formal basis. While they were all dependent on staff for toileting, they approached these interactions in a matter-of-fact fashion which conveyed little if any embarrassment. They also took the most positive view of the day centres of any of the users. At the start of our formal interview Norman said,

'I don't want you to say owt' bad about this place . . . , cos' I like it 'ere.'*

A female member of the group stated,

'I think it's great 'ere, I'd come on Saturdays an' Sundays if they were open.'* — Millie

All spoke of others in the clique as best friends. And while it is often stated that most informal friendship groupings have a leader (Hargreaves, 1975) none was obvious, although it may be that this role fell to Norman, because of his seniority in Contact generally and the fact that he was the only male in this grouping who used the centres every day of the week. All said they got on relatively well with the majority of other users, but some animosity was expressed toward the rowdier elements in Contact, notably Andy, Billy, Jamie and Spike, because they were occasionally disruptive and abusive towards them. In short, these users were by far the most consistent and well-adjusted members of the Contact group. Since they appeared to accept their dependent status with little difficulty I shall refer to them as the 'conformists'. They were relatively autonomous within the confines of the day centres, rarely showing any visible signs of emotional upset or depression, unlike some of the individuals in the two subdivisions discussed below.

The largest subdivision in the Contact group, subgroup C, numbering thirteen in all, had no visible subgroup affiliations. They suffered from a farrago of conditions ranging from muscular dystrophy to 'behavioural' problems. Only John, Gavin and Bruce were permanently confined to wheelchairs. All three had walked when they were younger. The remainder were all ambulatory, although four, Sheila, Karen, Barry and Elizabeth, used chairs when not in the centres. Five had experienced education in normal schools before the age of 11, but while Karen, Nancy, Wendy and Richard had all hated it, because of the bullying, John, who had been able-bodied before his accident and had been sent to a secondary remedial school because of his learning difficulties, told me,

> 'T' school were all reet, I gor'on wi'other kids an' that. It were just that I wa'nt any good at readin'.'*

Although in this grouping only Sheila had any academic qualifications and some could be regarded as 'slow' in certain areas, particularly literacy and numeracy, this should not be construed as an indication of the group's intellectual dullness. Gavin, for example was generally perceived as one of the brightest boys in the entire group. He and Elizabeth, who was one of his regular companions, often sat working through the computer instruction manual without help. Another boy from this faction, Bruce, despite a limited education owing to having spent much time in hospital, had an encyclopaedic knowledge of sport, especially football.

This was not applicable for others in this group, however. Barry for instance was regarded by everyone as a 'bit thick'. He was inseparable from his best friend, Henry, who took it upon himself 'to look after him'.* Henry was bright but extremely shy, preferring to stay in the background. According to senior staff, self-confidence had never been his strong point, but what little he had had been further undermined in 1985 when he was hit by a car while crossing the road. Karen had a similar disposition, and was drawn to socializing with the girls in the 'conformist' group but was frequently upset after these interactions, because she felt they put on her by asking her to fetch things for them, such as tea or coffee. She also had a chronic affection for James, which was seldom reciprocated and this only added to her general depression. Others in this group were prone to similar moods. Wendy was regularly distraught due to her living accommodation. Amy and Richard were similarly affected because they were nearly always excluded from informal user activities due to their 'babyish' ways. Both were subject to violent mood changes and would cry or sulk for long periods. On occasions this would mean sitting alone with their head bowed for five to sixty-five minutes, speaking to no one until one of the staff took an interest. Amy was also diagnosed as an epileptic and would frequently have one or more seizures after heightened activity or successive mood changes. When excluded from all other social activity, both Amy and Richard sought out the most severely impaired Contact members, particularly the three who were unable to talk. This provided them with both companionship and usually a positive response from one of the staff.

Those in the third subdivision rarely ventured out of the main Contact areas, nor out of earshot of senior staff. Wendy, for example, could normally be found sitting next to Jayne or Jackie. In terms of physical appearance, none of them wore 'trendy' clothes. In fact some were quite poorly dressed. By coincidence, this was a reflection of the fact that most were reputedly from the poorest families in the group. In many respects they were not as physically impaired as others in Contact, but in many ways they demanded a higher degree of attention from staff, who, in general, looked upon them as victims, not fully responsible for their predicament or their behaviour. In return many of them viewed staff in an almost deferential light. Elizabeth for example said,

> 'I don't know where we'd be without 'em. You've got to 'ave staff in case you get stuck or owt, say if you fell . . . , where'd we be then . . . .'*

Like subgroup B most of this group took a fairly positive view of day centre attendance, notwithstanding that Karen and Wendy claimed they would prefer to do something else, though neither knew what. Apart from Barry and Henry, none had any particular friends. They were the misfits, the floaters and the loners. Sometimes they were included in social interaction with others in the group. Clive, for example, would sometimes be found with the conformists and Sheila with the girls in subgroup D. On other occasions they were ignored. They were the 'silent majority' occupying the middle ground between the groups mentioned earlier and the remaining subdivision described below.

Those in the final subdivision, subgroup D, were distinguishable by their relative maturity and autonomy, both inside and outside the centres. As a result they were often less visible than the other subdivisions but were characterized by the similarity of their attitudes to the other users, the staff and the centres generally. Included in this grouping were the five who did not use social services' transport and therefore attended as and when they felt like it. This could be anything from three or four times a week on a regular basis in the winter to once a fortnight in the summer. This group included Joyce and Marilyn who only visited the centres in the afternoons, as well as Roger who was the oldest user in Contact and Billy who was the youngest. They were generally the least physically impaired.

All were ambulatory in the centres, although Billy and Joyce occasionally used wheelchairs outside.[4] Three of the group were adventitiously impaired and like Billy and Matthew had gone through normal education without interruption. With the exception of Molly, who was one of the least impaired users in the centres, all the congenitally impaired individuals in this faction had been separated for long periods from the parental home either through attending boarding school or residential colleges. All bar Jamie and Spike, who were by no means unintelligent, had some academic qualifications. And several had spent lengthy periods outside the centres either at college, on government-sponsored youth training schemes (YTS), or in work. This group also includes those people who had set up homes of their own as well as Spike and Roger, who had both left home before the advent of their impairments, Spike to join the army and Roger because he could not get on with his family.

Because of their relative autonomy, associations between members of this subdivision could take many forms, but when inside the centres they generally congregated together and away from the majority of Contact users, usually at the far end of the smaller of the two rooms at Alf Morris, or in the library at Dortmund Square. If several were sitting around a table and someone arrived who was considered part of the group, then a space would automatically be made for them, while the arrival of non-members would be ignored. These congregations normally only took place in the afternoon, because some of the principal members did not arrive until then. They would usually include one or two of the CAs, Pete, sometimes Annie, work permitting, and two of the female voluntary workers (VWs). This meant that on occasion some of these workers spent a disproportionate amount of time with this subgroup. If only a few of the group were present, then some of them would disperse to other parts of the centre and interact with other users or, more often than not, with staff. Matthew, for example, would regularly play dominoes in the lower building at Alf Morris with some of the older users and the male CAs. Philip often sat chatting to Bob, the activity organizer (AO) in charge of the carpentry workshop; and Joyce, Molly and Marilyn could be found talking with Eileen, the centre's hairdresser.

These individuals were also distinguishable from the others in Contact in their appearance. Unlike those discussed above, who had obviously been 'got ready' by someone else, they were clearly concerned about the way they looked, and wore clothes and make-up similar to those worn by their able-bodied peers. Billy wore sports shirts, jeans and trainers, Jamie sported a skinhead-style haircut and Spike draped himself in a black leather jacket covered in studs and the names of heavy rock bands. Philip, who was married, usually turned up in jeans, jumper and anorak, like most able-bodied young married men out at work. The girls in the subgroup were extremely fashion-conscious and took meticulous care over their clothes, make-up and hairstyles. Informal group discussions covered essentially the same topics as those of subgroup B, namely, leisure, peers and style, although gender differences were more prevelant. In addition, there was a definite tendency among the males toward the macho values generally associated with working-class youth subcultures. Conversations usually revolved around music, the opposite sex, "avin' a laff" and, when the girls were not present, violence and fighting (Hargreaves, 1967; Willis, 1977; and Brake, 1980).

Compared to those in the other subdivisions in Contact, however, they were far more discerning in their tastes. For example, a common topic of conversation for the 'lads' was the merits of particular heavy rock bands, a subject especially close to the hearts of Billy, Roger, Spike and Pete. The girls talked about individual rock stars. Mainstream top ten 'pop' was usually dismissed as 'rubbish'. Sex was frequently a subject for discussion, but it was talked about in a far more worldly manner. When the girls were not there the lads' conversation often turned to the physical attributes of the female day centre staff, particularly the young CAs, or sometimes Marilyn, who was generally regarded as the most attractive girl in the group, the day's page three girls, their sexual fantasies and their exploits. It was clear from the tone of these conversations that their (sexual) activities were not limited to fantasy. During this study Jamie experienced fatherhood and Spike and Billy both asked a number of the young CAs and Marilyn out. And Barbara, the 17-year-old VW, went out with Billy for six weeks.

When the girls were discussing this topic, they took a more moral approach (at least in my presence) emphasizing the virtues of chastity before marriage. Although they did discuss men in a similar vein to the lads, arguing for instance over their looks, they never spoke of other users or people who worked in the centres in this light. All the girls were adamant that they would never go out with anyone who was 'handicapped'. Marilyn, for example, only had eyes for one of the taxi drivers who she thought looked like Rod Stewart, a rock star.

Usually "avin' a laff" meant relating past experiences, discussing their social lives outside the centres, moaning about the day centres and 'takin' the piss' out of some of the staff, usually senior personnel outside Contact, and other users, including the elderly and some Contact members. These conversations, however, rarely went outside the subgroup. It was unusual for any of them to ridicule anyone openly.

The four most dominant lads in the group, Billy, Andy, Spike and Jamie, adopted what has been termed a 'delinquent orientation' (Hargreaves, 1975) or an overtly rebellious stance against formal authority. They often talked about violence, martial arts and their ability to fight. Sometimes these conversations erupted into displays of aggression and occasionally fights, usually over who was the "ardest", although these conflicts rarely went beyond pushing each other around. The ability to 'stick up for yourself' was important to all four. When these discussions got out of hand or attracted the attention of senior staff, other subgroup members, both males and females, normally moved away.

A general antipathy toward several of the other users in Contact was common to all in this faction. While individuals such as Charles or Gavin, whose physical impairments were judged severe, were accorded a great deal of sympathy and occasionally inclusion in group activity, others considered 'a bit mental' such as Amy and Richard and the 'conformists' group were viewed with universal disdain, both for their immaturity and perceived passivity. Billy, for example, who was only 17 himself, told me repeatedly how the others in the group,

> 'especially them in wheelchairs mek' me bleedin' sick. For most of 'em it's like they're 2 year old, you know what I mean. It's like they've never grown up, they want to be carried around like babies.'*

Many of the individuals in this faction experienced sporadic bouts of depression stemming directly or indirectly from their impairments. Billy was deeply upset by the fact that since leaving school he had lost all his able-bodied friends. Roger was constantly at odds with his family and desperately wanted to leave home. Throughout the study Philip was having marital difficulties and some of the girls were prone to periods of acute anxiety over their 'spoiled body image', a common concern for impaired women (Campling, 1979). Joyce, for example, would never have her photograph taken unless she was sitting down or when her lower half was out of camera shot. Because they discussed these experiences with senior and junior staff, both professionally and socially, it stimulated a higher level of empathy between staff and them, as opposed to others in Contact. This was apparent in both casual conversation with staff and in their interviews.

> 'Adolescent traumas are exacerbated by disability for all of them, fitting into a peer group, fashion, all the things that are important to all teenagers, they're all exposed to them, especially after coming out of special education and back into the community.... But for some, if they're born with it, there's a kind of an acceptance of the disability and its limitations. There's a realization that they're different but I don't believe it's as profound for them as it is for ... say Billy or Spike.'* — Jackie

Although interaction with staff was important to this group it did not alter their ambivalent view of Contact and the centres in general. All confessed to using the system because they felt they had no choice. These views were best summed up by Joyce when she was discussing her return after her two years at an able-bodied college.

> 'Well you get in like a Catch 22 situation. I was determined not to come back after I'd left college, but you get ... , you know, you get so down. When the holidays 'ave passed an' you're still sat there, an' you get so bad you can't even be bothered to answer the phone when somebody rings up. It gets that bad you can't be bothered to push yourself to do 'owt. Put it this way, if I 'adn't come back I'd 'ave gone off me 'ead.'*

Each of this subgroup's members nominated others in the group as friends, and all said it was unlikely they would use the service if the others did not attend. In terms of popularity, or 'sociometric status', Marilyn was by far the most popular girl in the group, due largely to her physical attractiveness. She received attention from males, both users and staff, which in turn attracted the females. Her sociability and her independence outside the centres, which provided constant new conversation topics, also added to her popularity. In addition, she was a regular attender.

Because some of the lads were frequently absent, it was difficult to assess who was the most popular and influential among them. If, for example, someone was missing for a while then they were automatically the focus of attention when they returned, since they usually had much to talk about. Although Jamie was held in high esteem by all the males because of his past (he had two convictions for assault), his independence, and his extrovert personality, he was not as popular as Billy. While both were often at the hub of group activity, due to their ability to make the others laugh by acting the clown or 'messin' about', Billy had the edge because of his youth and freshness. These attributes are valued by most individuals, impaired or otherwise.

While explanations for the behaviour patterns of the first and third subdivisions can only be drawn satisfactorily with reference to individual life histories and subjective physical and psychological impairments, an explanation for those of the second and fourth subgroups can be found by referring to two distinct but related factors. These are (a) the degree of impairment and (b) socialization. In relation to impairments, subgroup B were all similarly disadvantaged, both in terms of cause and degree. When compared with others in Contact, excluding those in subgroup A and some from subgroup C, such as Gavin, their impairments were relatively severe, particularly with regard to mobility. In contrast, those in subgroup D were the least overtly impaired, albeit their impairments were diverse. In view of the general tendency for like-situated individuals to identify with each other, a tendency which is particularly acute during adolescence, this pattern of 'in-group alignment' (Goffman, 1968) was almost inevitable.

Further explanations for these affiliations may be found with reference to users' life experiences prior to this study. This is especially important since others in Contact were similarly impaired, but not normally included in either of the two principal friendship cliques. Consequently explanations which rely on impairment alone may be considered inadequate.

Most of the members of subgroup B had remarkably similar biographies before their introduction into the day centres. Their dependent status had been learned through sustained interactions with their families, professionals, teachers and, most importantly, with each other. They had literally been socialized into a culture of dependence since they were born. For them dependence was normal and apparently not considered a major problem. Their transition to day centre user status was merely another stage in the continuum of their dependent career. Subgroup D, on the other hand, was composed of individuals who had either (a) spent long periods away from the family home in residential schools or colleges and/or been partially integrated into able-bodied society, as in the case of the congenitally impaired, or (b) been part of that society before impairment, as in the case of the adventitiously impaired. Normality for them was able-bodied normality, not dependence. Moreover, since the norms and values of this grouping were similar to those of non-impaired working-class youth subcultures generally, especially those in state comprehensive schools, there is an element of continuity here also. Additionally, since gender roles are particularly significant in these subcultures this may explain why gender-related behaviour within this subgroup was more pronounced than in the others discussed. While the cultural values of the conformists may represent a form of resistance to the negative perceptions generally associated with disability, those of subgroup D are clearly a form of resistance to the imposition of the disability label.

With regard to the reference groups, distinctions can be made between (a) the group of which an individual is a member for social categorization, such as the disabled, (b) the group whose norms and values the individual accepts, and (c) the group of which s/he is not a part but to which s/he would like to belong (Hargreaves, 1975). While the principal reference group for the conformists was each other, or the disabled, the primary reference group for subgroup D was the able-bodied. While subgroup B adjusted to day centre life with relative ease, subgroup D adjusted to it with reluctance. As a result the latter had generally devalued conceptions of self and were prone to the type of severe adjustment difficulties generally associated with coming to terms with a disabled identity during adolescence, hence their animosity toward other users, particularly those who represented for them the disabled stereotype, their affinity with some day centre personnel and their ambivalent attitude toward the day centre system as a whole.

With reference to Goffman's (1968) analysis of coming to terms with a devalued or disabled identity, the pattern of socialization experienced by subgroup B conforms to the first model identified, which suggests individuals with congenital impairments can be socialized into accepting a disadvantaged status during childhood, while the previous life experiences of the individuals in subgroup D were broadly comparable to the second, in the case of the congenitally impaired, and the third, in the case of those with acquired impairments. His second model concerns those similarly impaired but who are unaware of their disadvantaged position until later in life. The third relates to the adventitiously disabled and the re-appraisal of self after the onset of impairment.

The data in this section have shown that there were four distinct informal user subdivisions within the Contact framework. The first, due to the severity of their impairments, was dependent almost exclusively on staff, both for physical tending and social activity. The second was a distinct subgroup or clique, with its own values, culture and structure. This group conformed in many ways to the general view of the disabled and its members had normalized their dependent status. They took a positive view of staff, on whom they were dependent only for physical tending, since social support was provided by others in the group, the day centres and the majority of other users. The third subdivision was conspicuous by its lack of cohesion. Its members had no definite subgroup affiliations but innovated and adapted as the need arose. Although the majority were less physically dependent on staff than the others mentioned, several required higher levels of social support. The fourth subdivision was distinguishable from the others by its members' physical independence and relative maturity, both inside and outside the centres. Like the second grouping they had their own values, subculture and structure, but unlike subgroup B and the majority of other users, they had difficulty accepting the consequences of their impairments, namely, the dependent status. They therefore disassociated themselves whenever possible from those in Contact who appeared to accept the system without difficulty. Consequently, although they derived social support from each other, they were disproportionately dependent on staff for this function. They viewed the Contact group and the day centres with ambivalence. For them, the ritual of attendance was due to necessity rather than choice. These apparent differences were explained with reference to two distinct but related factors, namely, the degree of impairment and differential socialization.

These findings, particularly the dimensions and severity of impairment, the differential orientation toward self and others, and the tendency toward factionalism among Contact members, might help to explain why senior staff adopted policies of 'enlightened guardianship' which attempt to accommodate both the dependent and the not so dependent. If these findings are representative of young people with impairments in day centres and other institutional settings, and I believe they are, then they may also explain why there is still a prevalence of this policy in social provision generally, especially that which is aimed at this particular user group.

Conclusion

This chapter has looked at the individuals who constituted the Contact group. The evidence shows that although there was a high degree of homogeneity among Contact members with regard to cause and type of impairment, previous experience, economic and social disadvantage, which subsequently led to their day centre attendance, this homogeneity did not extend to their attitudes relating to their dependent status, day centre staff, and the service generally.

The data show that the overwhelming majority of users were from the manual working classes and the majority grew up in economically and/or socially disadvantaged households. Although there was some diversity in cause and severity of impairment among users, most were congenitally impaired and mobility was a major problem for the majority. There was a general lack of knowledge among respondents about their conditions. Many had spent long periods in segregated institutions such as hospitals, special day schools, and residential schools. Those who attended residential schools viewed the experience positively in relation to furthering their independence. Over half the congenitally impaired respondents had been on vocational/independence courses in colleges of further education and three had integrated into schemes for the non-impaired. Their efforts with regards to finding paid employment proved fruitless. Work experience among those impaired at 16 was conspicuous by its absence. None of those with acquired disabilities had ever been unemployed before the onset of their impairment. All the respondents were economically dependent upon the state and only five were independent from their families in terms of accommodation. Of these, two were living in residential institutions. In conjunction with other studies in this area, the data in this section underpin the general inadequacy of some forms of special education and the poverty of economic and social opportunities available to young people with impairments during adolescence.

Although unemployment is a tacit factor, three main reasons accounted for users joining the Contact group. Some apparently wanted to maintain long-established peer group relations. Others, although aware of the stigma attached to day centres, viewed attendance as preferable to the extreme social isolation encountered in the post-education period. The remainder, mainly the adventitiously impaired, believed it would assist in their rehabilitation. The data brought into focus the severity of the social isolation these users experienced in the post-education years, a problem which is common to many young people with impairments, and it showed how influential professionals were with regard to shaping their lives. I noted here that any criticisms directed at those responsible for introducing Contact members into the day centres should be set within this context.

The final section discussed the four principal subdivisions within the Contact user body as differentiated by degree of impairment and perceived dependence. Among these subdivisions were two friendship groups or cliques with apparently contradictory perceptions of dependence, day centre staff and the day centres generally. These attitudinal differences were explained partly with reference to the degree of impairment but also as a consequence of differential socialization of group members. I suggested that these contradictions may go some way in explaining why 'enlightened guardianship' was the management strategy adopted by Contact staff. Similar attitudinal differences were also evident in users' views regarding user participation and control within the Contact group. These subjects are discussed in detail in the ensuing chapter.

Notes

1 The Family Fund is a government fund administered by the Joseph Rowntree Memorial Trust for families caring for children with impairments whose needs fall outside statutory provision (Bradshaw, 1980).
2 Both Wendy and Paul were enrolled on the independence course for students with special needs which lasted one or two years depending on college staff's perceptions of need.
3 Margaret and Angela had both stayed in residential homes while their respective families had gone on holiday.
4 As his illness grew worse, Billy's use of a wheelchair increased steadily throughout the study period.

Chapter 6
Participation and Control

This chapter focuses on the level of user participation and control within the context of the Contact group in relation to structured activities, the organization and general running of the group, and social control. Attention will be drawn to the environmental limitations on the amenities available, particularly as reflected in 'swamping' by other user groups, the differing needs of the Contact members, and the tension inherent in the philosophy of social rehabilitation within an expressly voluntarist atmosphere in explaining the relatively low level of participation by users in formal activities. At the same time the data illustrate how staff encourage involvement in each of the areas of potential user participation. The evidence shows that the limited user involvement in formal mechanisms of policy formulation is largely due to the social divisions among Contact users and a belief by some that such involvement is futile because of the environment in which the group operates.

There is no formal constitution within the Contact format and control is exercised by senior staff through 'orchestration' or, when necessary, through supervisory means. The study shows that senior Contact staff are discretionary in their use of power to restrict user activity outside the day centres during opening hours and that this is an area of concern for several Contact members. Nonetheless discipline is not considered a problem within the group because, it will be argued, of users' socialization and their relative autonomy within the centres compared with the constraints imposed on them outside.

The level of user involvement in the provision and delivery of services for people with disabilities is now considered central by most writers concerned with the experience of impairment. The chapter begins with a brief overview of the recent research in this area.

User Participation and Day Centres

The origins of the growing demand for higher levels of user participation and control of services for disabled people is generally associated with the emergence of the Independent Living Movement (ILM) in the United States in the late 1960s.

The central issue for this movement's advocates was, and remains, how to achieve effective control over their own lives. The movement does not deny the limitations imposed upon individual activity by impairments, but maintains that those limitations are worsened by environmental factors and by those who provide required services. The ILM does not suggest that impaired people do not need help, but maintains that they should control the form that such help takes.

The first Centre for Independent Living was set up in Berkeley, California, in 1972 by a group of severely physically impaired individuals who took responsibility for the organization of the services they needed. By 1983 there were 135 similar institutions established throughout America, each offering a wide range of services from telephone advice lines to care attendants (CAs). Wedded to the 'traditional' American ideologies of radical individualism and consumer sovereignty, the political demands of the movement quickly found favour with the American Congress. In 1973 legislation was passed which provided services for individuals for whom vocational rehabilitation was not a realistic proposition. The Act also accorded priority to those 'most severely disabled', provided affirmative and anti-discriminatory programmes, and stipulated that there should be corporate compliance in architecture and transport (Williams, 1984). However, a number of authors have shown that these positive changes have not been spread evenly throughout American society and that they favour specific sections of the impaired community (Goodall, 1988).

Partly due to the universalistic policies of the British welfare state and the fact that its central philosophy traditionally viewed consumers as passive recipients rather than active participants, no national equivalent of the ILM has emerged in this country, albeit self-help and consumerism have become cornerstones of new right philosophy and recent government policy (Clode et al., 1987). British writers in the field, the late Paul Hunt, Finkelstein, Davis and Oliver, for example, have directed their attention toward the prevailing attitudes of the non-impaired population, who, they argue, view the impaired as needing care and protection. Hence the idea that people with impairments should be active participants and take control of their own lives has been slow to catch on (Goodall, 1988).

From an essentially Marxist perspective, Oliver (1983b) has discussed the politics of disability within the British context and concludes that because of the divisions within the disabled population in terms of age, social class, impairments and the reluctance by many to identify with disabled organizations, the emergence of a coherent political movement is unlikely. For Oliver these divisions are exacerbated by successive government policies, such as tax concessions to the blind but not to the deaf, mobility allowance to those unable to walk but denied to those who can, and higher pensions for those impaired at work. By adopting these strategies the state keeps in check the collective interests of the disabled population and their demands for more resources. Oliver accepts that the impaired have made considerable gains under Labour administations, but following Walker (1982) contends that social policy from the left has been consistently imposed from the top down by those in power rather than from the bottom up by those who need it. The much venerated Chronically Sick and

Disabled Persons Act of 1970 is seen less as a 'charter for the disabled' as liberal writers suggest (Topliss and Gould, 1981), than as a charter for professionals.

Like other writers from the left, Oliver views the traditional alliance between social democracy and liberal professionalism in a negative light, since it has hitherto failed to solve the problems of the working classes. From the perspective of the impaired, the radical critique of the professionals as applied to the caring industry is complicated by the fact that the vast majority of professional helpers are able-bodied and therefore open to the accusation that they can never understand what it is like to be disabled. It is argued for this reason that the 'enlightened guardian' approach is inappropriate and needs to be replaced by 'disabled action', involving full participation and control, or full participation in the administration of services for people with disabilities by people with disabilities. Because of the divisions outlined above, however, any foreseeable gains are only likely to be small-scale and at the local level (Oliver, 1983b).

Although progress has been slow, some tentative moves in this direction have taken place. Probably the best known example is the Derbyshire Coalition for Disabled People. Adopting the philosophy of the collectivist approach rather than the individualistic American variant, because the latter may lead to the monopolization of limited resources by impaired individuals, the coalition works in close collaboration with the statutory authorities to provide improved services for people with disabilities. After some preliminary difficulties emanating from the conflict of attitudes between the coalition members and the local authority, the Derbyshire Centre for Integrated Living has gone from 'strength to strength' (Oliver, 1987a). Although Derbyshire seems to be far ahead of other local authorities, there have also been developments elsewhere resulting from the shift toward community care. For example, some authorities have set up inter-departmental social services and health authority partnerships with the Community Volunteers Organization to coordinate and finance the latter's independent living schemes. These are consumer-orientated programmes which supply volunteers to work in the homes of disabled individuals. A pioneering Community Aids programme is flourishing in the London Boroughs of Islington and Wandsworth (Goodall, 1988) and the Cambridge Health Authority funded an experimental project where the primary aim was to set up a domiciliary care service for young disabled people living in the community, to improve their quality of life (Owens, 1987). Moreover, a recent survey by Crawley (1988) has shown that there has been a substantial growth of user participation and self-advocacy in Adult Training Centres (ATCs) and similar organizations for people with learning difficulties.

This general shift of emphasis has not gone unnoticed by those involved in the provision of day services for the younger physically impaired. The recent Royal Association for Disability and Rehabilitation (RADAR) report on this subject states:

> Day centres should encourage and assist users to develop physical, social
> and intellectual skills, including the ability to organize their own lives,

make their own decisions and function as members of their own community. Skills and knowledge will have to be imparted to users in areas such as the management of handicap, claiming welfare and other rights, social competence and emotional maturity (Kent *et al.*, 1984, p. 18).

From this perspective the role of day centres is essentially rehabilitative. The authors point out that any formal instruction should be carried out with a 'minimum didactic content' and that users should be 'encouraged' to participate fully in the planning and running of services. It is clear that Kent *et al.* place great emphasis on the type of activities provided by day centres in the drive toward heightened user participation and control, but they are somewhat vague as to what is meant by 'minimum didactic content' or how users should be 'encouraged' to get involved. These concerns provide the starting point for the next section which looks at the structured activities available to the Contact users and the methods used by staff to stimulate user participation.

Structured Activities and User Participation in the Contact Group

In a recent analysis of social control in a therapeutic community, Bloor (1987) referred to a collection of such practices as the relinquishment of direct supervision, the encouragement of patient autonomy, the provocation of patient dissent and the mobilization of patient culture as a 'treatment resource' by professionals as 'orchestration'. I shall now show that day centre staff utilize similar strategies to encourage user involvement in structured activities. Since any such user participation is relatively low, I shall argue that the strategies employed remain largely ineffective because of the contradictions inherent in the notion of didactic activity in an explicitly unfettered atmosphere. And although environmental factors contribute to this phenomenon I shall suggest that these activities are largely inappropriate for the users' needs since the majority view the centres as a social rather than a rehabilitative setting and that for those who do not, the formal activities offered are inadequate.

As noted in Chapter Four, the three day centres used by Contact originally were restricted to social/recreational-type activities and that it is only since Contact's inception that the shift toward services with an explicitly rehabilitative component really took hold. While senior staff have undoubtedly been influenced by the recent change of emphasis is social service provision, both Jayne and Jackie maintained that much of the stimulus for the activities offered within the Contact framework stemmed from the users themselves. Two notable examples were literacy/numeracy and music and drama. The desirability of the former within day centres for the younger impaired has been acknowledged since the Warnock Report on Special Education (1978) over a decade ago, but it is only recently that the value of the latter has been recognized in this type of establishment (Carter, 1988). Although they are still not available in many units, the Contact group has had access to both since 1985. The range of regular structured activities available during the study period is shown in Table 16.

Table 16 Structured activities available to the Contact Users

Time	Monday Alf Morris Centre	Tuesday Engineers' Centre	Wednesday Alf Morris Centre	Thursday Dortmund Square Centre	Friday Alf Morris Centre
4.00 p.m.		— —			
3.00 p.m.		Arts			
	—	Crafts — —	Music — —	— —	
2.00 p.m.	Discussion Group	Weight Training	Drama Discussion — — Group	Weight Training	
1.00 p.m.	--				
			Lunch		
12.00 p.m.	--				
			Music		Literacy
11.00 a.m.	Swimming	Arts	Drama		Numeracy
	— —	Crafts	— —		— —
10.00 a.m.					
9.00 a.m.		— —			

Note: Swimming and weight training were held at local sports centres, not in the day centres.

Source: official timetable for the period September 1986/July 1987

Woodwork, cookery and sewing were offered at the Alf Morris centre on Wednesdays and Fridays. There was also opportunity for an individually structured bridging course to prepare day centre users for further education, organized in conjunction with a local college. Also at this centre there were periodic visits from representatives from Disability Information and Advice Line (DIAL) to discuss benefits and changes in social services procedures etc.[1] There were also occasional visits to local places of interest, art galleries, exhibitions and shopping centres, as well as annual outings to the coast and a Christmas lunch. Finally, there were the semi-formal spontaneous pastimes such as quizzes, organized games, listening to music, watching television or socializing. While there is little consensus on what constitutes rehabilitative activity and there were substantial gaps in this timetable, these activities represent more than simply 'tea and bingo'.

According to Jayne and Jackie recent changes in the general approach to day services for the younger physically impaired have had specific implications for the two senior roles within the context of the Contact group. While the traditional functions of senior activity organizer (SAO) and activity organizer (AO) have been the conceptualization, organization and coordination of user activities, social or otherwise, there is now mounting pressure, albeit predominantly implicit, to 'encourage' activity in particular areas, notably those normally perceived of as heightening individual independence and self-help. This pressure comes from at least three sources — Mrs B, the Residential and Day Care Officer (RDCO) in charge of the centres; an increasing number of parents;[2] and some of the users. With respect to the users' families, other studies have focused on the concern expressed by parents over the services provided in day centres for impaired adolescents (Anderson and Clarke, 1982). The change of emphasis towards independence and self-help presents substantial difficulties for staff since it is generally agreed that Contact members spend three-quarters of their time socializing, either sitting around chatting or playing games, and that the voluntarist nature of the group should be maintained.

Strategies of encouragement were most visible when senior staff were attempting to orchestrate user involvement in explicitly educational activities. The techniques used can be related to the three ideal types devised by Hargreaves (1975) in his analysis of teacher/pupil relations — the 'liontamer', the 'entertainer' and the 'new romantic' approaches. The most typically used method resembled Hargreaves' 'entertainer' model. The central assumption of this strategy is that motivation is latent and ready to be tapped. Hence the teacher motivates the student by making learning fun or appealing to the eventual usefulness of what is being offered. In the day centre situation, however, where there were no sanctions involved, it is important to have a comprehensive knowledge of users' biographies if the method is to work, since staff have to capitalize on users' interests and must avoid making rash statements about the advantages of what is being offered.

An example of how staff try to make learning fun occurred when Jayne was encouraging users to join the literacy and numeracy classes. These subjects had initially been requested by two group members who wanted to improve their skills in these areas. Jayne chose a popular member of subgroup B, Millie, who she knew was interested in the subjects, elicited her compliance and then systematically went round her friends telling them Millie was taking part. If they showed any reluctance she emphasized Millie's enthusiasm and suggested it was bound to be more enjoyable than being left out. Similar approaches were made by Jackie when collecting names for swimming and weight training sessions at the local gym, although clearly here knowledge of users' physical abilities was imperative since some individuals were unable to take up these options because of their impairments. These techniques were used by Benjamin, the tutor from the local college of further education, to stimulate interest in the bridging scheme when he got Andy and Spike onto the course. Since neither was interested in education 'per se' he emphasized the social aspects of attending an able-bodied college, particularly the opportunities to meet girls.

After joining the group in January 1987, Patrick, Contact's AO after Jayne's departure, employed the same methods, but complemented them with techniques resembling the 'new romantic' approach, which suggests that students are naturally motivated and will participate if interested. Playing upon users' natural motivation he looked for areas of interest and turned them into didactic activity. Several of the lads had complained about the legs on the snooker table so rather than send them to the Carpentry Workshop for repair or put in a request for new ones, he set about repairing them himself and in the process elicited voluntary help from Billy, Andy and Matthew. The entire enterprise lasted eight weeks. Clearly this technique is limited, especially in view of the environmental and monetary constraints under which the group operates.

The models devised by Hargreaves also typify the strategies used by the four main tutors responsible for presenting formal activities to the group. Here, however, there was evidence of the traditional 'liontamer' approach where students are literally told what to do and how to do it. Hilary, the arts and crafts teacher, used these techniques in her classes on Tuesdays at the Engineers' day centre. She has been at the unit since it opened and her ideas reflected those of the Officer in Charge (OIC), Mrs W, who held the view that 'idle hands make idle minds'.*

'People need guiding or they'll do nothing. I don't believe that's good for them. They need stimulus. Everybody needs stimulus. Nobody's ever told them, you see, that they can do anything well, so they don't do anything at all. So I provide the stimulus. I know some of them don't like it but...'* — Hilary

The arts and crafts classes began as soon as the users arrived and continued throughout the day. Although 'compulsory' was not a term used in the day centres, there was no alternative other than to sit and do nothing. In 1985, five users were coached to GCE O level standard and sat the exam, but many of the group resented Hilary's approach and saw the subjects as a waste of time with little point to them despite the fact that some of the finished artefacts, such as teapot stands, plaster of Paris ornaments and the like were sold to supplement the group's amenity fund. As a result of general disinterest Tuesday was the lowest attended day of the week apart from Friday when there was a deliberate policy in the system generally of limiting user numbers so that staff could spend time on routine paperwork and maintenance. Of the moderately impaired only Billy and Matthew went to the Engineers' on Tuesdays, the former because there was no one at home and his parents preferred him not to be in the house alone and the latter because he had to attend in order to do weight training later in the day. When weight training changed days in February, Matthew stopped going to the Engineers'.

It is notable that the Engineers' centre and arts and crafts were popular with the girls in subgroup B, although they did not like Hilary's methods.

'It's alright there, there's always something' to do. I like art, but you shouldn't be told what to do, it shouldn't be like school should it?'* — Margaret.

Senior Contact staff appeared to have little control over the situation at the Engineers'. They were aware that it was unacceptable to many of the group but consoled themselves with the fact that it was productive in terms of tangible results.

The ability to achieve visible results was the main reason why a more traditional approach was also adopted by David and Prudence, the two tutors responsible for the music and drama group. In this case, the pressure for its adoption did not come from management, as was the case at the Engineers', but from some of the users. Originally when music and drama instruction started in 1985, the two teachers opted for the relaxed technique of the 'new romantics'. The principal activities were loosely structured, usually involving individual and collective discussions, and there were group renderings of favourite pop songs using a multitude of percussion instruments. Roger, who first suggested Contact include this facility, used it as an opportunity to practice his electric bass guitar. In 1986, however, when the group was opened out to all Alf Morris users, it was joined by three members of Insight, the group serving those 25 to 45, who wanted to perform a 'proper play' or revue in front of the entire centre. This idea appealed to the majority but a formal play was out of the question since many of the original members could not read. After much disagreement the two tutors took control and decided upon a semi-improvised fantasy revue involving music and mime based on Peter Pan. This was unacceptable to the newcomers so they left. After six weeks, three of the Contact members, including Roger, also left because they were 'fed up' doing the same things week after week. In the event the remaining five members along with David and Prudence planned, produced and performed a twenty-minute show in front of the entire centre at Easter and repeated it in a local nursery school one month later. This achievement was unimagined six months earlier when the idea was first suggested.

Such methods are not appropriate, however, for other activities provided in the centres. Maggie, who took the literacy and numeracy classes on Friday mornings, adopted the more relaxed individually structured approach because of the nature of the subjects she taught and the fact that if she exerted any pressure students walked out.

'You can't push them, their concentration is very poor. The group I have on a Monday at evening classes [able-bodied] are also young and not an unsimilar age group to this group. But these youngsters seem to have difficulty sitting down and getting on with it. They want more breaks, they're distracted much more so than the able-bodied ones that I know. It's very rare that they'll start something at the start of the class and plod their way through it. They'll do a bit, then it's gone.'*

The relaxed atmosphere of Maggie's classes achieved success in the sense that they are regularly attended, but often individuals would not bother to go in if they did not feel like it. The classes were held in the smaller Contact room and averaged between six and ten regular students each week. They included all the girls in subgroup B and usually Karen, Amy and Richard from subgroup C. There were ten on the official register. Often there was scant evidence of academic activity. Books were got out but little work was done. Students would sit around chatting, leave if they felt like it and not come back if they found something more interesting to do. Rather than a forum for serious didactic activity these classes resembled a relaxed social gathering of close friends. Matthew, who had been to a normal school, described the classes as follows,

> 'Well I don't know what it is they're supposed to do in there. I think it was supposed to be English but they were just sat about talkin', an' some of 'em were drawin' when I went in. Well that's not English to me, they don't do owt in there.'*

Inspection of some of the users' books showed that work was actually done. Some users had written letters to pop stars and others were doing elementary arithmetic. But because they were individually structured and proceeded at the students' own pace, the classes appeared disorganized and the results paltry, particularly from the perspective of someone who had had a 'normal' education. However, considering the subjects, the lack of literacy skills amongst the majority of users, their antipathy to formal controls and school in general, it is doubtful whether the classes could or should proceed in any other fashion.

While these examples can be interpreted in a number of ways they do illustrate the problems facing teaching staff in a voluntary situation with students having varying expectations and abilities. In order to stimulate user participation, Hilary, the arts and crafts tutor, had adopted traditional methods which proved relatively productive but unpopular with the majority of users. The second example of the music and drama classes shows how similar methods were deemed necessary to solve the conflict of expectations among participants. The strategy produced results in this case as well, but user participation diminished. The final example illustrates a different strategy which besides stimulating achievement can secure prolonged user participation because it is individually structured and the user sets her/his own pace. A major factor in the explanation for the success of this latter technique is that it can accommodate didactic interaction within a social environment.

Participation in vocational activities at the centres was limited by environmental factors and 'swamping' by the elderly. Although senior staff were aware that several Contact users saw moving around as beneficial since it prevented boredom, some felt that travelling from centre to centre each day inhibited the development of interest and concentration. Individual or group projects could not be continued the following day, equipment and materials had to be limited to what could be carried from unit to unit and there was no area in any of the centres where the group could leave work unfinished. Even at Alf Morris the two rooms used by the group were used by others when Contact was not there.

'Swamping' by the elderly was particularly relevant to activities such as woodwork, sewing and cookery. These three subjects were open to all day centres at the Alf Morris centre. But since the facilities for each were limited, only accommodating ten users at a time, competition for places was intense. Inclusion in the woodwork group, for example, was determined on a first come, first served basis. A waiting list was posted outside the carpentry workshop and prospective candidates were expected to enter their names on it. Several Contact users said they would like to do woodwork, and this included a number of females, but they chose not to because the carpentry workshop was always full of 'old men'. A number of girls said they would like to do sewing but only if they could do it within the confines of the Contact group and with their friends. Cookery was provided exclusively for Contact members during the long summer school holidays (July to September), at the insistence of Jayne, because of its importance in relation to independent living. But even here enthusiasm was often low unless the weather was poor and there was little else going on, despite the fact that only seven user respondents said they could cook.

Although there was a difference of opinion among the respondents as to the reasons, users also appeared to have little interest in the sort of discussion groups generally seen as furthering mutual support and understanding among impaired adolescents. The more able in the group felt they 'couldn't tell us anything we don't already know' or they were 'depressing', while the remainder said that they did not like them because they made them feel inadequate. For example,

'I don't like discussions, 'cos I never know what to say an' I feel stupid.'* — Henry

These divisions were also evident when the centres organized the two visits by the representatives from DIAL to discuss the future changes in social security benefit payments due to come into force in April 1987. Although Jayne and Jackie stressed their importance on several occasions, only nine Contact members attended, and three of those were the most impaired members of the group, who were pushed in by staff. Among those who did not, some said their parents looked after their benefits while others claimed to know about the changes already.

Based on the data provided in the user interviews, it is clear that the majority of Contact users saw the day centres as a social setting rather than a site for rehabilitative activity or training. As shown in the last chapter, many of the group entered the units purely for social reasons. They represented 'somewhere to go' to get 'out of the house' rather than somewhere to learn. Social interaction with peers was characteristically more important for the user respondents than educational or vocational activity. Although only eleven were happy with the activities offered, most of the remainder's comments concerned the limited resources rather than the type of activities provided. Major concerns for many of the males related to the relatively poor quality of the pool and snooker tables and the need for more sports facilities. A minority of both male and female respondents said there should be more computers. Everyone wanted more trips and outings.

Only eight respondents suggested that the centres should provide more activities which were specifically concerned with independence training or rehabilitation. Only one of these, Tony, was non-ambulatory and not from subgroup D. Along with Joyce, Andy, Jamie and Matthew, he felt that the centres should provide more educational facilities and structured independence training.

None of these four wanted these activities for themselves. Tony felt he did not personally need them as he was still at residential college, only using the day centres in the holidays. The other three considered themselves independent already. But they all believed that such activities were important for the rest of Contact and that the staff should take a more prominent role in promoting them.

> 'I think they should have more independence courses, not for people that have been on 'em like me, but to make people realize they can do things for themselves. I mean this place hasn't got to be the end of their universe.'* — Joyce

> 'There should be a mixture of the facilities what they've got already but more on the independence side. To push the people who get mollycoddled, them who are mollycoddled by their parents. Like they're not grown up. I don't think they should be pushed into it but they should be encouraged by staff.'* — Jamie

These views were shared by the other three in this group, Marilyn, Roger and Spike, but they believed that the activities should also be organized around the needs of the moderately impaired as well. Spike suggested that there should be facilities for learning to drive and car maintenance and Marilyn felt that the centres should do more to help the younger impaired find work. None of these users, however, could offer any advice as to how staff should encourage users to participate in the type of activities suggested. Like the rest of their Contact peers, they were adamant that 'people shouldn't be forced to do things'.

This section has focused on some of the problems associated with the implementation of structured rehabilitative activity within an unreservedly voluntarist atmosphere. I have shown that Contact users have access to rehabilitative and social activity and that there is some pressure on staff to direct users toward the former. Since user involvement in these areas is low, staff utilize their knowledge of users' biographies and employ strategies which allow them to emphasize the social element of the activity rather than its didactic content. This is important as shown by the three examples taken from the formal activities. Although environmental considerations may be significant and the preponderance of the elderly is a crucial factor in the explanation for low user involvement in vocational activity, it is clear that most of the Contact members see the day centres as sites for social rather than didactic activity. This may be explained with reference to the users' life experiences before entering the centres and their motives for entry (see Chapter Five). The work ethic, deferred gratification and independence are outside the frame of reference for the majority of users, the lifestyle and activities available in the centres represent an extension of what they experienced at school and/or in further education. For them rehabilitation in the literal sense is inappropriate. For the remainder who consider themselves independent already, the structured activities available are incompatible with their needs. Rehabilitation therefore can only proceed on an individual basis. If, however, the central function of the Contact group is to become more rehabilitative than social, then there will have to be a radical reformulation of group and day centre policy generally.

User Participation in Policy Formulation in the Contact Group

It is often argued that one of the major factors explaining apparent passivity and apathy among day centre users is that they are not involved in the planning and running of the services they need. For example,

> Day to day management of the centres seems in many instances to proceed without regard to the aims and aspirations of the users. Often lip service is paid to participation in the planning and running of services when in fact participation is limited to peripheral issues such as trips and social events (Kent *et al.*, 1984, p. 15).

Kent *et al.* maintain that although the official rhetoric of organizations sponsoring day services often espouses a desire to achieve maximum consultation between users and staff, the internal regimes of centres usually conform to traditional bureaucratic procedures, similar to those discussed by Weber (1948), where communication is essentially one-way and policies are fairly intransigent. One of the principal reasons for this is undoubtedly economic. Organizations which run day services, particularly local authorities, have since the 1970s come under increasing pressure from central and local government to control costs. This is invariably reflected in the policies of senior day centre staff, whose primary loyalty will be to their employer rather than to users. Hence the majority of centres offer few opportunities for user participation.

There are a few notable exceptions such as the Primus Club in Stockport where the users control the budget and hire and fire the staff and the Wigstone Centre in Leicestershire which has a committee composed of staff and users. The committee is responsible for the general running of the centre, albeit the control of the budget remains with the local authority (Kent *et al.*, 1984). But the most frequently quoted example of user participation in day centre management is the Stonehouse at Corby (Tuckey and Tuckey, 1981; Anderson and Clarke, 1982; Oliver, 1983a, Kent *et al.*, 1984). Bob and Linda Tuckey, the social workers responsible for setting up the unit in 1973, which was originally planned as a centre for the handicapped and elderly, developed what was in effect a community centre. While concentrating on the needs of the physically impaired, Stonehouse adopted an open door policy toward others in the community, including relatives and friends of users, parents of handicapped children and people with special needs, providing that they were below 50 years of age and intellectually capable of organizing their own lives in the centre.

For policy-making the Tuckeys developed a system of 'community meetings' with little formal structure where everyone was involved. But as more people began using Stonehouse this type of system proved unworkable.

> When the numbers grew what tended to develop was a sort of factionalism with groups of members veto-ing initiatives from others through self interest rather than rationality. As it was impossible to achieve consensus for a period the direction of the centre was lost (Carr, 1987, pp. 1–2).

In response a formal constitution was drawn up and the principle of user participation was incorporated into it. The management committee is now composed of at least nine annually elected users and has control of the centre's finances and internal policy. Committee meetings are held at least once a month and the committee is responsible for the convening of the six annual community meetings, where all Stonehouse users are present, as well as the yearly general meeting where the committee's annual report and the audited statement of accounts are presented (Stonehouse Association Constitution, 1985; Carr, 1987).

In an earlier paper concerned with user participation in day centres for the elderly, Jewell (1973) identified the principal difficulties he encountered when setting up a similar structure. The first, which he referred to as 'misrepresentation', concerns the situation where committee members fail to understand that they represent the whole user body and only put forward their own ideas. The second problem relates to the tendency for committee members to view themselves as privileged members of the day centre community. They become the 'committee elite'. The third focuses on the interaction between committee members and the rest of the users. Jewell contends that user committee membership can aggravate existing rivalry and conflict between users. Finally, he points to the dangers of staff manipulation, where staff use their 'professional expertise' to impose their own ideas rather than implement those of the users thus rendering user participation meaningless. He highlights the level of skill needed by staff to avoid these difficulties and concludes that there is considerable pressure on staff to avoid them altogether and run the centres themselves. The following shows that user participation in policy formulation in the three centres where the research was carried out was primarily concerned with 'peripheral issues' and was characterized by factionalism, misrepresentation and aggravated divisions within the user body. Consequently 'enlightened guardianship' rather than 'disabled action' retains its prominence within both the centres and the Contact group.

Excluding the Contact group, in each of the three day centres studied there were five separate users' committees, one for each of the unit's principal user groups. Each committee had its own formal constitution and was independent of the others. Committee members were elected annually and meetings were held daily at the Alf Morris and Engineers' centres and monthly at Dortmund Square. Senior staff involvement was not compulsory unless requested by members. The length of the meetings varied depending upon the agenda, although according to most observers the average was between thirty minutes and an hour. The minutes of each meeting were recorded by appointed members and submitted for the OIC's signature, in order to ensure that any complaints, comments or suggestions were duly noted by those in authority in the event of their absence.

On the basis of general discussions with senior staff and several users as well as a brief appraisal of the committee's minutes, it was evident that the main subjects discussed at these meetings were 'peripheral issues' such as trips, social events, day centre meals, the younger staff, the amenity funds and how they were spent. Generally it was felt that there were not enough outings organized by the centres. There were constant references as well to the poor quality of the food provided in the day centres and occasionally committee members complained about the conduct and demeanour of some of the younger CAs, usually those on government training schemes. At Alf Morris disquiet was expressed over how the amenity fund was allocated. As with Contact each user group collected amenity funds for the 'little extras' to make day centre life more comfortable and supplement the cost of outings, but these subscriptions were submitted to a communal fund for the benefit of the whole centre. And although access to the accounts was available to all users, as were the benefits of the funds, some of the user groups, notably Insight, felt that each group should be responsible for raising and spending their own money. Although reasonable in principle, this presents a problem for management as the funds are topped up by the proceeds of activities organized by each user group and the sale of products made in the centre's workshops. Since some groups, such as the younger relatively fitter Insight group, are more capable of raising finances than others, autonomous control of funds would inevitably produce inequalities. This problem was still unresolved when the study concluded.

Based on informal conversations with users (excluding Contact members) it seemed attitudes concerning the value of the committees varied considerably. While some felt that they did a fairly good job, a substantial minority pointed out that the same people were on the committees year after year and argued that they were unrepresentative of the users as a whole and looked after their own interests rather than the users generally. This group did concede, however, that most people were not interested in the committees or committee membership. Some suggested that their activities were irrelevant as the real power base lay outside the centres in the social services central offices. They also felt that even if the committees had more influence, it would make little difference to the majority's attitudes towards participation.

It was significant that in none of the centres were there any representatives from Contact on these committees despite the fact that the group constitutes nearly a third of the overall number of users at Alf Morris on Mondays and Wednesdays, and almost half at both the Engineers' and Dortmund Square on Tuesdays and Thursdays. Any contribution to centre policy from the Contact members had to be made either by senior Contact staff or individually. This is explained by staff with reference to the group's history.

'Because of the way it's developed, it's a unit in a unit if you like. It comes down to the organization of the Contact group and us. They're autonomous in that they have their own staff, their own budget, their own transport etc. and that's why none of them sit on our committees.'
— Andrew, OIC at Alf Morris

Contact has had its own users' committee in the recent past. Only the newcomers Paul and Clive knew nothing about it. There was some confusion, however, as to what form the committee had taken and what function it had performed. There had never been a formal constitution and like the other committees in the centres, it had never had access to or control of the group's budget, or control over the staff. Its primary role seems to have been the formulation and development of group activities, social events and the provision of a forum for committee members to air their grievances. It is clear that although others who have since left the group had sat on the committee, its principal members had been the most independent, notably Joyce, Marilyn, Andy, Jamie and later Billy. All five cited the general lack of interest by other users as the main reason for the committee's demise.

After his formal interview, when this subject had been discussed, Billy twice attempted to resurrect the committee 'in order to get a few things sorted out'. + His primary concerns were the poor condition of the snooker tables and the need for more outings. The first meeting, on 21 January 1987, was conducted with the full cooperation of both senior staff, and all the group, both users and staff, were present. It was opened by Patrick who introduced Billy and asked the assembly to listen carefully and consider seriously what he had to say. Billy told the group that he thought it was a good idea to get a new committee together since the old one had all but disappeared. He offered no other reason for this proposal than his complaint about the snooker tables. After some persuasion on his part he managed to scrape together four reluctant nominees besides himself. These were Joyce, Andy, Gavin and James. The latter two accepted their nomination with extreme reluctance.[3] There was no policy statement, mention of a formal constitution, or even an agreed date for the first committee meeting. Little more was heard of the committee until almost six months later.

On 1 July 1987 Billy again asked for a group meeting but gave no specific reason why, other than vague statements about 'gettin' things movin''. + Of the nineteen users who were present that day only twelve attended. Norman, Angela, Sally, James, Millie, Margaret and Karen elected to stay sitting outside in the sun. When I asked why they were not participating, Margaret replied,

'It's only Billy, we don't want to listen to 'im, 'e's only called it so's 'e can tell us what 'e thinks we ought to do'. +

James added,

'I don't want to sit in there listenin' to Billy . . . , nobody else will say anythin'. It's only Billy that wants it. It it 'ad been Jackie or Patrick who'd've called it, it'd be different. It's only Billy 'an we 'ear enough of 'im the rest of the week'. +

The meeting was held without these users. It lasted three-quarters of an hour and when it broke up there was much animosity between its organizer and the people who did not join in.

Because of non-participation by the majority of users, factionalism and the general failure of the users' committee, regular group meetings were initiated shortly before this study began. There were three between July and December 1986 and four between January and July 1987. These were open forums chaired by one of the senior staff and were usually attended by the entire group. They were all held on Wednesdays at Alf Morris since this was the best attended day of the week. The main subjects discussed were forthcoming activities or outings and various comments, suggestions and complaints made by users.

The subjects discussed at the first meeting I attended (2 July 1986) related to the forthcoming arrangements for the annual trip to the coast and the centre's closure during the holiday period. The second (3 September 1986) covered the programme of structured activities for the coming session and the proposals for the Christmas outing. At the third (22 October 1986), staff outlined the final arrangements for the Christmas festivities, including the annual Christmas lunch. Normally at these meetings there was little user involvement other than to pass comment on what staff had said. There was seldom any reference to the group's finances unless a user suggested buying a particular game or record with the amenity fund. In this case the suggestion was offered for approval.[4] At the last of these meetings conflict erupted when Jamie suggested an alternative venue for the proposed Christmas outing.

On the basis of several informal conversations with users, Jayne and Jackie suggested that the group use the same hotel as the year before since it had good facilities (such as disabled toilets and few steps) and the cost was the same as the previous year (£5.00 per head for a four-course meal). At the beginning of October each user had been given a letter for her/his parents outlining this idea and no one had proposed any alternative.

At the meeting Jackie outlined the proposal, pointed out that no one had voiced any objection and asked for comment. After approximately one minute's silence she stated,

'Do I take it everyone's happy with this idea then?' +

Several people nodded and began quietly talking amongst themselves. Then Jamie interjected,

'We don't want to go to the G . . . .Hotel again. Why can't we 'ave it on a night at a place with a proper disco?' +

Jackie replied,

> 'But they had a proper disco last year.' +

Jamie,

> 'That disco was rubbish. Why can't we go somewhere like the B. club?' +

Turning to the rest of the users who had remained silent throughout Jackie enquired,

> 'Does anyone else want to go to the B. club?' +

Jamie replied,

> 'Me, Joyce, Marilyn an' Billy think we ought to do somethin' different this year.' +

Joyce interjected sharply,

> 'Don't bring me into it, I know nothing about it.' +

Marilyn agreed that Jamie's suggestion was a good idea. Billy said he 'wasn't bothered' and turned to Spike who looked at Jackie and said it did not matter to him either as long as there was a bar. But Jamie continued,

> 'They won't say owt but I know they'd like a change.' +

Jackie restated that the hotel was well suited to the physical needs of the group, the cost of the lunch was low and there was no charge for transport since the outing would be during the day and users could use that provided by the day centres. Without these considerations some of the group would not be able to go. Jamie protested that since the event was only once a year users could afford a little more and that if they couldn't, then the money could come from the amenity fund. Jackie pointed out that there was insufficient money in the fund to supplement everyone and it would be unfair to subsidize some and not others. The two argued for several minutes while the rest of the ensemble remained silent. Jackie then concluded by stating that the Christmas lunch was for the entire group and that for the reasons stated it was probable that not everyone would attend if the venue and time were changed. She proposed that the arrangements stay as they were and that Jamie organize an evening function for those who wanted it. No one else offered any comment and some of the group began to move away.

The general feeling among all the users immediately after this meeting was that Jackie's plans were fine. Some of the group were sure that they would not be able to attend an evening outing, either because they could not get helpers or because of parental restrictions, and said that Jamie was just 'showing off'. Whether or not he was trying to elevate his status in front of the rest of the group (and myself) by challenging Jackie's proposals is open to interpretation. Certainly his friends and the two CAs Annie and Pete said that they would go to both events if he organized an alternative, but he never did. Jackie was reluctant to comment but pointed out that Jamie had not mentioned it earlier although he had known about the planned Christmas lunch for some time.

Assuming that Jamie's intentions were real, this example illustrates the dangers of both factionalism and misrepresentation within this type of setting. It is clear that he had not considered whether the change of plan would be acceptable to the rest of the group or whether it would be practical. Although he had a specific venue in mind he had made no preliminary enquiries if the club could, or would, accommodate thirty or so impaired people immediately before Christmas, or how much it would cost. This type of incident not only aggravates the significant divisions between Contact users, but draws attention to the centrality of the staff role in policy formulation. These points are reflected in the data from the users' interviews.

Seventeen users felt that group committees and meetings were an ineffective method for influencing policy. Non-participation was attributed to their domination by a vocal minority, and some of this group were clearly intimidated by that minority. Consequently they preferred to go directly to senior staff. The remainder believed that they were ineffective because the majority of the users did not appear to them to care what happened in the centres. Joyce, Andy and Jamie attributed this to socio-psychological factors, arguing that the majority had not been taught to think for themselves by either their parents or their schools. Marilyn took a similar view but suggested that the situation was made worse by chronic boredom after protracted periods in the day centres. Billy, who was relatively new to the group, took a less charitable view suggesting it was because 'most of 'em are thick'.* The remainder believed that mechanisms for user representation were simply cosmetic and/or unnecessary. Spike, for example, whose mother and father were on separate committees at Alf Morris, said that their only function was 'to make the members feel more at 'ome'.* Others such as Robert and Charles believed that staff were well trained and did their best to accommodate everyone's needs. Any limitation on what was available was due to the economic constraints on the system as a whole.

It is clear that the limited user participation in formal mechanisms of policy-making within the Contact group, if not the centres as a whole, is largely due to the significant social division within the Contact user body rather than staff manipulation. As a result of the tendency toward factionalism, misrepresentation and the aggravation of existing differences between users, these mechanisms appear to discourage user involvement in policy formulation instead of stimulating it. This situation could be improved by the implementation of a formal constitution and more direction from staff, but this might be viewed in a negative light by users since it could be interpreted as an infringement of their individual autonomy. In the meantime senior staff were endowed with both the legitimacy of their official role within the group and the popular support of the majority of users.

Social Control in the Contact Group

The previous section has shown that the variation in personality, impairments and attitudes among the Contact users is a major factor in preventing 'disabled action' or power becoming a reality within the context of the Contact group and the day centres generally. As a result, power, which is an embedded feature of day centre life, as in all social life (Sharpe, 1975) rests firmly in the hands of senior day centre personnel. This is important as it is often suggested, particularly since the ascendance of the 'new criminology' during the 1960s and 1970s (Downes, 1978), that agencies concerned with the treatment and care of deviant or disadvantaged groups, including the physically impaired, maintain 'hegemonic and manipulative control' of their 'clientele' in the normal process of daily interaction. This is sometimes referred to as the social control thesis. However, in an analysis of social control in a therapeutic community for the mentally ill, Bloor has shown that although power cannot be ignored, its impact need not be intentional (Lukes, 1974) and that although frequently associated with the manipulation of interaction, social control is not an embedded feature of social life. Rather it is

> a particular attribute of a given superordinate status which may or may
> not be asserted in interaction as the superordinate chooses (Bloor, 1987,
> p. 319).

Following this train of thought I shall show that within the context of the Contact group and the day centres generally, social control was not a significant component of staff/user interaction. It was only one among staff's repertoire of tasks and when necessary was exercised through a combination of orchestration and supervision. Discipline was not considered a problem but this was attributable to external factors rather than the activities of day centre staff. I shall begin by looking at the constraints on user activity in the centres and the strategies used by staff to maintain order.

I have already stated that the principle of individual user autonomy is sacrosanct within the day centres and the Contact group. It follows that apart from implicit and occasionally explicit constraints on the younger users' movements, which are imposed by other users rather than the staff, and the pressure to participate in 'constructive' activity on Tuesdays at the Engineers', every effort is made by staff to ensure that an unfettered atmosphere prevails. This was particularly visible in relation to the delivery of services. It is an important consideration because for people with impairments the body is the principal site of oppression, both in form, since a disabled person is seen as disabled first and a person second, and in respect of what is done to it (Abberly, 1987).

The general practice in all three centres adheres closely to this principle wherever possible. There were no bathing or toileting routines for the convenience of the staff. Under normal circumstances it was up to users to decide as and when these services were necessary. This policy could only be frustrated by extreme staff shortages but this never occurred during the study. Users were responsible for the administration of any drugs they needed, although it was not uncommon for staff to be told by a parent or guardian to remind individuals not to forget to take them. Since April 1987, each user has had access to any files or documents kept by the social services which concerned them as individuals.[5] Contact users, however, gained access to such data several years earlier because a number of them, notably Joyce, Andy, Jamie and Marilyn, expressed concern over the right of staff to keep this type of material. Sharpe (1975) reported the same concerns among similarly aged residents in a therapeutic community for the mentally ill a decade earlier. Contrary to the practice prevailing in 1985, senior Contact staff gave them access to this information. But according to Jayne, as was the case with the residents in Sharpe's study, they were more interested in the principle of the right of concealment than in the actual documents.

The policy regarding transport was less flexible for other day centre users than it was for Contact members. The service provided for the former conformed to the 'traditional' model, which has been subject to criticism for its inflexibility (Kent *et al.*, 1984). Individuals requiring transport were collected from their door by a specially adapted social services vehicle at a specified time (between 8.30 and 9.30 a.m.), brought to the centres and then taken home in the afternoon (at approximately 3.30 p.m.). Users were faced with one option, and obliged either to take it or leave it.[6] Transport was arranged through consultation with senior day centre personnel.

The situation was less rigid in relation to the Contact group. Because of its ad hoc development, its peripatetic policy and the recent economic and political constraints on social services spending, it had never been assigned a permanent transport facility. Consequently Contact subcontracted to local taxi firms for this service. Apart from the fact that travel by taxi carries no stigma, unlike travel in social services' vehicles, they gave users a greater sense of control, were individually radio-controlled, and only carried one or two users and their wheelchairs at a time, whereas social services' minibuses carried up to eleven. Although initially organized by either Jayne or Jackie, once in operation users had direct access to the taxi firm via the telephone if they wanted it. They also allowed greater flexibility in terms of collection times. Joyce and Marilyn, for example, preferred to use the centres only in the afternoon, which would not have been possible had they used social services' vehicles. There was also a rehabilitative function to this policy in that it enabled users to become more familiar with commercial transport other than that 'provided' by the Local Authority.

There was no evidence of a general policy statement or constitution outlining a set of rules and procedures relating to users' behaviour in the centres. None of the staff interviewed said they had ever seen one. Directives relating to internal policy seem to have been issued on a purely ad hoc basis and were dependent on the interpretations of the senior staff in each unit. A good example concerns their views regarding users' freedom to leave the centres as and when they chose. While it was clear there was some official policy in this area there was confusion as to what form it took. Two of the OICs, Andrew from Alf Morris and Sandra at Dortmund Square, held the view that users were not free to leave the centres temporarily unless accompanied by a member of staff. Since there was rarely a surfeit of staff this was seldom possible on an individual basis. Consequently users were effectively confined to the centres during the day.

'This applies to everybody. This is a clear directive from above if you like. We are not a drop-in centre, So that means necessarily . . . , that if somebody's down on our register say, Tuesday, then by and large, we expect them to be here on a Tuesday. They have, or are expected to, show that commitment.'* — Andrew

His explanation for this policy was as follows,

'If people were allowed to come and go as they please, administratively it would be a terrible headache, because of the constraints of the building if you like. You're talking about insurance, fire risk, all those sorts of things.'*

It is clear that these two OICs put other considerations above user autonomy as far as this issue is concerned. One probable reason is that if users go out alone and anything goes wrong, such as a road accident for example, then senior staff are held responsible by the social services department. Andrew and Sandra clearly prefer to contain users rather than take the risk. Despite the fact that she is subject to the same constraints, however, Mrs W at the Engineers', who is reputed to be a 'stickler' for regulations, adopted a more flexible approach.

'As long as they pop their heads round the door and tell me where they're going and when they come back. Because we're held responsible for them while they're here you see. If they don't turn up at home at night, someone's going to ring up and say, "Oh but they were left in your care for the day". You see we're also responsible to their families.'* — Mrs W

Clearly Mrs W puts user autonomy before other considerations. Her statements brings into focus a further dilemma regarding this issue which is particularly pertinent to those working with the younger day centre users living with their parents or guardians. Who should they be accountable to, the users or their families? The problem is made worse when staff are acutely conscious of the former's need for autonomy and the latter's concern for their offsprings' welfare.

In a discussion about this issue Jayne stated,

'It's been put to me that if anyone goes out of the day centre and anything goes wrong it's on my head, nothing's been written down mind you. But it's a difficult one because there's the families as well. You see I don't think we should have any say in it really. I mean in most cases we're talking about twenty to thirty year old people.'*

There was no clear policy in Contact with regard to this issue. Although officially the group was subject to the policies favoured by the OICs in the host centre, Jayne and Jackie adopted a flexible approach in response to the demands of the more able Contact members, which gave individual users considerably more freedom. In general those not reliant on social services' transport used all three centres as and when they felt like it. As for the remainder, several often went out without a member of staff. The only apparent rule concerning this group was that those wanting to leave the units should tell staff when and where they were going. Although this policy is inconsistent in that it allows some users more freedom than others, there was little objection to it by the majority of Contact members.

This can be attributed to a number of factors. Firstly, because several of the group were dependent upon wheelchairs for mobility, travelling any distance without transport or an ambulate companion who can push was almost impossible.[7] As the social services' transport facility, whether a specially adapted minibus or a subcontracted taxi, only included travel to and from the centres, users wanting to go out during the day had to pay for transport themselves. Since taxis were expensive and mobility allowances were grossly inadequate (Disability Alliance, 1987), few could afford it. Secondly, a number of the group stated that they would not leave the centres unless they were accompanied by a member of staff. Some of these respondents, Margaret, Sally and Angela, for example, said in separate interviews that they would not trust other users to push them due to the fear of being 'tipped out' of their chair by accident. Barry and Henry, both with unsteady gaits, maintained they would not go out without staff because of the 'dangerous roads'. Four others said they could not go out owing to their disabilities. These included Billy, Paul and Karen because they couldn't walk very far without help, and Bruce because he 'takes fits'.* In answer to the question 'who said you can't go out?' Billy and Paul said they just took it for granted. Karen and Bruce said they had been told by their respective parents. Nancy also stated that day centre staff had been told by her father that she was not to go out unless accompanied by one of the staff. This was later confirmed by Jayne. When asked if she would inform parents if any of the users went out alone, she said she would avoid it at all costs because it would damage relations within the group. Since none of these users left the centres during the study unless with a member of staff, it is fair to assume that the knowledge that parents might be informed if they did was enough to prevent it occurring.

A third point relates to the practice of informing staff when leaving the building. All those who used day centre transport felt it was a legitimate request, some because they were aware of the responsibility senior staff bore regarding this issue, and others because they felt certain people in the group were not capable of looking after themselves and therefore staff should provide guidance.

> 'I think we should ask staff. It should be up to them whether people go out or not, 'cos some people might think they can go out and really they can't. It should be up to staff whether they think you're capable of doin' it. I think if staff let people do what they like outside, I think there'd be a lot of accidents. There's gotta be some control over it. If they can let you go out they will.'* — Curt

This view was not shared by those individuals not dependent on social services' transport who used the centres as and when they pleased. They felt it was childish to have to tell staff when they were going out and what time they expected to be back. For example, Molly, who is keen on art and got on well with Hilary, the arts and crafts tutor at the Engineers', stopped attending on Tuesdays because she objected to being 'treated like a little kid'* by Mrs W who reminded her to inform someone in authority when she was leaving the building one lunchtime.

Within the context of the Contact group these differences, in terms of some users' apparent freedom to go out at will while others were not, provoked a degree of animosity from a minority within the group. It was not, however, directed toward staff but at those who

> 'just seem to do what they like'* — Margaret

The issue of whether or not users should be allowed to leave the day centres at will is a critical one since it is central to any philosophy which purports to encourage user independence and self-determination. Although there is some confusion concerning official policy on this issue, the interpretation of senior staff at Alf Morris and Dortmund Square clearly involves a denial of user autonomy and a negation of that philosophy. While it is likely that this view is determined by external factors, such as limited resources and family considerations, it is patronizing to users in that it assumes they are unaware of those considerations. The interview data show that they are not. It is unlikely, however, that the flexible policy adopted by Contact staff on this issue was conceived without knowledge of these factors. By allowing users to define their own situation it may be said that they are encouraging user independence. The principal difficulty is that such a policy re-emphasizes the significant differences among Contact members.

The maintenance of social order in the day centres was considered a non-issue by most of the staff respondents. There was no formal disciplinary code relating to users and there were no official sanctions other than contacting users' families, where applicable. If an individual was consistently disruptive they could be referred to another institution where there were enough staff to cope with such behaviour. This was rationalized with reference to the predominantly social atmosphere in the day centres and the principal social characteristics of the majority of users they catered for, namely, that they were elderly and/or lonely and that they came because they wanted company, not to cause trouble. All three OICs interviewed suggested that their primary concerns in this area were preventing individuals from smoking in spaces where it was supposedly proscribed or trying to uphold appropriate standards of table manners and personal hygiene. When necessary the responsibility for this function fell on the shoulders of the SAO/AO in charge of each section. Neither of these issues presented much of a problem in the Contact group. Only one of the users, Jamie, smoked, and although it was reported that there had been difficulties with specific individuals and hygiene in the past, they were infrequent and did not occur during the study.

Behavioural norms in the day centres were subject to abstract principles of 'common sense', or what Jackie referred to as 'the general rules of society,* which were said to be determined by the users themselves. However, in the Engineers' and the Dortmund Square day centres, what was viewed as acceptable was clearly determined by the elderly and was a constant source of consternation for both Contact users and staff. Within the Contact format, all the respondents agreed that certain types of behaviour were unacceptable. These included shouting, swearing, overt rowdiness and fighting. Since some of those within the group were occasionally prone to this type of activity, notably the lads in subgroup D, senior Contact staff employed a number of techniques to control it. In the broadest sense these involved disruption avoidance strategies, or orchestration, and crisis management, or supervisory control. These techniques were not mutually exclusive but inter-related and implicit in the rehabilitative and supervisory components of senior staff's roles discussed in Chapter Four.

The first of these strategies refers to the tactics employed by senior staff to stimulate, motivate and perpetuate user participation in particular activities analogous to those referred to earlier in this chapter. This involves educational and vocational as well as social activities. Consequently this function is also performed by CAs and VWs when they are organizing what I have termed semi-formal social activities such as quizzes and organized games. Senior staff employ a number of techniques to control unacceptable behaviour. Disruption or crisis management involved one of three distinct but related tactics depending on the nature and the gravity of the misdemeanour. These were straightforward requests, reference to a higher authority, and exclusion.

The first, straightforward requests, was the most commonly used technique and was applied when relatively minor infringements of social norms occurred. These requests were usually legitimized with appeals to abstract moral principles rooted in common sense and culture, collective interests and group loyalties — usually those of the Contact group as a whole rather than subgroup affiliations or the day centres generally. A common example, which does not relate to general disruption or to one of the lads, concerns the problem of congestion in the ladies toilet and the corridor outside the Contact rooms at Alf Morris. As noted in the last chapter, users, notably the girls from subgroup B, would frequently congregate in one of these locations, causing problems of access for users and staff. Usually this meant Jayne or Jackie pointing to the inconvenience caused by it and asking those responsible to move elsewhere. For example,

'Come on girls, you can see nobody can get past. I thought you had a bit more common sense than this.' +

Such requests normally met with protestations about the limited space available to Contact users but usually it was enough to get the girls to move.

Patrick utilized appeals to an abstract masculine moral code when asking male users to curb their language.

'I usually get 'em on one side and speak to 'em man to man. Say if it's about swearing for example. I just tell 'em if they're going to use language like that, an' we all do, then they should keep it down, especially in front of girls.'*

Boisterous behaviour was not unusual within the Contact areas at Alf Morris, albeit it was uncommon on Tuesdays at the Engineers' and on Thursdays at Dortmund Square. This is attributable to the spatial constraints and the general atmosphere at these latter centres which results in the more disruptive members of the group not attending or, when they do, only staying for a short while. Staff saw users' boisterous activity as a normal part of adolescence, something that should be expected, especially when considered in relation to the constraints placed on most of the group at home. Such activity, however, occasionally became unacceptable, such as when the usual noise levels increased and/or when other users began to leave the immediate vicinity where the incident was occurring. A number of the group, normally those with low status, Karen, Richard or Amy for example, sometimes told staff when proscribed activity was taking place.

The most common location for disruptive behaviour was around the pool table in the smaller room at Alf Morris and more often than not involved one or more of the lads from subgroup D, Billy, Andy, Jamie or Spike. Arguments often erupted over who was to play next, despite staff's efforts to organize a rota system, or whose shot it was. Most of these disputes were sorted out fairly quickly by those involved, but occasionally they broke out into open conflict which invariably involved swapping insults or threats and inevitably involved swearing at a higher volume than normal.[8] When this happened CAs sometimes intervened using references to senior staff as a deterrent. For example,

'Can't you shut up, you'll have Jayne in here'.

Normally these or similar appeals fell on deaf ears because of their peer group status and lack of authority. However, such requests were not usually ignored when they came from one of the senior staff, although they were rarely addressed to individuals. Most requests of this nature appealed to the collective interest and/or group loyalties, such as,

'Can you tone it down in here please, you'll get us a worse name than we've got already, we have enough trouble as it is.'

Sometimes one of the protagonists would attempt to elicit staff's help to sort out any conflict or protest their innocence, but usually these interventions stifled the disorder. Compliance may be attributable to a desire to please staff or a respect for commonly held values, as is likely with the first example involving the girls. But I believe it is more often because further disruption would provoke further involvement from staff. It resembles what Hargreaves has referred to as 'expedient compliance' (Hargreaves, 1975). Although members of subgroup D adopt what resembles a 'delinquent orientation' in that they present an overtly rebellious stance toward formal authority, all were aware of the sanctions available to day centre personnel. Both Jamie and Spike claimed that they had been both threatened with exclusion because of their overt aggression prior to my joining the group.[9] While the effects of exclusion from the centres were important, in terms of loss of friends etc., I suggest that their compliance was also due to their awareness of the importance of senior staff as a readily available professional resource which they could not afford to alienate.

If an individual was continually disruptive, staff took the view that there was some underlying cause and the miscreant was invited to account for her/his behaviour in a semi-formal setting, usually in the Contact office with only one or other of the senior staff present. This action was not rationalized by staff as part of the control mechanism but as part of the rehabilitation process. It occurred twice during the study, first, when Jamie's verbal aggression became an almost regular feature of his personality, and secondly, when Billy became sullen and argumentative. After one counselling session Jamie's behaviour was ascribed to socio/economic factors, specifically relating to housing and financial worries associated with his impending fatherhood. In the event Jackie contacted a social worker on his behalf and his anti-social behaviour declined. Billy's problems were explained in socio/psychological terms relating to his loss of able-bodied friends when he left school, his worsening impairment and his lack of knowledge concerning his disease. Staff attempted to resolve these difficulties, firstly by contacting his parents, so that he could discuss his illness with them, secondly, by organizing a series of individual counselling sessions, and thirdly, by the formulation of group projects with him in mind, namely, the snooker table project and a lengthy indoor games and sports tournament. This involved all the group, males and females, where each user played everyone else in the group at every indoor game available. Billy was in fact the overall winner. In this instance orchestration was the result of crisis management rather than a disruption avoidance strategy.

The second technique for crisis management, reference to a higher authority, was used for more serious norm infractions, two instances of which occurred during the study period. Both involved the same individual, Andy, and because of the seriousness of the misdemeanours, both involved the OIC at Alf Morris. The first arose because one of the girls accused Andy of interfering with her sexually against her will. Because this is a serious accusation both parties were asked to give an account of the incident in the manager's office. What actually happened is open to speculation since at her interview the girl changed her story and Andy denied the whole incident. In the event staff took the view that something had occurred but because the girl did not wish to make a fuss no further action was taken other than Andrew, the OIC involved, giving Andy a warning that any future incident would warrant investigation. The second example took place six months later and followed a similar pattern but involved a users' family. Nancy's father rang the OIC at Alf Morris because he said his daughter had told him Andy extorted money from her by force. In the subsequent office confrontation she maintained that her father had misunderstood and that she had lent Andy had the money, following which the matter was closed.

The ritual of being asked to account for behaviour in a formal setting performs at least three specific functions. Firstly, it emphasizes that certain types of behaviour are considered more serious than others. Secondly, it acts as a formal reaffirmation of staff's superordinate status within the day centres. This is important because most senior staff deliberately try to foster a social relationship with users. And thirdly, it is a confirmation that in the last analysis there is an unequal distribution of power within the system and that staff can, if necessary, use that power to impose sanctions on users. It is important that this ritual act as a suitable deterrent since both the main sanctions available to staff, contacting users' families and exclusion, have negative implications for both parties. For example, contacting users' families on a regular basis not only causes unpleasantness for the individual concerned but also damages the carefully nurtured staff/user relationship and social atmosphere in the centres. With regard to exclusion, the fact that the miscreant uses the centres through choice has obvious implications. From the staff perspective, because this process involves a protracted process of consultation with the RDCO, other agencies and professionals, and the careful scrutiny of all the relevant data, internal policies may be seen wanting and senior staff viewed as incompetent. Consequently it is in their interest to avoid it where possible.

This section has shown that in the day centres generally and the Contact group in particular social control, or the manipulation of interaction by day centre personnel, was not a prominent feature of the staff/user relationship. This was evident in the internal policies relating to the delivery of services. User control was restricted with regard to transport although here Contact members had more flexibility than other users. This was due largely, however, to accident rather than design. One area of concern, since it is central to the ethos of user autonomy, relates to users' freedom to leave the centres at will during opening hours. Official policy on this issue appeared arbitrary and subject to interpretation by senior staff. Only one of the three OICs concerned adopted a flexible approach to this issue. The other two advocated containment. In contrast, Contact staff favoured a discretionary approach which allowed users to take responsibility for their own actions. The result was that some users were able to take advantage of this freedom while others were not. This highlights the external environmental, economic and social constraints imposed on the majority of Contact members, and the significant differences among users in terms of impairments, abilities and attitude. This disparity could easily be minimized by an input of resources into the centres, such as more transport and staff for example.

Social order in the centres and also within the Contact group, was based on commonly held values and norms. Control in both was subject to normal power relations inherent to the division of labour. Authority rested in the superordinate status of senior personnel and was dispensed when necessary through a subtle combination of orchestration and supervisory control. Boisterous social activity was not unusual in Contact but discipline was not considered a major problem. It was apparent that socially disruptive behaviour was usually perpetuated by the lads in subgroup D and was normally controlled by staff through appeals to abstract moral values and common sense. But while these appeals may have carried weight with particular individuals I suggest that compliance was based to some degree on mutual reciprocity, since senior staff represent a valuable resource for Contact users. Staff generally attributed excessive anti-social behaviour to external force. In response staff orchestrated rehabilitative activities which partially resolved individual problems and alleviated further disruption within the group. When 'serious' crises occurred staff employed tactics which re-emphasized their authority before exercising negative sanctions. This is important since the two main sanctions available to staff, contacting users families and exclusion, have negative effects for both parties.

Conclusion

The first section of this chapter has shown that user involvement and control of services for disabled people is now considered central to contemporary thinking. It is suggested that progress in this direction is inhibited by traditional professional attitudes and the significant divisions within the disabled population. Consequently any advances are likely to be small-scale and at the local level. In relation to day services for the younger physically impaired, recent research has recommended that institutions provide rehabilitative activities which encourage user participation and control. The empirical data show that although the structured activities offered to Contact users were limited by environmental and other factors, particularly swamping by the elderly, they fell broadly in line with this philosophy. User participation, however, was low despite staff's efforts to orchestrate it. This was due to the explicitly voluntarist policy in the centres since users appeared to prefer social rather than didactic activity. While the environmental limitations of these activities clearly contributed to this phenomenon, the users' lack of motivation in these areas is due to earlier life experiences, so that for the majority rehabilitation was inappropriate, and for the remainder the facilities offered were inadequate. This highlights the contradiction inherent to a policy which encompasses both social and didactic activity within an expressly voluntarist framework.

Discussion of user involvement in the formal mechanisms of policy formulation in the system has highlighted the user committees which existed in the three day centres studied. Their power did not include the control of finances or staff. Rather, they were primarily concerned with social isssues and relatively minor complaints. These bodies were prone to factionalism and misrepresentation which aggravated the social divisions between users. As a result their value was undermined. Although a users' committee existed in the Contact group before the study began it was abandoned in favour of semi-formal group meetings which included all the Contact members. However, a tendency for factionalism and misrepresentation by a vocal minority within the group remained and extended to these group forums. As a result existing antagonisms between Contact members were exacerbated and the authority of senior Contact staff remained unchallenged.

The principle of user autonomy and control was given precedence in relation to the delivery of services within the centres by senior staff but was limited with regard to transport and freedom to leave the building during opening hours. Although this policy may be rationalized in a number of ways with reference to administration, family constraints or the users' best interests, it involves an explicit denial of user autonomy and a negation of any philosophy which purports to encourage social rehabilitation. Contrary to this policy Contact staff adopted a discretionary approach which allowed users to make their own decisions. This policy highlights a number of points which include, firstly, users' awareness of the external constraints on their mobility outside the day centres, secondly, the extent of these constraints, environmental, economic and social, and thirdly, since some of the group were able to leave the units as and when they chose, the differences in terms of impairments, abilities and attitudes among Contact members. While this policy facilitated higher levels of user freedom, it further accentuated those differences.

Behavioural precepts within the centres were kept to a minimum and while there were some environmental constraints on Contact's activities, social order was not considered a major problem. Disruptive behaviour was sometimes evident within the group but was normally controlled by staff through a combination of orchestration and supervisory control. During the study period anti-social activities were only perpertrated by the most independent male members of the group. These were interpreted by staff as caused by external socio-psychological factors and controlled through the orchestration of rehabilitative activities. In the case of 'serious' misdemeanours staff resorted to strategies which emphasized their superordinate status and authority rather than the imposition of negative sanctions. This was due to the fact that the principal sanctions available to staff have negative implications for both them and the users.

In the final analysis it is clear that higher levels of participation and control by Contact members were inhibited by a number of environmental and social factors which I believe can only be resolved by a radical reformulation of internal policies that clarify the social and rehabilitative function of the centres. This may mean abandoning voluntarism within the units and the imposition of some form of formal constitution which demands a greater degree of commitment from users. Whether or not such controls would be acceptable is open to speculation since individual autonomy is one of the principal attractions of day centre use. This may be more understandable with reference to the following chapter which looks at the constraints on that autonomy outside the centres in the community at large.

Notes

1 Representatives of DIAL visited the day centres twice during the study period.

2 Shortly after Paul joined Contact Jayne was visited by his parents who wanted to make sure he did not waste his time during the day.

3 Jamie was absent from the centres on this occasion because he had just become a father and Marilyn refused to join the proposed committee although she was nominated.

4 The amenity fund accounts were posted on the unofficial noticeboard immediately above the tea trolley in the main Contact area at Alf Morris, but few of the users ever looked at them.

5 It is likely that this is one of the reasons why some referral agents, for example social workers, are reluctant to provide substantial information on day centre referrals.

6 Those who could use public transport were given the full cost of the bus fare to and from the centres.

7 Research shows that at best about 25 per cent of wheelchair users can push themselves more than 200 yards in an average urban environment (Segal, 1986).

8 Although it was reported that fights have ensued after this type of incident, none occurred during the study period.

9 This was denied by senior staff, notwithstanding that both Jamie and Spike had been warned about their aggressiveness by senior day centre personnel.

Chapter 7
Integration into the Community

This chapter is divided into two main sections. The first concerns the environmental and social barriers to integration which confront people with disabilities in the community and illustrates the extent to which the Contact users are disadvantaged in these areas. The second covers their leisure and social activities outside the units and highlights the level of social isolation many experience in the domestic sphere. The data underpin the importance of the day centres as a nexus of social activity for participants and show that the majority do not expect to leave the system in the foreseeable future. I conclude, therefore, that to varying degrees many of these users will become dependent on the day centres and as a result their disadvantages will be compounded.

Barriers to Integration and the Contact Group

I will first outline the major environmental and social barriers to the integration into contemporary society of people with disabilities, and secondly, show how these obstacles are encountered by Contact users when outside the day centres. The data is based both on observed examples of individual and group interaction and on user interviews. Where appropriate I will draw attention to the visible changes in users' behaviour during these encounters and show how these experiences reinforce their dependent status.

Bowe (1978) has indentified six major barriers to the integration of people with disabilities into society. They are architectural, attitudinal, educational, occupational, legal and personal. Bowe illustrates the first of these, which includes all aspects of the physical environment including braille notices for the blind, printed signs for the deaf, correctly sited elevator buttons, modified public transport accessible to people with limited mobility and access to all public buildings, by discussing the problems associated with government buildings in America. He records, for example, the number of schools not adapted for pupils in wheelchairs and shows how getting legislation for an architecturally barrier-free environment through Congress is considerably easier than putting it into practice. A similar difficulty exists in Britain. This is evident from the increasing number of guides put out by organizations representing people with impairments which show that access to many public buildings and amenities such as theatres and libraries, which the non-impaired take for granted, is almost impossible without prior notification to the appropriate authority. The report by the Committee on Restrictions against Disabled People (CORAD, 1982) stated that many people with impairments perceive access difficulties as 'the most fundamental cause of discrimination'.

The basis for Bowe's second category, attitudinal barriers, is historically and culturally determined and enmeshed in the ideologies and policies of national governments and institutions (see Chapter Two). As noted earlier, we sanctify the minority of 'super-cripples' who transcend the limitations of their impairments but relegate the majority of like-situated individuals to a life of relative poverty and social isolation. These practices perpetuate the negative attitudes associated with disability among the general public. They include perceptions of the disabled as 'less than whole' (Dartington, Miller and Gwynne, 1981), a threat, objects of ridicule, pitiful, or eternal children (Hurst, 1984). Usually on first encounters people with overt disabilities are viewed by the non-impaired as abnormal. Consequently these interactions are problematic for both parties.

In a study of data derived from encounters between the able and the visibly impaired, Davis (1964) identifies a two-stage process before normal relations ensue. The first stage is designated as 'fictional acceptance' and denotes the initial interface where distant cordiality prevails and the question of impairment is overlooked. The second stage occurs when the subject is brought out into the open and the disability enters the conversation in a 'non-stigmatizing way'. Only then can normal relations proceed and it becomes possible to admit to the interaction the restrictions which the impairment imposes. Bowe comments on covert rejection occurring since politeness does not permit overt negative reactions and describes experiments which show how the non-impaired espouse opinions that they do not hold to avoid giving offence when conversing with the disabled. He notes the falseness and awkwardness of these encounters. Other sources have drawn attention to the extent of the 'does he take sugar'? syndrome (Hurst, 1984) where remarks are directed to a third party and not directly to the person with an impairment. It is also important to note that overt hostility and rejection are not uncommon. Individuals with visible impairments are occasionally refused admission to public amenities because of their impairments and sometimes made to feel unwelcome by entire communities (Mills, 1988).

Educational barriers are those which operate to segregate children with impairments from their non-impaired peers into special schools. This applies in further and higher education as well as in basic schooling. And despite the plethora of criticism directed at the policy of segregation because of the consistent failure of special schools to provide an adequate education, both the number and percentage of children in special education in the British Isles continues to rise (Booth, 1981; Barton, 1986; Tomlinson, 1985). Barton echoes Tomlinson in suggesting that the gradual expansion of special education can be best seen as a political response to a critical dilemma facing the education system and society generally, namely, the need to control the expanding surplus population (Barton, 1986). The situation in further and higher education is equally dismal. Thomas (1982) maintained that many universities and colleges were inaccessible to disabled students. In a recent survey of provision for students with disabilities in further and higher education, Richard Stowall provided evidence to show that this is still the case and reports that,

> Despite the recommendations of the Warnock Committee in 1978 that all colleges should have and should publish, a policy on the admission of students with special educational needs, fewer than 1 in 5 colleges have a formal policy. Those that have tend to be the major providers for students with special educational needs (Stowall, 1987, p. ix).

Obstacles to paid employment, Bowe's fourth category, are many and various. The Disabled Persons (Employment) Act of 1944 laid a framework for the provision of employment rehabilitation and resettlement schemes and provided legislation which gave people with impairments legal rights to paid work by obliging those employing more than 20 workers to recruit at least 3 per cent of their workforce from the disabled persons' register (Oliver, 1983a). Despite these legal rights, unemployment among the disabled remains disproportionately high when compared with that among the non-impaired. Prosecutions for non-compliance with the Act against employers are few. There have only been ten since the Act became law in 1944. There is substantial evidence to suggest that even within government departments quotas are not filled (Thomas, 1982).

There are conflicting explanations for this situation. It has been suggested, for example, that many people with impairments do not register as disabled because of the stigma associated with disability and/or because they feel that registration can harm their future prospects. One source has suggested that the majority of civil servants who work in the employment resettlement and careers services believe that the Act is unworkable and that they favour the repeal of its mandatory features and a return to a voluntary policy. Organizations representing the disabled, on the other hand, take the opposite view, arguing that the Act is too weak and should be strengthened. There is also clear evidence to show that government officials consistently attach more importance to the views of employers than they do to the representatives of the disabled population (Stubbins, 1983). In a society dominated by the economic rationality of the market place, the disabled are among the most vulnerable sections of the community. Even when employment is offered it is often low-paid demeaning work, and the match between abilities and occupations is frequently unbalanced. As well as unemployment many people with impairments have to contend with under-employment (Thomas, 1982).

Bowe's fifth barrier relates to the legal obstacles which confront disabled people. On a similar theme Thomas (1982) has asked why it took so long for the Chronically Sick and Disabled Persons Act to reach the statute books and why an important report such as 'Integrating The Disabled' was published as late as 1974.

There is also a gap between legislative intent and action. The much vaunted Chronically Sick and Disabled Persons Act, the cornerstone of statutory provision for people with impairments, sought to give people with disabilities the right to live in the community by providing the appropriate support services. Local authorities were obligated to perform two specific tasks which were (a) to inform themselves of the number and needs of disabled people in their area and (b) to publicize their available services.

Section 2 of the Act lists services which should be provided for those whose needs have been assessed. These include practical assistance in the home, recreation facilities, free or subsidized travel, social services support for carers and families, aids and adaptations and so on. It is regarded by some, notably Topliss and Gould (1981), as a 'charter for the disabled', nothing less than a public testament to the social rights of disabled people. They argue that the passing of the Act and its subsequent publicity has increased public awareness of the problems associated with disability and changed attitudes toward people with impairments. Others contend that this unprecedented media attention has had the opposite effect. Public interest in the subject has waned, it is suggested, because many non-impaired people now believe that all the needs of the disabled are met by the Act (Simpkins and Tickner, 1978). The reality could not be further from the truth.

In 1979 one commentator maintained that Section 2 of the Act was in effect only Section 29 of the National Assistance Act of 1948 'writ large' (Keeble, 1979, quoted in Oliver, 1983a). The same author notes that while the Act promises much, careful analysis of Section 2 reveals that provision is not mandatory and nor is it free. The Act's implementation has been hindered by a number of factors such as the reorganization of local authorities and the health service during the 1970s, the successive economic 'crises' and the discouragement by central government of local authorities' attempts to initiate parts of the Act, particularly those which involve a large capital outlay. Consequently there is much regional variation in services.

One attempt to clarify this piece of legislation, conducted by the Royal Association for Rehabilitation and Disability (RADAR), concluded that despite some limited success in specific areas, it is clear that given the 'current' economic climate and the uneasy relationship between central and local government, the Act is neither implementable nor enforceable (Cook and Mitchell, 1982). Subsequent developments, namely, the successive re-election of right-of-centre governments with a definite bias against state-sponsored welfare systems, an avowed intent to reduce state spending and an ambivalence toward local authorities which borders on paranoia have exacerbated these problems still further. The result is that some authorities have begun to withdraw services which were hitherto provided (Ernstoff and Howe, 1988).

Thomas (1982) maintains that while there are still legal barriers confronting disabled people, such as the requirement on some job applications for applicants to disclose specific illnesses such as epilepsy, the most important hurdle is the complexity of legislation rights, allowances and claiming procedures. Claiming welfare benefits is now so difficult that a new professional known as the Welfare Rights Officer, has emerged to act as intermediary between the layman and the law (Simpkins and Tickner, 1978). The situation has become progressively worse in recent years with the tedious successive changes to the already complex state-sponsored social security benefit schemes, and the introduction in April 1988 of the Community Fund, which marks the end of statutory payments and a return to a means-tested discretionary system (Lynes, 1988).

The final category in Bowe's (1978) typology is the personal barrier. He comments that adventitious disability results in problems of daily living, reduced social status, decreased income and lowered perceptions of self. Life-long impairment, he argues, is frequently associated with an inferior education and preparation for life as well as segregation from the non-impaired. Bowe contends that the stress of coming to terms with the harshness of the non-impaired world makes the congenitally impaired attribute their misfortune to their impairments. Within this context, 'passing' as normal or non-impaired becomes an over-riding preoccupation.

Goffman (1968) used the term 'passing' in his analysis of the interactions between the 'stigmatized' and the 'non-stigmatized'. It refers to those situations where the former on initial encounters with the latter deliberately conceal information about specific aspects of their social identity which they feel will be discrediting. From this perspective to be disabled is to be a 'shamed' person. However, while there are a number of techniques for passing available to individuals with less obvious impairments, such as epilepsy, passing for the overtly physically impaired is more problematic.

Thomas adds a further dimension to Bowe's typology, the professional barrier to integration. It is the result of what he terms the 'professionalization of handicap'.

> Handicap has become the happy hunting ground of many professional interests. Handicap is the province of the medical specialist, the educational psychologist, the social worker, the welfare rights worker, the residential care worker, the special teacher, the health visitor and the occupational therapist. Each cadre of professional concern develops its own cognitive style of appraising handicap with its in group jargon, house journals, specialist training and shared value systems (Thomas, 1982, p. 182).

One source has estimated that there may be as many as twenty-three different acredited helpers involved with people with disabilities (Brechin and Liddiard, 1981). This situation not only presents problems stemming from inter-disciplinary communication, and to some degree rivalry, but it also contributes to the process of mystification (Wilding, 1982). Each specialization tends to accrue to itself a code of practice which gives professional respectability and status to its work and its practitioners and distances these tasks and those involved in their execution from everyday life. As a result the lay person, because s/he does not feel able to act on his/her own, will become reliant on the 'specialist' skills of the expert. Any individual impairment is reinforced by a dependence on professionals. This process leads to an abdication of responsibility where interest, concern and skills are lost forever (Wilding, 1982). In addition, the professionalization of handicap enhances the social distance between the 'normal' community and people with disabilities by reassuring the former that specialist help is available for those perceived as different. Consequently that difference is perpetuated.

The existence of all seven barriers taken together means that there is considerable pressure on individuals with impairments to accept a dependent role, and that it is problematic for them to seek integration (Hurst, 1984). How these obstacles effect the individuals in the Contact group is discussed below.

Environmental constraints become apparent as soon as the users leave the day centres. The importance of these constraints can be judged with reference to the last chapter and the fact that most Contact members do not leave the buildings without being accompanied by a member of staff. This is because each centre is located in a normal urban environment which is not geared to people with mobility difficulties. Excursions into the surrounding community are therefore a precarious experience both for the users and their helpers. Pushing wheelchairs is not as easy as it looks. It is extremely tiring and it demands a great deal of skill and concentration, particularly in a busy urban environment. This is partly due to the fact that many people who rely on wheelchairs are overweight, but more importantly because of the delicate and intricate manoeuvres that are necessary to negotiate uneven pavements, curbs, parked cars and busy roads.

Of the numerous examples I observed, one of the most memorable occurred at the Dortmund Square centre shortly after I joined the group as participant observer, when Joyce asked me to take her in a wheelchair to the central lending library. I was surprised by her insistence that she use a chair since it is something she is normally reluctant to do. The reason, however, became apparent as soon as we left the building. I had anticipated few problems since I had some experience of wheelchair pushing inside buildings, and the library is only ten or fifteen minutes' normal walking distance away from the centre. However, the journey there and back, not including the time spent in the library choosing books, took an hour and twenty minutes. This was due to the difficulties I encountered negotiating the uneven pavements in the city centre, moving up and down curb edges — there are eight vehicle access points and three main roads to cross on the way to the library building which means twenty-two separate manoeuvres — and the problems getting in and out of the library itself.

The library is on the first floor of a large Victorian structure and is only accessible via steps, apart from a side entrance normally reserved for service deliveries. On arrival at the building I had to leave Joyce sittng outside while I went in to arrange for these doors to be opened. After about 5 minutes I returned with a security guard who let us in. A young caretaker apologized profusely for the general inaccessibility of the building and escorted us through what was obviously storage space. We had to ascend four steps to reach the lift to the first floor where the young man and I had to lift Joyce and the chair. The lift itself was designed for transporting goods and not operable by someone in a chair by themselves. The actual library was clearly not designed for people with impairments. There was barely enough room for someone in a chair to get through the doors, and the chairs and tables situated around the bookshelves were arranged in such a way as to render independent movement by a wheelchair occupant impossible. Although Joyce expressed some anger at this state of affairs she was evidently embarrassed by the situation. She assured me that she would return to the library as she enjoyed reading but never did during the study. What started out as an attempt by her to enjoy an activity most people take for granted ended in frustration and disappointment. What is also disturbing about this incident is that arguably one of the most important resources for people with limited mobility, namely, a public library, is so obviously outside their reach. But environmental barriers are not only problematic for people who are unable to walk without help.

Frequently when out with Andy, Jamie or Spike I was surprised by the problems they had when negotiating stairs or getting on or off buses, and the way in which these experiences exposed their vulnerability and transformed their personalities. When in the day centres all three strive to present a self-assured exterior, only rarely asking for assistance and often recounting exploits in the outside world which emphasize their relative independence. Outside, however, they are quiet, pensive and visibly concentrating on geting to their destination without mishap. This is particularly evident when they are in close proximity to large numbers of non-impaired people, such as in shopping centres, or when they are travelling by bus. For individuals with an unsteady gait being 'brushed past' by someone in a hurry can be a harrowing experience. It can often lead to them being knocked over which may result in broken limbs. Getting on and off buses is also a major problem because of the height of the step. It is frequently made worse by harassment by bus drivers and other passengers who seem impervious to these difficulties. None of the lads will travel by bus if there is standing room only. Andy's predicament on public transport is compounded by his epilepsy. Travelling by bus can sometimes induce an epileptic seizure which invariably means he is dispatched to the nearest hospital by well-meaning but ill-informed bus drivers or passengers. This occurred once during the study period.

Environmental considerations have a significant bearing on the activities of the entire Contact group. They are one of the principal concerns confronting users and staff when planning trips and outings. As well as the difficulties relating to transport and the number of helpers required, they limit where the group can actually go and what can be achieved when they get there. Sixteen users were permanently confined to wheelchairs and five often used them outside the centres, so a comparable number of helpers was needed for outings into the community. In a group discussion regarding the proposed annual outing (2 July 1987) I was struck, for example, by the lack of enthusiasm by a number of users for a proposed trip to a national leisure park. After a number of enquiries it became clear that several of the group held a view similar to that expressed by Curt immediately after the meeting was over.

'What's the point of me goin' somewhere like A . . . T . . . [leisure-park] where there's loads 'o rides an' stuff like that that I can't go on. I don't wanna go anywhere like that 'cos it only meks you feel sick 'cos you can't go on owt. I'd rather stop at 'ome.' +

I accompanied the group on four outings during participant observation. The first was on a trip to a country pub for lunch which included twenty-four users and ten helpers (10 July 1986). The second was to a newly opened shopping precinct in a nearby town and only consisted of eight group members and four staff (30 July 1986). The third visit was to a large national photographic exhibition (14 August 1986). Only seven users and four day centre personnel went on this occasion. My final excursion with Contact included six youngsters and three helpers and was to a large local pottery (16 September 1986). On each outing we encountered difficulties stemming from the physical environment.

Although access outside and inside the hotel on the first trip was generally good, the toilets were inaccessible to wheelchair users. At the shopping mall the only access from the car park, which was in the basement of the complex, for people unable to walk, was via the loading bay. Once inside, getting in and out of some of the shops and boutiques was almost impossible for individuals with mobility problems. Moreover, although the entire precinct spanned three storeys, there was only one lift which could only hold two wheelchair users and their helpers at once. Ambulatory shoppers, in contrast, are well catered for by escalators and staircases. Consequently much of the day seemed to be spent waiting to go from one floor to the next. The restaurants in this structure are all self-service and again inaccessible to individuals confined to a chair. All the menus are located high above the self-service counters and are virtually unreadable to anyone with visual problems or reading difficulties.[1]

A similar situation confronted the group at the photographic exhibition which was also a multi-floored affair. Here there was no elevator, but a special chairlift attached to the main staircase which only held one individual at a time. It had to be operated by an appointed attendant. Again a lot of time was spent waiting around to use this device. While there were few difficulties with access at the pottery, because of the limited space in the workshop only two wheelchair-bound users and their helpers could go round it at once. This meant the group was split up and half the afternoon consisted of lounging about in the foyer doing nothing. On each of these occasions both users and the authorities concerned looked to senior staff to resolve these problems.

On the first outing helpers had to assist users from their chair into the toilets. Although this type of interaction is normal and accepted by both parties in the day centres, it was evident that the individuals concerned, particularly the users, were embarrassed because it occurred in a public place. In the shopping mall, the photographic exhibition and the pottery, senior staff occupied a central role, organizing lifts, meals and so on, in order to complete the visits inside the allotted time.[2] Indeed, although users were given every opportunity to go off on their own, they never ventured away from helpers.[3] While this may be partially due to their lack of experience in the community at large, the attitudes of the general public were almost certainly a contributing factor.

It was obvious on each of these outings that the able-bodied were not accustomed to interactions with the overtly physically impaired. At the restaurant, for example, the hotel waiting staff without exception addressed all their enquiries to the most visibly non-impaired on each table. And although some of the staff insisted that they make any enquiries to the individual concerned, it tended to continue throughout the meal. It was noticable that some of the less visibly impaired, namely, Richard and Amy, were happy to speak for their contemporaries, but it was evident that several of the others were not used to such encounters and were clearly intimidated by the situation, hardly speaking during the entire lunch.

At both the shopping mall and the photographic exhibition I was conscious of the way non-impaired people stared at individuals in the group or turned away quickening their step to avoid eye contact. At each venue the officials concerned, the restaurant manager, the guides at the photographic exhibition and at the pottery, directed all their conversation to the senior staff, virtually ignoring the users and the younger helpers. At the shopping mall the lift operator commented to me on the lack of facilities at the precinct, and almost as an afterthought asked my wheelchair-bound companions, Bruce and James, in a maternalistic tone, which I considered would be inappropriate for an 8-year-old, if they were having a 'nice time'. When we had moved away I asked them both if such situations bothered them. Bruce shrugged his shoulders and said nothing, James replied 'it doesn't bother me, you get used to it', and Bruce agreed.

It may be argued that more than one visibly impaired individual in a public place is bound to stimulate these or similar reactions from the able-bodied since such situations are unfortunately relatively rare, but the same type of behaviour occurred on each of the numerous occasions I was out with only one member of the group. For example, Bruce and I went to a large record shop to buy some records. It was clear by the way the other occupants of the store stared at us that someone in a wheelchair browsing through record sleeves was not an everyday event. When Bruce had selected what he wanted to buy I pushed him to the counter. Despite the fact that I stood immediately behind him and he was holding his proposed purchase, the shop assistant looked straight at me and asked, 'Does he want this?' I replied that I did not know but it might be wise to ask him. She took the record jacket out of Bruce's outstretched hand and said in a louder than normal voice, 'Do you want this then?' Bruce's face flushed with embarrassment and he simply nodded. The girl took the disc from the shelves behind her and placed it in the sleeve, put it in a bag and stated the price wihtout lifting her eyes from the till. She took Bruce's money, put it in the open drawer and passed the record and the change to me, over Bruce's head. I motioned for her to give it to my companion. Clearly distraught she did so and turned away, and we left the shop. Outside Bruce seemed unperturbed by the incident and made no comment.

It is clear that he and the others in the group are used to this type of interaction. Data collected from a number of informal conversations with a cross-section of the group about this subject suggest that although the majority tend to gloss over such incidents many are still affected by them. As Roger commented,

> 'I used to get annoyed at first, but that sort of thing happens all the time, so you tend not to bother. It doesn't make any difference if you say anything anyway, some people just don't want to know. They've got their ideas and nothing'll change 'em'. I still get annoyed, but what's the point?' +

On two occasions during my time in the centres individuals in the Contact group were openly verbally abused by members of the general public. Both incidents took place at the Alf Morris centre in the summer when they were outside the building unaccompanied by staff. The first incident occurred when a number of youths shouted insults and obscenities relating to disability at several people sitting outside enjoying the sun and the second, when Sheila was crossing the yard after returning from the sandwich van. Three young men approached her and asked her if she was 'mental'. She said she was not, but they demanded proof. She became upset and began to cry and the youths began to laugh. When she moved away they started to make fun of the way she walked. She was deeply upset by this experience and spent the rest of the day in silence. Several of the Contact group could recall experiences when they had encountered overt hostility from the non-impaired because of their disabilities. In the formal interviews twelve respondents referred to such incidents. For example, in June 1986 Marilyn came home early from a holiday at a well-known seaside resort on the south coast because of the prejudice and negative attitudes she and her impaired friend Sharon had encountered in discos and pubs.[4]

Roger told me of an occasion when he was out with his mother in a local park and they were verbally abused by a gang of 'skinheads'. He said that when he and his mother retreated and she threatened to call the police the gang began to throw stones at them. Jamie stated that both his convictions for assault were caused by his retaliation after someone had made derogatory remarks about his impairment or called him names such as 'cripple', or 'spaz' (short for spastic) and this claim was verified by senior staff. The negative effects of these experiences are neutralized to some degree by sharing them with others in similar situations, namely, in conversations with other day centre users, and/or the psychological support provided by staff, whether it be through normal everyday interaction or specially arranged counselling sessions.

I was constantly reminded of the limited education many of the Contact users had received and the very real problems this created for subjective autonomy and integration into normal society. Their inability to read, for example, has already been mentioned in relation to relatively simple printed items such as menus, but it has clear implications in other areas, such as finding work, claiming benefits, housing and so on. And this in turn reinforces their dependence on others, particularly those in an 'official' helping role. The extent of the educational barrier to integration is also evident in their frequent inability to handle money. Most of the Contact group are not responsible for their own financial affairs. Such matters are left to their parents. In fact for many handling money is a major problem. When I was asked by users to go to the shops for sandwiches or sweets, for example, some individuals would ask for an item costing less than 50 pence and give me all the coins they had, unsure if they had given me enough.

A memorable incident which illustrates this point occurred when the group was returning from an outing by coach and stopped at a service area for something to eat. While some of the group asked staff to get their food, others decided to get their own. Barry was one of the latter. He collected items valued at £2 75p. When he got to the cashier he gave her a one pound coin, which was all he had. It was plain from the expression on his face when the girl told him this was not enough that he had no idea of the cost. His subsequent silence during the rest of the journey indicated the level of embarrassment this incident caused him.

I noted in the last chapter that some effort is made by senior staff to encourage users to overcome these problems through education and that part of this policy involved a local college. After one visit it was clear that the facilities at this institution were inappropriate for individuals with the degree of impairment of many of the Contact group. I went to the college with Billy after he had been persuaded by Jayne and Benjamin to give the bridging scheme a try.[5] The college is a multi-storeyed building providing courses for 8,000 full-time and part-time students. There are a number of steps up to the main entrance, no classrooms below the first floor and only two small lifts. The ground floor accommodates student common rooms, a refectory, staff rooms and offices. The rooms in which the course was being taught were at the back of the building on the first floor. To get to the classes students had either to ascend a number of steps before entering the building or use a side entrance. Once inside they had to negotiate two flights of stairs or wait for the lift, cross a large foyer which was usually full of people and then pass through a series of narrow corridors. Although Billy had initially expressed some enthusiasm about going to college he was clearly shaken when he got there. When we got back to Alf Morris he said to Jayne,

'Why can't I do it 'ere? I don't really fancy it there.' +

His reasons for the change of attitude were never given.

As noted in Chapter Two the very existence of day centres is largely the result of the occupational barriers facing disabled people.[6] The idea that day centres are 'the last resting places' (Kent *et al.*, 1984) for people excluded from the world of work was clearly reflected in the practices of those who worked in the careers services during this study, such as Disability Resettlement Officers (DROs). Indeed, when planning the study I was told by one DRO that day centres were for the 'cabbages who wouldn't or couldn't fit in anywhere else'. Senior day centre staff were also aware of this attitude among this particular group of professionals, as the following makes clear.

'Unfortunately social services is seen as the last option, it's seen as the end of the road.... When we started I thought we had a fine relationship with the careers service. But they don't seem to have the interest, we only hear from them when they want to make a referral.'*
— Jayne.

'DROs, I know they're there, but they don't come in unless they're making referrals. The only way people [users] have contact with them is if they take themselves off down to the job centre and ask to see one.'*
— Jackie

Any information relating to employment in the centres only came in via the users themselves, or through the efforts of the day centre personnel. Senior staff frequently circulated data relating to jobs among users. Jayne, for example, told the group of the plans for the new sheltered workshop three months before it actually opened. She received this information from the social services department, not the careers service. Most of the more able users, however, were put off working in this unit because 60 per cent of the workforce were to be mentally handicapped. One of the group did sucessfully apply for a job there but only stayed six weeks. The only individual to break through the occupational barrier, Marilyn, did so through her own volition, although she acknowledged her debt to the staff for providing motivation and practical assistance in the form of references and help with application forms.

Few of the Contact users seemed aware of the legal constraints on people with disabilities. From the data derived from informal conversations with users and staff it was evident that the majority leave their financial affairs to others, usually their parents. Other studies have noted that many similarly impaired young adults are ignorant where their benefit entitlements are concerned (Anderson and Clarke, 1982). This did not apply to some of the moderately impaired members of the group. All expressed concern over what were, at the time, impending changes to the state welfare system. Joyce and Marilyn discussed in detail the implications for the latter in relation to loss of benefit and reassessment when she decided to look for work. Andy was especially critical of the assessment process for eligibility for mobility allowance, a benefit for which he does not qualify, despite his awkward gait and his difficulties on public transport. And Jamie is all too aware of the restrictions imposed on disabled people by state officials. Not only did he and his girlfriend have considerable difficulty finding out what assistance was available to them before the birth of their child, they were also forced to attend a 'case conference' where their competence as parents was critically assessed by doctors, social workers and others before they were allowed to keep it. It is inconceivable that this situation would have arisen if they had been non-impaired. With such considerations in mind it is not surprising that many of the Contact users experienced low self-esteem, limited motivation and a lack of confidence, synonymous with what Bowe termed the personal barrier to integration.

It was evident that of the six users who had become impaired at sixteen or after, at least five experienced adjustment difficulties. Apart from Billy whose problems have been documented in earlier chapters, Roger, Charles, Spike, Philip and Robert all ascribed the difficulties they encountered in their daily lives to their impairments. The only other individual disabled after sixteen, John, appeared to have adjusted fairly well to his paralysis although he did cite regaining the ability to walk as his only ambition. However, he rarely complained, was always cheerful and although he was not affiliated to any particular user clique, was relatively popular among the others. His 'successful' adjustment may be explained by the fact that he had attended special schools since the age of eleven because of his inability to read, so in a sense he had already been socialized into a dependent role.

With regard to the others mentioned above, Roger's only goal in life had been to play the bass guitar in a rock 'n' roll band. The onset of his illness at 25 had undermined that completely since he was unable to stand up straight, had limited control over his hands and became tired very quickly. Before his impairment he had lived independently from his mother, had been a dedicated follower of fashion and had had a string of girlfriends. He had since returned to the parental home, although he did not get on with his stepfather, because he could no longer look after himself. He was also aware that his condition, the cause and name of which were unknown, was degenerative. He was frequently prone to bouts of overt depression.

Charles suffered similar moods but his were exacerbated by his limited communicative abilities. His only aim was to make 'a complete recovery', despite the fact that his condition had remained constant for the past ten years. Prior to this he had led a completely normal life. He had had an apprenticeship with a well-established engineering firm and had looked forward to a prosperous and happy future until his motorcycle accident rendered him speechless and almost completely paralysed from the neck down.

Spike, on the other hand, had adjusted relatively well to his incapacities. The fact that his impairments were modest in comparison to others in the group and that his mother and stepfather were both impaired have probably helped. Within the Contact format he was seldom visibly depressed but often aggressive. Some senior staff within the centres ascribed this behaviour to his frustration because of his impairments. He had an unsteady gait, had difficulty controlling his hands, and spoke, as he put it, 'as if I'm always pissed'. He said, however, that he had 'enjoyed' violence before his accident, had collected militaria, practised the martial arts and joined the army as soon as he could. But although he was one of the most autonomous members of Contact he stopped going to college because he could not take the ridicule directed at him by the able-bodied students.

'People was treatin' me like a freak, not teachers, kids. Like when I walked down the corridor an' they walked past, cos' I 'av a funny way of walkin', they'd laugh an' some of 'em'd call me names as I was passin', like freak. So I packed it in.'*

Throughout the study Philip was experiencing severe marital difficulties which he clearly believed were the direct result of his impairment, although he said this was not the view his wife held.

> 'Well there's been quite a lot of argy bargy at home just recently. It's been a mixture of me wife wantin' me to do things around the 'ouse, an' sometimes I just think I can't do 'em. I just think they're beyond me. I put it down to me disability an' she puts it down to laziness. It's somethin' we've tried to get over, we were seein' a marriage guidance counsellor at one time. We're not seeing' 'er now though.'[7]*

Since 1984 Robert had relatively few problems integrating into the community, because it was something he did not attempt. His 'blindness' was the result of a car crash when he was 20, after which he regained some of his self-confidence and went out alone. But in 1984 he was knocked down by a car. He then rarely left the family home unaccompanied other than to go to the day centres. While there he did not move about without a 'guide'. He hardly ever involved himself in any activities, formal of otherwise, only spoke when spoken to, and admitted that he had little interest in anything since his accident.

With regard to the congenitally impaired users, the difficulties associated with the personal barriers to integration were most apparent in those who were relatively moderately impaired and able to walk. Those in what I termed subgroup B did not appear to manifest any adjustment problems. I ascribe this to a number of factors including the degree of their impairment and their socialization. Analysis of their individual biographies shows that they have on the whole been sheltered from what Bowe (1978) describes as the 'stress of confronting a harsh world' by their parents, their education and the day centres. Their protracted affective interdependencce throughout has also provided them with an effective psychological defence mechanism against lowered self-perceptions which is mutually reinforcing on contact with the able-bodied world.

Because they were all wheelchair users their activity outside the day centres was extremely restricted. And since these devices act as signifiers of their dependence, when interactions between them and the non-impaired occurred, they were conducted upon firm foundations. There were none of the ambiguities and negotiations associated with encounters between the less visibly impaired and the normal. This accords with Goffman's (1968) account of the importance of what he termed 'stigma' symbols for minimizing uncertainty in confrontations between the impaired and the non-impaired. Furthermore, as there is a general resemblance between a wheelchair and a child's pushchair (Hurst, 1984), they were more likely to stimulate feelings in the non-impaired of overt pity or perceptions of the wheelchair users as eternal children, rather than outright rejection or hostility. The consequences, therefore, are potentially less psychologically destructive, particularly if such perceptions are all the individuals concerned have known. It is significant that none of the people in subgroup B reported having experienced first-hand the extreme negative attitudes toward the disabled described by other Contact members.

Those in what I termed subgroup C hardly ever left the day centres without a member of staff and when they did their behaviour was decidedly subdued, and in specific cases withdrawn. For those such as Gavin, who was confined to a wheelchair, this was probably due to environmental limitations and the severity of his illness, but for the remainder it was due to a life-long experience of impairment and negative discrimination. Several had been subject to patent animosity by the non-impaired. For example, Karen, Barry, Nancy, Richard and Wendy each had distinctly unpleasant memories of ordinary schools which had a profound effect on their self-esteem. Barry spent much of his formal interview telling me how he was 'picked on' when he went out. Karen felt that she was an object of ridicule in her neighbourhood and Wendy frequently spoke of how she was bullied in the children's home where she lived. They all, apart from Nancy, complained of being stared at when they were out in the street. And since their impairments were overt, 'passing' as normal was out of the question. Consequently each, to varying degrees, had opted for withdrawal as a safeguard against further emotional damage.

Withdrawal was not the general strategy adopted by the remaining members of the Contact group — Joyce, Andy, Jamie, Molly, Matthew and Marilyn. But passing was also out of the question since their impairments were clearly overt. Despite their relative independence, both inside and outside the day centres, integration into able-bodied society was nonetheless difficult and the ensuing psychological consequences equally debilitating. While they identified with the norms and values of the non-impaired community, many of their attempts to integrate into it had met with failure and disappointment. As noted above, all have experienced some rejection and hostility from the non-impaired. The cumulative effects of these experiences have had a significant impact on the individual consciousness of each. It found expression in their attempts to distance themselves from others within the Contact group who appeared to accept their dependent status willingly, and their general ambivalence toward day services. For example Molly told me in a discussion about friends,

'I wouldn't be seen dead with some of this lot in 'ere outside. They're pathetic.'*

As his formal interview drew to a close Andy told me,

'I'm not like most of 'em in 'ere you know. I only come so's I can get a job wi' the social services.'*

He has been a Contact member for the past six years. Matthew stated,

'I don't know why I come 'ere really 'cos I'm not really disabled, not like

some of 'em in 'ere. When me uncles ask me why I come, I tell 'em cos'
I 'ave to cos' me doctor says so.'*

There was also a very real belief by some of these individuals that the experience of
impairment was worse for them than it was for others in Contact, particularly
those in wheelchairs.

'I think some of the members in the group, them in wheelchairs, I think
they've been brought up with, I don't know how to explain it.....
They've been brought up as though their handicap's not a bad thing to
live with. They've never actually been in the street and had the mickey
taken out of them. They've never been in the street and been made fun
of. If I walk down the street people will notice. We walkers have alot
more to put up with because as soon as people see someone in a
wheelchair they think "Oh that person is handicapped". They don't
understand if you've got a walkin' problem.'* — Marilyn.

The emotional consequences of these perceptions were manifest in occasional
moodiness, aggression and depression. One of the most memorable examples of
the latter occurred shortly after I had joined the group on a full-time basis (14 July
1986) when Joyce arrived in a particularly depressed state. She spoke to no one
unless they addressed her first and looked as though she might burst into tears at
the minimum provocation. I found out from her best friend Marilyn that she was
upset because it was her birthday. Later that day I began a conversation with her
and after her mood appeared to improve I told her I knew it was her birthday and
that I found it difficult to understand why she was so unhappy about it since she
was still young. She replied,

'You might do Colin if you were disabled.... What have I got to
celebrate, what have I got to look forward to? Another year in this place?
I don't want to be stuck here for the rest of my life, and end up like
some o' them down there [elderly users].' +

She was only 25 years old.

The fact that many of the users were directed into the day centres by
professionals provides evidence of the professional barrier to integration, if only
because the centres are clearly discriminatory, although such arguments should be
offset against professional awareness of the extreme social isolation many young
disabled people experience in the community at large. However, apart from the
initial referral, there was little involvement by professionals once individuals were
in. This was explained by senior staff with the claim that most agencies see the day
centres as 'dumping grounds' for people with nowhere else to go. Throughout the
first nine months' participant observation there was no evidence to contradict this
view. But in March 1987 a social worker for physically disabled children began to
visit the group on a regular basis at Jackie's request, normally once a fortnight. In

July 1987 an occupational therapist was appointed by the Social Services Department whose responsibilities included the Contact group. Up to then the only involvement users had with these workers was either direct or through the day centre staff.

Only a minority of the users appeared to have definite views with regard to professionals. Some, such as Paul, for example, expressed antipathy toward those who work in the careers services for directing them into the day centres rather than finding them work. Billy and Nancy were particularly critical of doctors for their failure to provide adequate information regarding their impairments.[8] Several of the group, particularly those with acquired impairments, appeared to have a high regard for the medical profession, though they viewed other professionals such as social workers with polite indifference and occasional disdain.

Many users had little knowledge of what services were available and some were clearly intimidated by officialdom. During this study, their own and their families' involvement with other agencies was usually mediated through one or other of the senior day centre personnel. While it may be argued that their reliance on staff in this way merely sidesteps the central issue, since they are still dependent on a group of formal helpers, it is generally accepted that many people's needs go unmet because they find dealing with professionals and professional agencies difficult (Glendinning, 1986). It is also important to note that any involvement by day centre personnel in this regard was invariably instigated at the users' request.

This section has focused on the seven major environmental and social barriers to the integration of people with impairments into 'normal' society, architectural, attitudinal, educational, occupational, legal, personal and professional, and the consequences of each in relation to the Contact users. The evidence shows that architectural and/or environmental considerations are of primary importance in (if not the most important factor) restricting users' movements outside the centres. This applies to both individuals, and to the Contact group as a whole. This is applicable not only to the more severely impaired members of the group who are unable to walk, and rarely leave the units without an approved helper, but also to those who can. The examples provided show that as a result of the physical difficulties encountered by users outside the day centres, the behaviour patterns of the most overtly autonomous members of the group were altered and that their vulnerability was exposed. Besides undermining individual self-confidence and esteem, this helps to perpetuate the essentially negative attitudes associated with disability among the able-bodied, particularly those which suggest that all the impaired are dependent and helpless. It was evident that the most common attitudes encountered by users during initial interactions with the non-impaired were consistent with this view, encompassing covert pity and the 'does he take sugar?' syndrome and rarely passing beyond 'fictional acceptance'. It was also apparent that overt rejection and discrimination are not uncommon. The extent of the educational barrier facing many Contact members was reflected by their illiteracy and inability to handle relatively small sums of money. By focusing on a visit to a local college of further education I demonstrated the difficulties facing disabled people who try to overcome these limitations in an 'ordinary' educational environment, With regard to occupational obstacles, I suggested that the very existence of the day centres is evidence of the lack of occupational opportunities available to the individuals in the Contact group and that the lack of involvement by the careers service in this system undelines this view. Several Contact users have confronted the complexities of claiming procedures and the legal constraints imposed upon people with impairments and have found the experience highly stressful. The most extreme example was Jamie's and his girlfriend's confrontation with state bureaucracy in relation to their parenthood.

With regard to the personal barrier to integration, the data suggest this is less of a problem for those born with significant impairments, who have been socialized into accepting their dependent status and have been sheltered to some degree from able-bodied society, than for the majority of Contact users. Those with acquired disabilities all experienced problems of daily living which resulted in lowered perceptions of their own worth as human beings. The remaining congenitally impaired members of the group, particularly those who were 'moderately' disabled and able to walk, appeared to experience similar feelings. But while some reacted to these emotions with varying degrees of withdrawal, others expressed ambivalence toward the day centres, and animosity toward their impaired contemporaries who appeared to have accepted their disabled identity.

The evidence shows that professional involvement in the day centres during participant observation was limited and that apart from an almost unanimous antipathy toward the careers service, users' views on this subject were inconclusive. This was probably due to the fact that most Contact members and/or their families' dealings with other agencies were usually conducted at their own request, through the day centre personnel.

In sum, this section has drawn attention to some of the material and social problems encountered by the Contact users in the community at large and has shown how these experiences affect their behaviour and reinforce dependence. The following section focuses on their leisure and social activities outside the day centres.

Leisure/Social Activities and the Contact Group

It has become increasingly apparent in recent years that the sociology of leisure is a relatively neglected area. This may be due to the general view that leisure is linked to the social and ideological superstructure of society rather than the economic base. Cultural norms and values socialize us into the belief that work is good and idleness reprehensible (Parker, 1975). We perceive leisure as a marginal period of recreational activity which can only be legitimately enjoyed in conjunction with work. Consequently the long-term unemployed, who ought to be able to adjust to a life of leisure, usually find it difficult (Fagin and Little, 1984). Although people with impairments have consistently been excluded from the world of work it is only within the last decade or so, since unemployment in Britain reached unprecedented levels, that serious consideration has been given to the problem of giving meaning to a life without paid employment.

The phrase 'significant living without work' entered the vocabulary of professionals in the field of disability and rehabilitation after the publication of the Warnock report in 1978. In keeping with the general shift toward self-help the report stated,

> We believe that the secret of significant living without work may lie in handicapped people doing far more to support each other, and also in giving support to people who are lonely and vulnerable (quoted in Kent and Massie, 1981, p. 33).

This suggestion fails to take stock of the very real problems facing people with disabilities and is unrealistic since most individuals with impairments capable of voluntary work will almost certainly be seeking employment in the open market.

Kent and Massie further report that there have been a number of proposed solutions to this problem, such as quasi-legal substitutes for paid employment, work-type activities undertaken for people without a proper job, and the instigation of some form of training for unemployment. There are, however, distinct dangers in educating people, particularly those with impairments, for unemployment. They suggest that the most obvious is that professionals will decide when a child is young that s/he is unsuitable for work. Her/his education will then reflect this view resulting in a self-fulfilling prophecy, which produces a downward spiral in professionals' expectations about the potential for achievement of disabled people. These authors rightly point out that if significant living without work is to become a real option in the future and not merely an elaborate way of disguising a life without purpose lived in comparative poverty then it must not be a lifestyle reserved exclusively for the disabled. From what is termed an 'interactionist standpoint' Coe summarizes the situation well.

> Only when the able-bodied cease to look for employment will I stop advocating the need for the handicapped to obtain satisfactory paid employment (Coe, 1979, quoted in Hurst, 1984, p. 216).

At present individuals with impairments facing a lifestyle of long-term unemployment also face a life of relative poverty which often adds to any problems of low motivation, lowered self-esteem, and social isolation. This is generally reflected in the pattern of leisure and social activities they pursue.

There are a number of studies which show how non-impaired young adults spend their leisure time. Two notable examples which involve large representative samples are the National Child Development Survey of 16-year-olds (NCDS) and the Isle of Wight study of 14-year-olds (Rutter, 1979). Both confirm that in the mid-teens the amount of peer group contact outside school is very high, both in terms of the number of times peers are seen, and in the number of friends seen in an average week. In the Isle of Wight survey, less than 10 per cent of the sample were reported to have had no peer contact in the previous week, while over half had three or more contacts. Although less than 30 per cent claimed to be a member of a gang, almost half were members of clubs, and at least a quarter had visited a club at least twice in the previous week. Over 70 per cent said they had a special friend and three-quarters of these were on visiting terms with these friends. Few of the sample went out regularly with their parents, over one-third never went out with them at all and only 10 per cent once a week (reported in Anderson and Clarke, 1982).

With regard to the use of leisure, the Rutter study showed that watching television was a very common way of spending time. This underlines Parker's assertion that this is the leisure pursuit which takes up more time for more people than any other. Reading was another common activity. Less than a quarter of the sample said they rarely read books. This was also a popular leisure activity among the respondents in the Isle of Wight study. Going to the cinema was also a regular pastime, nearly half averaging at least once a month while a quarter went two or more times. Engaging in outdoor activities and sports were also popular activities, nearly 50 per cent of the respondents in the NCDS survey playing 'often' and one-third 'sometimes'. It was reported that very few of the young people said that they felt lonely 'often' while 60 per cent said that they never felt lonely.

There are relatively few studies of how young people with impairments spend their leisure time. Three important exceptions are Dorner's (1976) analysis of teenagers with spina bifida, Rowe's (1973) study of young people with cerebral palsy, aged 18–30, and Anderson and Clarke's (1982) study. Rowe found that nearly 20 per cent of his sample had never been out of the house at all other than to go to their Adult Training Centre (ATC) in the preceding week. He found that 60 per cent of his respondents would have liked to go out more. They cited transport and access difficulties to places of entertainment as the main causes of their confinement. Rowe stated that those who could drive were emphatic about the difference this had made to their lives. In general, watching television and listening to music were the most common activities named. Reading was not popular. A quarter said they found reading difficult. Over half of the Rowe sample claimed to have a hobby but this included listening to records which is often a solitary passive activity.

The Dorner survey found that most of the teenagers interviewed had friends although these relationships were limited to school or college. Those in special schools saw no friends at all in the evenings, on weekends, or during the school holidays. Social isolation in this study was closely related to mobility difficulties and virtually all those affected were perceived as socially isolated.

Anderson and Clarke compared the leisure and social activities of 33 able-bodied and 119 physically impaired adolescents between the ages of 14 and 18. Of the physically impaired respondents, 89 had cerebral palsy and the remainder spina bifida. Sixty-three were, or had been in ordinary schools and the rest in special education. In general they found that the youngsters with disabilities spent far more time engaged in passive solitary activities such as watching television or listening to music than their able-bodied peers. Few had well-established hobbies with which to occupy themselves 'constructively'. Reading was less prevalent among the impaired than the non-impaired, which the authors attribute to the difference in literacy skills between the two groups. In comparison to the non-impaired, a large number of the youngsters with disabilities belonged to a club. But most were members of clubs specifically for the disabled and over a third of these were school-based and closed in the holidays. The authors contend that this type of club membership is due to the impaired individual's need to compensate for their lack of peer contact. The benefits of club membership in relation to integration into the community were therefore limited.

They found that although those with a background in ordinary education were a relatively mobile group, they had a very limited social life when compared with the non-impaired. For example, a third said they hardly ever saw friends outside school. This applied to only 10 per cent of the able-bodied. They were also much more likely to go out with siblings or parents than were the latter. This also applied to those from special schools. Nearly three-quarters of the sample with impairments normally went out with one or more members of their family, while the non-impaired almost always went out with peers. Of those in special schools 60 per cent never socialized with their friends outside school, over half had never been to a friend's home and only a quarter had made such a visit in the last month. The researchers concluded that the overall degree of handicap, especially related to mobility, was closely linked to the amount of social contact the teenagers had. The more mildly handicapped led the more active social lives.

The difficulties experienced by those in special schools were said to be compounded by two other factors, First, the majority only had friends who were themselves impaired. Therefore on both sides of the relationship there were difficulties in making social contact. And secondly, those from ordinary schools, impaired or otherwise, had friends living within walking or wheeling distance from home. It was evident, however, that fewer of the impaired from normal schools, in relation to their non-impaired peers, had a particular friend. These writers contend that apart from mobility, no particular impairment seemed to influence peer relationships although those with speech difficulties tended to be more solitary with fewer peer contacts. They concluded that the majority of the impaired teenagers suffered high levels of social isolation (Anderson and Clarke, 1982).

A more recent analysis which compared the lifestyles of impaired and non-impaired young adults, was that conducted by the Paediatric Research Unit at the Royal and Devon Hospital between 1983 and 1985 (Brimblecomb *et al.*, 1985). This research focuses on the lives of 511 young adults aged between 16 and 25, 385 of whom had been labelled as handicapped or disabled because they had one or more physiological, sensory and in some cases, cognitive disorders. The study demonstrated that in this particular age group the non-impaired are three times more likely to be living independently from their parents, employed, and married, than their impaired contemporaries. They also found that social isolation was widespread among the latter. Although these researchers did not cover leisure activities in detail they showed that three times as many handicapped people as non-handicapped never went out socially in an average week and almost double the percentage of cases (52 per cent as opposed to 28 per cent) went out on two days or less. Only 3 per cent of the able-bodied resepondents never went out with friends. Brimblecomb and his colleagues found that the impaired young adults sampled were less likely to be involved in 'normal' social activities, such as going ot the pub, generally associated with people in their age group. As a result many felt there was a 'shortfall' in one or more areas of their social lives. These included lack of friends, social facilities and transport. As a result they had a poor self-image. In contrast to the non-impaired twice as many of the disabled respondents said

> that they often felt lonely, miserable or that life was not worth living, three times as many of them were not able to say they often felt happy (Brimblecomb *et al.*, 1985, p. 63).

It is important to note that similar experiences are also encountered by other socially disadvantaged groups in the same age range excluded from the world of work. Willis' (1985) recent study of the social condition of young people in Wolverhampton aged 16 to 24 found that social isolation was invariably the outcome of long-term unemployment. Willis shows that unemployed young people are less geographically mobile than their employed contemporaries, though this was obviously not due to subjective impairments but rather to a lack of money. Over half of those interviewed said that they could not afford to go out. The study shows that their leisure and social activities were radically different from those of their employed peers, being far less involved with commercial forms such as cinemas and discos, for example, and much less structured. The author concluded that there is an overall tendency for the long-term unemployed to be less active and more housebound.

The most common activities among this group were watching television and listening to music, and they were much more socially isolated than their employed contemporaries. Willis shows that for those out of work 'even courtship loses some of its social centrality'. He concludes that in many ways the young unemployed have been thrust into a new social condition of 'suspended animation' between school and work since many of the old traditions have frozen or broken down. Instead they experience a period of relative poverty and dependence on the state. This new social condition is characterized, Willis says, by some or all of the following: alienation (which he defines as feelings of separation from society, and suspicion of its main agencies and centres of power), depression and pessimism about the future. Whether or not this is a new phenomenon, or whether it will be a permanent feature of British society in relation to the young non-impaired, is open to speculation, particularly in view of the 'greying' population and the shortage of labour that this will inevitably cause in the not too distant future. It is, however, similar to that experienced by the young people with impairments in the studies already discussed and most if not all of the individuals in the Contact group.

The data provided by the formal interviews clearly show that the majority of users had few hobbies, spent most of their leisure time in the family home, were reliant on their families for social activity and had little or no contact with their able-bodied peers (see Table 17). Fourteen of the sample said that they had no hobbies whatsoever other than watching television or listening to music. Matthew, Paul and Gavin collected stamps, and the latter said he spent most of his time at home playing with his computer. Karen and Angela cited needlework as their primary leisure activity but while Karen enjoyed sewing and embroidery, Angela confessed that she probably would not bother if it was not for her grandmother who 'was always goin' on' about her doing something 'useful'.'* Jamie and Bruce said that they were keen football supporters. Both followed a specific team, but neither regularly went to matches, although they had been to important games in the past with members of their respective families. Four of the sample, Joyce, Andy, Sheila and Marilyn, said that they were avid readers. The three girls preferred biographies and romantic novels while Andy opted for science fiction and horror stories. Joyce and Marilyn also cited cookery as one of their favourite pastimes. In conjunction with her mother and sister, Molly bred, trained, and showed pedigree dogs, and Richard said that his main interest outside the day centres was looking after a pony owned by a friend of his mother's. Roger was the only respondent who played a musical instrument but admitted his interest had waned because he could no longer play as well as he once did. When he was not at residential college, Tony was a keen radio ham and a member of a local radio club. This did not, however, involve face-to-face contact or his leaving the family home.

Only three of those sampled were members of clubs not directly associated in some way with disability. Nancy was a member of a Bingo club, which she says she was only allowed to attend with her father, and Jamie and Spike were members of local working men's social clubs. Many of the respondents, fourteen in all, regularly went to clubs for the disabled. Norman, James, Curt and Elizabeth occasionally attended a local sports centre on Tuesday evenings when the facilities were reserved exclusively for people with disabilities.[9] But while Elizabeth went because she enjoyed weight training, the others said that as far as they were concerned it was a site for social activity rather than keeping fit.

'I only go for the bar an' the food, I'm not interested in sport or owt' like that.'* — Curt

This club has also been regularly used by at least six others in the past but none of them were attending during the study. Twelve of the respondents attended one or both of the local Physically Handicapped and Able-Bodied (PHAB) clubs on a regular basis. The clubs met each week. One was located in the local special school where most of the group were educated and the other at the Alf Morris day centre. This was a temporary location in the case of the latter since the property normally used by this club was being renovated. Both were closed in the school holidays.

Margaret, Norman, Gavin, James and Millie went to both almost weekly. The remainder only used the club located at the Alf Morris complex. Angela was a

Table 17   Leisure and Social Activities of the Contact Users Outside the Day Centres

Name	Hobbies	Clubs	Average outings per week	Where Users go	Who Users go out with
Margaret	TV/music	PHAB	2	Pubs/S'club	Family
Tony	Amateur Radio	Radio Club	2	Pub/S'club	Family
Joyce	Reading Cookery	—	2	Pub/Meal	Friends
Billy	TV/Music	—	2	Pub/Meal	Family
Andy	Reading	PHAB	7	Mother's/Pub	Alone
John	TV	—	1	Pub/S'club	Family
Sheila	Reading	PHAB	—	—	—
Jamie	Football	S'club	1	Pub/S'club	Family/alone
Sally	TV	PHAB	—	—	—
Karen	Sewing	—	1	Church	Family
Molly	Breeds dogs	PHAB*	2	Pub	Family/alone
Matthew	Stamps	—	1 (14 days)	Pub/S'club	Family
Paul	Stamps	—	1	Cinema/meal	Family
Gavin	Stamps C'puter	PHAB	—	—	Family
Norman	TV/Music	PHAB/DSC	2	Pub/S'club	Family
Barry	TV/Music	—	—	—	—
James	TV/Music	PHAB	1	Pub	Family
Henry	TV/Music	—	1 (14 days)	S'club	Family
Marilyn	Reading Cookery	—	3/4	Pub/Disco Meal	Friends/ alone
Bruce	Football Music	PHAB	1	S'club	Family
Nancy	TV/Music	Bingo	—	—	Family
Angela	Sewing	PHAB	2	Pub/S'club	Family
Millie	TV	PHAB	1	S'club	Family
Richard	Pony	—	1	B'sitting	Alone
Wendy	—	—	—	—	—
Curt	TV/Music	PHAB/DSC	1	—	—
Roger	Bass guitar	—	—	—	—
Elizabeth	Weight training	PHAB/DSC	2	Pub/S'club	Family
Charles	—	—	—	—	—
Spike	TV/Music	S'club	2	Pub/S'club	Alone
Philip	TV	Headway	—	—	—
Robert	—	Headway	1 Monthly	Meal/Pub	Family
Clive	TV	—	1 Monthly	Pub	Staff and residents from home

Key
DSC = Attends disabled sports club
*   = Is a member but does not attend

Source: user interviews

regular user of these facilities until March 1987, but was subsequently stopped by her parents because she had a number of severe epileptic seizures while there. Others in Contact including Paul, Barry, Henry, Wendy and Clive, also expressed an interest in going to one of these clubs. According to Wendy and Clive, the only reason they did not go there already was that they were not able to get transport. Both lived in residential institutions. Surprisingly even Matthew and Roger said that they had considered going along to see what the clubs were like simply 'to get out of the house more'. However, the other moderately impaired users sampled were extremely critical of these organizations. All said that they had attended at some stage (invariably when they first heard about them, shortly after joining Contact) but said that despite their name, Physically Handicapped and Able-Bodied, they were mostly frequented by people with impairments and that the only non-impaired people there were helpers. Moreover, the age span of the membership included small children and 'old people', and the clubs closed at 9.30 p.m.

> 'It's just like comin' to a day centre only at night. If I come 'ere durin' the day I don't want to come back an' see the same people at night.'* — Marilyn

> 'It's dickie that place man. They're all dickie that go there you wouldn't catch me goin' there.'* — Billy

Two of the adventitiously impaired respondents, Philip and Robert, were regular visitors to a self-help group for people with head injuries called 'Headway' which met once a month at the Dortmund Square day centre. Both said that they had found going to this club helpful for coming to terms with their impairments.

It is clear that without these organizations the social lives of most of the sample would have been even bleaker. Indeed, ten of the respondents said that they never went out at all and one girl, Karen, said that her only excursion out of the family home other than to the day centres was to church. Parental influence cannot be ignored here since her father was a lay preacher. Two went only once a month and two once every fortnight. The remainder averaged once or twice a week, apart from Marilyn whose tally was three or four, and Andy who said he went out every night, albeit five or six of these were trips to his mother's house.

For those who went out more than once during the week, this usually meant a visit to the pub or social club in the evening, usually Fridays or Saturdays, and at Sunday lunchtime. Only one respondent, Paul, said that he 'sometimes' went to the cinema. This alternated, he said, with going out for a meal. Joyce, Marilyn and Robert also cited eating out as one of their social activities. But Marilyn was the only member of the group who regularly went to discos or night clubs. Only seven of those interviewed said that they regularly went out without family and all were ambulatory. Joyce, Andy, Marilyn, Richard and Spike said that they hardly ever went out with kin, although Richard's only social activity outside the home involved babysitting at a friend's house on Saturday nights. Jamie and Molly both said that they went out with members of their respective families as well as by themselves. The rest only went out with siblings or parents or, in Clive's case, with people from the residental home where he lived. Whether or not the majority of users would have chosen these locations for socializing is open to speculation, since the data clearly show that they were normally only 'taken out' by someone else.

Although the quality of their social lives was a bone of contention for all the users interviewed, it was clearly more important to some than others. The individuals in subgroup B, for example, were apparently less dissatisfied with their

social situation than the rest of the group. They were all regular visitors to one or
more of the clubs for the disabled, and were less critical of them than others in
Contact. This may be explained with reference to the factors discussed earlier,
particularly their limited mobility.

However, the individuals in subgroup C felt that they should be going out
more. Wendy put it this way,

'A young girl like me should be goin' out. My life's just wastin' away. I
never go anywhere. I should be goin' out like the others in the house
[children's home].'*

Wendy's lack of social activity cannot be attributed to mobility problems since,
although she had a limp, she had little obvious difficulty walking. Moreover, as
she lived in a children's home, where others in the house did go out, her social
isolation may only be explained with reference to social rejection by the non-
impaired and/or psychological factors, or the personal barrier to integration.
Indeed, she had no ready explanation for this phenomenon unlike others in the
sample. Paul, Karen, Barry, Henry and Nancy, for example, all cited their
parents' over-protectiveness as the principal reason for their lack of social activity
outside the parental home.

'I think I should 'ave more freedom than what I've got, I'm 20 years
old. If I ask to go out me dad says to me, "no we daren't let you go out
in case you 'ave an accident an' end up in 'ospital''. I mean it gets above
a joke I never go anywhere. I might as well be 50. It's not really fair is
it?'* — Nancy

This situation was particularly disturbing for someone like Karen where rigid
parental controls were not extended to her younger sister.

'I'd like to go out more, but me mum doesn't let me, she says I'll get
poorly. It's not fair 'cos me sister goes out an' she's younger than me.
She goes out but I can't.'* — Karen

None of the interviewees, apart from Joyce and Marilyn, could name current
friends their own age, who were not involved in the day centres or clubs for the
disabled, either as users or helpers. With regard to able-bodied friends Joyce
maintained that she had a girl friend she saw 'quite regularly' whom she met at
college and Marilyn said she had several friends in the pubs/discos she used.
Andy, Jamie, Matthew and Spike all said that they 'knew' people who were not
disabled, but would not consider them friends.

Apart from Jamie and Philip, only three of the sample, Sheila, Norman and
Angela, said that they had a regular relationship with a member of the opposite
sex. Sheila said she was 'going out' with an able-bodied helper from one of the
PHAB clubs[10] and Norman and Angela were officially engaged.

The majority of the respondents had few plans or ambitions for the future and many seemed to view their prospects with obvious pessimism. As noted above, those respondents who acquired impairments after the age of 16 only had ambitions concerning their lost abilities. Although fifteen of the others wanted a job, they all saw this prospect as highly unlikely. Jamie said that he would like to set up his own jewellery business. A further six nominated getting a girl/boyfriend. The rest said that they had no ambitions because they felt there was little point.

> 'If you don't have ambitions you don't get disappointed. I don't like thinking too far ahead because the future frightens me. I don't like thinking I'm gonna do this or that cos' nearly always I've been disappointed. The things I want, friends, family, someone to love me, seem miles away.'* — Joyce

Although at various points during the formal interviews and during participant observation many of the user respondents had expressed a desire to leave the day centres, in response to the question 'are you likely to be leaving the day centres in the foreseeable future?' nineteen said it was unlikely. While some seemed resigned to this prospect without undue visible concern, others were clearly worried by it.

> 'I might have a couple of quick breaks if I get fed up, but I can't see it really [leaving the day centres]. I can't see me leavin' it altogether. It's better than nothin'.'* — Curt

> 'It's alright but, I thought to myself, our group is for the 16-to-30-year-olds. There's some that goes on 'til you're 40 an' there's some that goes up to 80, an' if I go on 'til I'm 30 somebody'll say "you've got to go on to the next one". I don't want to end me days in 'ere.'* — Paul

Of the remainder, only Jamie, Molly and Marilyn were sure that their attendance would cease, Jamie because of his family commitments, Molly because she was simply 'fed up with the place' and Marilyn because at the time of her interview she had applied for the job which she subsequently got. The rest could not give a definite response.

This section has looked at how the users in the Contact group utilized their time when not in the day centres. It identified the level of social isolation many of them experienced in the domestic sphere and underlined the importance of these units as a forum for social interaction. It began with an appraisal of recent theoretical analyses of leisure and concluded that how we perceive leisure is culturally determined, but that generally it is viewed as a marginal activity which can only be enjoyed in conjunction with work. Hence the long-term unemployed experience considerable difficulty adjusting to a life of permanent idleness. With regard to people with disabilities, following Kent and Massie (1981), I noted the added dangers inherent in the notion of 'significant living without work', namely, labelling by professionals, separation from the rest of society, relative poverty, and lowered self-esteem.

Empirical studies of how non-impaired teenagers spend their free time show that generally there is a high level of peer group contact and that although passive activities are not uncommon, social activity usually involves commercial forms and participation with others. The data also demonstrated that during the mid-teens most individuals are relatively autonomous from the family in relation to their use of leisure time and social isolation is unusual. In contrast, studies of young adults with impairments show a high level of dissatisfaction regarding their social lives. Outside formal institutions, teenagers with disabilities have few peer contacts, are more likely to be involved in solitary passive activities only and are almost entirely dependent on the family for social activity. As a result they experience extreme loneliness. The data show that there is a correlation between limited mobility and social isolation and that between 16 and 25 years, non-impaired young people are three times more likely to be living outside the family home, employed, and married than their impaired contemporaries. It was also noted that the experience of unemployment is in some ways similar for both non-impaired and impaired young people with regard to their use of leisure time, but that for the latter it is likely to be a permanent way of life.

The empirical evidence collected during the present study regarding leisure and social activities of the majority of the Contact group largely corresponds with the findings outlined above. Relatively few of the respondents had specific hobbies or interests with which to occupy their time. And apart from the day centres and clubs for the disabled, most users had few if any contact with peers, impaired or non-impaired. Apart from these activities, almost a third of the respondents had no social contact outside the parental home whatsoever and over three-quarters of the sample never went out without a member of their family ot guardian. Although there was a degree of dissatisfaction among all user respondents with regard their social lives, it was most acute among the more moderately impaired respondents. Notwithstanding that their only social activity revolved around specialist clubs and/or their respective families, those individuals with severely restricted mobility appeared less dissatisfied than the others interviewed. While not applicable to all, several of those who were able to walk ascribed their lack of social activity to parental control. Only two of the sample had non-impaired friends, and only five claimed to have permanent relations with the opposite sex. In this instance, therefore, it is not necessarily the more mildly physically impaired who lead the more active social lives.

The majority of the respondents had few plans or ambitions and viewed their prospects with an unmistakable air of pessimism. Although several were evidently deeply unhappy about the situation, most did not expect to leave the day centres in the foreseeable future. For the majority, due to circumstances largely beyond their control, the day centre system and the Contact group in particular represented the only real opportunity for social activity outside the family home.

Conclusion

In this chapter I have examined the problems encountered by the Contact users outside the day centres. The first section looked at the seven major environmental and social barriers to integration which confront people with disabilities generally, and illustrated the extent to which the Contact users were disadvantaged in these areas. The evidence reaffirms the general view that environmental factors are the major barrier to normative integration. They affected not only individuals in Contact, but also the activities of the group as a whole. I then noted the awkwardness and unease which proliferates in social interactions between Contact users and members of the general public outside the day centres, and in addition, that overt rejection and hostility were not uncommon. This section brought to light the very real disadvantages Contact members experience as a result of their inadequate education. The most telling indictment of that education is that many individuals in the group cannot handle relatively small sums of money. Although day centre attendance itself is verification of the lack of employment opportunities open to Contact members, I drew attention to the dearth of involvement by the careers service in this system. It was shown that the excesses of the legal and bureaucratic constraints on people with disabilities were most acutely felt by the more autonomous members of the group.

In terms of self-perception, it was evident that the cumulative effects of these phenomena has had unmistakable consequences for all Contact users, although the experience of impairment was apparently less problematic for some than it was for others. Although those with acquired 'severe' impairments appeared to experience problems of adjustment, the data suggest that among the congenitally impaired integration was relatively more emotionally disturbing for individuals with 'moderate' physical impairments than it was for those with severe conditions. This underlines the pressure on individuals to adopt a dependent status and the general view that it is easier to accept dependency rather than reject it. This section concluded with reference to the professional barrier to integration and how day centre staff helped to circumvent this particular problem.

The consequences of these considerations in relation to the users' leisure and social activities was demonstrated in the second part of the chapter. The majority of the group spent most of their time outside the centres, engaged in solitary passive activities, had little or no peer contact and were almost totally dependent on their respective families for social activity. Consequently there was a disturbingly high level of social isolation among most Contact users. The negative effects of this isolation were mitigated to a degree for some by their use of the specialist clubs for the disabled associated with the day centre system. It was apparent that while there was a definite discontent among all the sample concerning their social lives, it was less conspicuous among those individuals who appeared to have accepted their dependent status and attended these clubs regularly. But without exception dissatisfaction concerning social activities was highest among the less severely impaired members of the group.

In the final analysis this chapter has shown how environmental and social factors in the wider community impose constraints on the activities of all the users sampled, and in turn reinforce disadvantage. The data also show how day centre attendance helps to alleviate some of the negative effects of that disadvantage as it brings users into easy contact with a range of resources not readily accessible for people with mobility problems. In addition, by focusing on the excessive levels of social isolation experienced by the majority of the Contact group and their desperate need for social interaction, this chapter underpins the importance of these units as a forum for social activity. In view of these considerations it is highly probable that many of the users will, to varying degrees, become almost exclusively dependent on both day centre staff and the system as a whole. In the majority of cases this is an unwanted dependence which can only have a debilitating effect on their already limited self-confidence and self-esteem. Although in the present social and political climate it is debatable whether or not this disturbing situation can be avoided, one possible solution is discussed in the final chapter.

Notes

1 This state of affairs is even more alarming considering the recent construction of this shopping complex. It was officially opened in 1983.
2 Users had to be back at the day centres at 3.30 p.m. for their transport home.
3 None of the more independent members of the Contact group went on the last three outings discussed.
4 Sharon was only marginally impaired with a slight limp. She only attended special school at the primary level, had a job in a bank and owned her own car. She has never been a day centre user.
5 I was recruited to provide the physical support Billy needed when walking. When he visited the college he was still relatively ambulatory and did not want to go in a wheelchair.
6 The extent of the occupational barrier is patently manifest in the work experience of the Contact users discussed in Chapter Five.
7 Philip's marriage broke up shortly after the study period finished. He subsequently went to live with his parents.
8 During the study Nancy was having treatment at an out-patient clinic at a local hospital for high blood pressure. She said she had never been told what caused this condition or what consequences it might have for her in the future.
9 This is the same sports centre used by the Contact group for swimming and weight training.
10 This was later confirmed when he accompanied Sheila to the Christmas lunch. However, although not physically impaired it later became apparent that Sheila's boyfriend had attended a special school for children with learning difficulties.

Chapter 8
The Demise of the Contact Group

The empirical research was concluded in July 1987. The following account is based on a number of separate visits I made to the day centres between January 1988 and March 1989 and an informal but lengthy discussion with the Residential and Day Care Officer (RDCO), Mrs B, responsible for the service in April 1989. I shall outline the changes which occurred within the group during this period in chronological order and comment on these changes with reference to the conversations held with some of the users and staff during these visits.

Developments

In 1987 the composition of the Contact group changed dramatically. As noted earlier, Jamie had all but left the group by April due to his family commitments, Marilyn started work in the same month and Molly, whose attendance had progressively declined as the study drew to a close, stopped using the service altogether after July. In addition, several of the older Contact users were directed toward the Insight groups. I was told by senior staff that there were two main reasons for this policy. The first was that it was felt by senior staff that these users had outgrown the services provided within Contact and would benefit from mixing with slightly older individuals who were relatively more independent. It is said that the majority of Insight members had acquired impairments, were not dependent on their parents and generally took a more pragmatic approach to self-determination within the centres. Secondly, there were a number of prospective users in the younger age range waiting to join Contact. Whether or not this was the primary reason for this decision is open to speculation but three new members did join Contact in August 1987. These were the three boys who visited the group with the party from the local college of further education during the study period (see Chapter Five).[1]

The first two to move to the Insight group were Spike and Philip, both of whom perceived the change positively. They felt that they had outgrown the Contact format and welcomed the opportunity to interact on a regular basis with people who were 'more mature'. + Next to go were Andy, Matthew, Roger and

Charles, but unlike Spike and Philip who joined the Alf Morris Insight group, they were directed toward a similar unit at Dortmund Square. Although the decision to leave was 'mutually agreed' between them and staff, it was evident that the idea had initially been suggested by the latter. It was also evident that it had met with some resistance from Matthew and Roger because of the limited resources at Dortmund Square. Notwithstanding that senior staff were reluctant to comment on this point, I believe the decision to direct these users toward Dortmund Square rather than Alf Morris was because the former was undersubscribed while Alf Morris was not (see Chapter Four). In addition to these departures, Gavin contracted pneumonia in October and died in hospital.

With regard to the staff, the training programme for all newly appointed care assistants (CAs), whether on government-sponsored training schemes or employed on a permanent basis, was reformulated in July 1987. From this date no staff without previous experience of work with the physically impaired were allowed to start work in the centres prior to completion of a three-day induction course. Condensed into three full days, this course was in effect the training scheme which up to this point had been split into six separate training periods. It was generally agreed by all the staff that this was a far better arrangement.

In 1988 the system of recruiting staff through government-sponsored training schemes stopped. I was told by one activity organizer (AO) that this was because the centres were fully staffed and there was no real justification for employing any more. The change was generally regarded as a good thing since several of these workers 'were more trouble than they were worth'. + It is notable, however, that, with the exception of Annie, all the government-sponsored CAs who took part in the study were subsequently taken on by the Authority when their year-long contract finished, either for similar work in the day centres or in local residential homes.

In January 1988 Jackie started a self-advocacy and assertiveness training class specifically for Contact users at Alf Morris in conjuction with a tutor from the local college of further education. Participation was voluntary and the class ran for just over two months. It subsequently folded through lack of user support. While two or three Contact members, particularly Joyce, Billy and one of the three new males, were extremely enthusiastic about the project, the others who took part apparently lost interest after the first month or so.

The most profound change occurred in May 1988 when the Contact group effectively ceased to exist having moved to a newly modernized day centre specifically designed for younger users aged between 16 and 45. The new centre is situated in a quiet suburb about five and a half miles from the middle of the city. The building originally housed a training centre for the mentally handicapped and stands in the same grounds as a residential home for the elderly. Although there are no stigmatizing signs outside this area, both units are relatively isolated and reached only by a quiet cul-de-sac leading from a busy main road. The nearest shops and amenities are approximately half a mile away, clearly out of reach for people with mobility difficulties.

Internally the centre has been completely refurbished and adapted to the needs of the physically impaired. It houses a plethora of facilities and amenities including a well-equipped computer workshop, games room, cafeteria and lounges. Transport to and from the unit is provided by the local authority in a social services' specially adapted 'red bus'. The policy of using local taxi firms to transport users to and from their homes has been virtually abandoned for economic reasons. It seems that taxis are now used only as a last resort. Users' views regarding this issue were inconclusive. While some, such as Joyce, were extremely critical of the change, others were apparently placated by the fact that because the new centre is allocated a bus of its own, vehicles are no longer full of 'old people' when users are picked up or taken home.

Known as 'The Resource Centre for Disabled People', the unit is open from nine in the morning till nine o'cloock at night and offers a six-day service. Sunday is the only day it is closed. Although giving users a greater choice of when they attend, this choice is limited for those who are reliant on social services' transport which is only available at specific times of the day.

There are twenty-one permanent staff employed at the unit. All work shifts. Several, including Jackie, Rick, Denise, Patrick, Sean and Maria, previously worked with the Contact and Insight groups. According to a publicity handout printed at the unit's opening, the general aims of the centre are to provide (a) an appropriate forum where younger people with impairments can meet for social interaction, skill development, education and rehabilitation, (b) a centralized information service for users, their principal carers, and other professionals involved in rehabilitation, and (c) opportunities for people with and without impairments to share knowledge, experience and leisure activities.

To promote these aims the centre offers a wide range of services and activities both inside and outside the building similar to those offered by the Contact group, including sports facilities (at the same sports centre previously used by Contact), further education (in conjunction with the same colleges discussed in Chapters Six and Seven) and youth club evenings in partnership with national Physically Handicapped and Able-Bodied (PHAB) clubs. In addition, the centre boasts facilities for individually structured social and life skills programmes, information and advice and informal carers' support services. It also offers easy access to a recently developed community care support service specifically aimed at the younger impaired, jointly funded by the local social services department and the health authority, which includes a doctor, a social worker, a physiotherapist, occupational and speech therapists. Although these professionals are not located in the centre, I was told that they work closely with Resource Centre staff. In addition, the centre provides facilities for users to study and acquire office skills on a two-year Royal Society of Arts (RSA) training scheme supported by European Economic Community (EEC) funding. On completion students are promised assistance with finding appropriate employment.

As in the Contact group, eligibility for user status at the new centre is dependent upon both age and physical impairment. When I visited it in March 1989 there were ninety users on the unit's register and only twenty-three were from the original Contact group. As well as those who moved on to the two

Insight groups or who left for personal reasons, three other user respondents who took part in the study, Tony, Wendy and Clive, no longer used the day centre service because they had moved out of the Local Authority's catchment area.

In order to obtain all the available ex-Contact users' reactions to these developments I went to the Alf Morris centre to talk to Spike and Philip, and Dortmund Square to see Andy, Matthew, Roger and Charles. It seems Spike's use of the centres had gradually dropped off since he left Contact. When the Resource Centre opened Philip left Insight and transferred to the new unit and immediately enrolled on the RSA office skills course. He is particularly enthusiastic about the course because he is learning something which he considers useful, and there is the hope of a job at at the end of it. Although initially Matthew and Roger were opposed to their move to Dortmund Square, one year later they appeared relatively happy with the situation. Both said they got on well with other Insight users and the Dortmund Square staff. One of the main reasons for this change of attitude is undoubtedly the recent inclusion of sports facilities in Dortmund Square's list of activities. Both Matthew and Roger are keen on weight training. In response to the question 'would you like to move on to the new Resource Centre?' both said they were happy where they were. A similar response came from Charles. Andy, on the other hand, uses both Dortmund Square and the Resource Centre as and when he feels like it, although officially he is now a member of Insight.

On both occasions when I visited the Resource Centre there was plenty of user-centred social activity in progress, and there was clearly a warm friendly atmosphere throughout. Everybody gave the impression that user/staff interaction was distinctly positive. It was also clear that the longstanding social ties between some ex-Contact users had not been severed by Contact's demise. For example, on both visits Margaret, Norman, James, Curt, Millie and Angela from subgroup B were sitting together, and Barry and Henry were busy playing snooker. Most of the ex-Contact users I spoke to seemed genuinely enthusiastic about the recent developments. Norman, for example, told me how he was 'a bit worried at first' but had since decided that the new centre was 'alright because nobody bothered you' + . Even Joyce, who was especially despondent about the future when the empirical research finished, saw the Resource Centre in a relatively positive light, if only because of the RSA course and the chance of paid employment when it is completed. These reactions, however, are not surprising considering the quality and extent of the facilities available within this centre, the general expansion of services by the Local Authority for this particular user group, the influx of new users — all in roughly the same age group — and the fact that the majority of the more critical Contact members, particularly those in subgroup D, either stopped using the centres altogether or were located elsewhere. One notable exception, however, was Billy.

Billy's involvement with the Resource Centre has declined markedly since it opened. On both occasions when I visited the unit he was absent. It seems he now only attends to join in activities which he is particularly interested in, namely, weight training and judo. This is in contrast to his daily attendance throughout participant observation, irrespective of what activities were offered. In addition, according to the other ex-Contact users, his behaviour has become more aggressive and volatile. He is said to be increasingly critical of others, both users and staff, as well as the service generally. Although the reasons for this apparent dissatisfaction are likely to be many and complex, I believe that part of the explanation must lie in the fact that his two principal friends, Jamie and Spike, no longer use the centres and his illness has apparently deteriorated to the point where he is now totally reliant on a wheelchair.

With regard to the issues of user participation and/or user involvement in policy formulation, it was evident that little had really changed. In terms of activities, the principle of user autonomy was still given priority and user interest in explicitly social activity predominated, at least among ex-Contact members. When talking about the RSA course, Sheila, for example, said that she and a couple of the others had only 'stuck it for a week' + because it was just like school. When I suggested that this may be the best way to learn, she replied that she was not interested if it meant being told what to do all the time. Neither Philip nor Joyce felt that the course was too demanding, or that the tutors were excessively authoritarian.

With reference to user involvement in the general running of the centre, Jackie suggested that individuals do help out but nothing was formalized and it should be mentioned that on both occasions when I rang the centre to arrange my visits a user answered the telephone. However, she also pointed to the difficulties in trying to 'change the habits of a lifetime' + and said that participation was limited. At the time of writing there was no written formal constitution in the centre and user involvement in policy formulation, as in Contact, took the form of group or 'community' meetings. Jackie pointed out that user interest in these forums was still poor and that although staff had tried on a number of occasions to organize a users' committee, so far they had failed. She also said that getting individuals involved within the context of the Resource Centre framework was far more complex than it had been in Contact as there is no longer a clearly discernible group identity. This may be explained with reference to a number of factors. At the new centre, unlike the others studied, users are not formally organized into specified user groups according to age or day of attendance. Moreover, because of the extended opening hours many people attend at different times of the day and on different days of the week. There has also been a rapid expansion of the centre's users, the majority of whom only use the centre for particular activities.

Discipline is apparently less of a problem at the Resource Centre than it was in Contact. This can be explained with reference to at least three important factors. Firstly, all the users and staff at the centre are relatively young. No longer are the needs of the younger users swamped by those of the elderly. Secondly, the rowdier and more disruptive elements from the Contact group have either left or do not attend the Resource Centre on a regular basis. Thirdly, there are few spatial constraints on users' movements in or outside the centre. Those who are able use the unit as a 'drop-in centre', while those who are not can take advantage of the spacious grounds which surround it. Moreover, because the centre is located so far away from the local shops and amenities, staff do not have to worry about users leaving the centre's grounds, simply because there is nowhere for them to go.[2]

This point clearly brings into focus one of the most important limitations of the Resource Centre, namely, its isolation. Because of the unit's location attendance completely removes users from the rest of the community. This problem is compounded by the extensive facilities available within it, since it has been noted that large well-equipped centres tend to discourage users from using or seeking to use those which are available to the general public (Carter, 1981).

It was evident that the Resource Centre staff were aware of these problems. I was assured that all those involved in the delivery of services, including the RDCO, had expressed concern about them within the Department. The decision to locate the centre in its present site, however, was taken at the executive level for reasons of limited finances and growing consumer need. Within the budget available the Authority was presented with only two options. The alternative to the site chosen was centrally located but could only accommodate twenty users at a time. In view of the fact that the new centre was fully subscribed in the first year, this decision is understandable. But since it is generally acknowledged that segregating the younger physically impaired from the rest of the community on a regular basis perpetuates difference, stigma and dependence, any economic gains made by it are likely to be short-lived (see Chapter Nine).

Several senior staff also pointed out that despite recent developments, general perceptions of the day centre service with regard to this particular age group had not really changed. Many informal carers and most other agencies outside the local authority's social services department still tended to see the Resource Centre as simply 'somewhere to go' for people who because of impairment could not be fitted in anywhere else. The careers services, for example, were conspicuous by their non-involvement in the Resource Centre project. Only a matter of weeks before my second visit a party of 16-year-olds from the Christy Brown special school, who were clearly perceived by users and staff as potential users, had visited the new unit 'to have a look around'.

Conclusion

After participant observation was concluded a number of important changes occurred within the context of the Contact group and the day centres generally which not only underpin the study's general conclusion, discussed in the following chapter, but also raise a number of questions which demand further study.

Prior to the group's demise several of the Contact members either left the centres altogether or were 'directed' elsewhere. While Contact staff were instrumental in the successful rehabilitation of at least two of the former, Jamie and Marilyn, it is unclear if this is true for the remainder. Although directing individuals into another user group may not be construed as strictly rehabilitative, since the motives for this policy are unclear and users are not leaving the day centre system, the data suggest that from the users' perspective the effects were positive. But how long will this perception last? The training programme for the newly appointed care staff has also been transformed. While this change is viewed positively by staff, it raises the question how it will affect staff/user interaction (see Chapter Four). A final question is how user/staff relations will be affected in the long term by the submergence of the relatively small Contact group within the much larger Resource Centre framework.

The development of the Resource Centre project and the expansion of services for the younger physically impaired must be seen in a relatively positive light, particularly in view of the economic and political constraints under which local government currently operates, because it signifies official recognition by the authority's policy-makers that the needs of this user group are distinct from those of the elderly. However, the data suggest that there are a number of significant factors which, rather than promote independence and integration for Resource Centre users, may accomplish the reverse. These include the centre's transport and admission policies, the general philosophy of the unit and, most importantly, its location. When juxtaposed against the substantial environmental, economic and social barriers to integration facing young people with impairments in the local community generally (discussed in detail in Chapter Seven), these considerations make it difficult to reach any conclusion other than that the positive aspects of the Resource Centre project will be relatively short-lived.

Notes

1   The girl in the party chose not to attend for reasons unknown.
2   I noted in Chapters Six and Seven how Contact users with mobility difficulties were all too aware of the environmental barriers confronting them in the wider community.

Chapter 9
Summary and Conclusion

Introduction

This study was undertaken against a background of increasing awareness of the extreme socio/economic disadvantage experienced by young people with physical impairments, the general criticisms levelled at professional helpers engaged in the process of rehabilitation, the emergent demands by some sections of the disabled population for increased participation in, or control of, services which purport to cater for their needs and the general lack of empirical research in day centres for the younger physically impaired. In this conclusion I shall first summarise the implications of findings in respect of the three principal themes outlined in Chapter One, namely, the role of the day centre for the younger physically impaired, the nature of the helper/helped relationship within the day centre environment, and the extent of user participation and control. I shall then outline a number of policy recommendations which relate to both the day centres studied and provision generally for this particular user group. I conclude that current policies which effectively disable young people with impairments are no longer simply morally unacceptable. They are economically inept.

Summary and Implications

From the data collected during participant observation it was evident that the Contact group provided a range of services and activities which gave many of the users a degree of autonomy and independence unavailable in the community at large. It was also clear that a minority of the relatively moderately impaired Contact members who no longer needed those services would stop using the centres while the majority would not. In addition, because the facilities within the Contact framework were limited in their capacity to provide these young people with the necessary motivation, skills, and opportunities to achieve the same levels of autonomy and independence outside the centres as well as in, it was also evident that their attendance would almost certainly be long-term and that as a result their already substantial disadvantage would be compounded, if only because of the stigma generally associated with day centre use.

Although the evidence presented in Chapter Eight reported that there had been a number of important changes in the day centres after the main study was completed, I do not believe that they undermine this general conclusion. Indeed, the majority of the users still using the service in 1989 were unlikely to benefit from the expansion of services subsequent to participant observation, given the substantial limitations of the new Resource Centre. These include the general role of the new unit, which broadly speaking is analogous to that adopted by the Contact group emphasizing the social over the re/habilitative aspects of day centre use, its admissions and transport policies and most importantly, its size and location. I suggested that rather than making integration into the community easier these considerations are likely to make it more problematic. Moreover, since the experience of many of the users outside the day centre environment is limited to the family home, partial institutionalization, whereby users come to accept that life outside the domestic sphere is limited and preferable in an institutional setting, is also likely to ensue. This has particular significance for the user group studied, those aged between 16 and 30, since many are disproportionately dependent upon ageing parents or guardians. Consequently, there is a very real danger that partial institutionalization may lead to institutionalization proper, where users come to accept that for people with impairments life inside an institutional setting is both acceptable and inevitable.

Moreover, while it may be true that due to the degree of oppression experienced by young people with disabilities, the voluntary nature of day centre use and the general lack of resources in this type of provision, partial if not total institutionalization is to some degree unavoidable for many, these tendencies have serious negative implications for both the users concerned and policy-makers generally. Besides being contrary to the users' best interests, since most of the available data regarding this issue suggests that individuals with impairments prefer to live in a domestic environment rather than a residential setting, this runs counter to the general ethos of community care which is to ensure that people are 'helped to stay in their own homes for as long as possible' (Griffiths, 1988, p. 28).

The tendencies towards institutionalization have particular significance for policy makers, both at the local and national levels, who are charged with the responsibility for the provision of services for the growing numbers of younger people with impairments.

One solution to this problem, suggested by one of the staff who took part in the study, would be to abolish day centre provision completely for this particular user group. However, besides being unacceptable to the general population (West *et al.*, 1984), particularly those with first-hand experience of disability, any social and economic gains made by such a policy are only likely to be short-term, given the disabling effects of the social isolation experienced by many young people with impairments and the inevitable consequences for informal carers. Such a policy is likely to stimulate a greater demand for residential care rather than less and relatively sooner rather than later.

Moreover, in view of the apparent divisions among the younger impaired it may be argued that no single solution is possible and that there needs to be a range of options provided. Apart from the problem of who should decide which of the options is most suitable for potential users, such a policy would encourage differentiation, perpetuate ambiguity and do relatively little to promote integration.

A more acceptable approach would be for day centres to adopt a more pragmatic approach to rehabilitation and integration similar to that advocated by Kent *et al.* (1984). But while there have been tentative moves in this direction by some local authorities, the general perception of day centres remains ambivalent. Consequently there needs to be a definite clarification of the day centre role. I believe this can only be achieved by the formulation of a consistent and coherent national policy which provides the appropriate resources and impetus to determine a shift away from philosophies of 'warehousing' and 'enlightened guardianship' toward 'horticulturalism' and 'disabled action'.

It has been shown elsewhere that because the traditional or 'warehousing' approach to day centre management is founded upon essentially negative views of people with impairments, it provides little more than a respite for informal carers and a forum where people with impairments can meet others in a similar situation (Kent *et al.*, 1984). As noted earlier, while these are important goals, they do little to promote user independence and integration.

On the other hand, while this study demonstrates clearly the main strengths of 'enlightened guardianship' in providing a variety of facilities within a limited set of resources and giving users a degree of individual autonomy, it also brings into focus the fundamental weaknesses of this approach, namely, that its scope for providing users with the skills and opportunities to achieve higher levels of self-determination outside the day centre context is restricted to the most able.

Because 'enlightened guardianship' as was observed to operate in the Contact group is founded on both negative and positive perceptions of impairment and incorporates both 'warehousing' and 'horticulturalism', its objectives are vague and lack clear direction. Consequently, although the facilities provided within Contact included both social pastimes and rehabilitative activities, there was relatively little scope for staff guidance. This has particular significance for young people with impairments, especially those congenitally impaired whose experience of life outside the family home and/or institutional settings is severely limited and whose motivation, aspirations and expectations regarding self-determination are already low. It is also accepted by many that a lack of direction is contrary to their needs. For example, in their study of adolescence and physical disability Anderson and Clarke stated

> What the young people lack is the continued guidance and support which they need throughout the later years in school and in the post school period, to help them understand what opportunities are in reality available, not so they merely accept passively the low status society often offers but so they can begin to construct for themselves a satisfactory life, despite the problems posed by the handicap and society's response to it (Anderson and Clarke, 1982, p. 353).

As a result of this lack of direction, it may be said that 'enlightened guardianship' encourages users, albeit implicitly, to accept passively their disadvantaged status. Moreover, while this ideology acknowledges the drives for independence and autonomy, the boundaries for achieving these goals are determined by 'able-bodied' reality. And since able-bodied reality oppresses people with impairments, autonomy and independence are generally restricted to the confines of the day centre. This was clearly evident by the degree of freedom users had within the centres and the constraints imposed on them outside.

Because 'enlightened guardianship' incorporates negative and positive perceptions of the disabled and accepts the needs of both the dependent and the not so dependent, there are inherent contradictions in this ideology which inevitably undermine any progress towards user participation and control. This was elaborated in Chapter Six. As a result 'enlightened guardianship' has inherent coercive and controlling overtones which, although absent during participant observation, came into play subsequently when a number of users were 'directed' elsewhere, some, albeit a minority, against their will.

In addition, because 'enlightened guardianship' encompasses notions of 'significant living without work', a concept which is reserved almost exclusively for the impaired, in a world where work determines both economic and social status, day centre use inculcates in many people the seeds of a descending spiral of personal expectations and self-esteem which is difficult to break. Although the deleterious effects of this process were alleviated to some degree by the changes which took place in the centres during 1988–89, it is probable that they will re-emerge when the novelty of these changes wears off. The only way this and the other problems outlined above might be resolved within the day centre context is by the complete abolition of this approach in favour of a shift toward 'horticulturalism' and, where possible, user control.

As noted earlier 'horticulturalism' is founded on perceptions of people with impairments as 'really normal'. It is favoured by both rehabilitation professionals and representatives of the 'disabled population' from both the left and the right of the political spectrum. Its aim is self-determination and independence, which for people with impairments is generally taken to mean the ability to devise and control their own lives in exactly the same way as does the rest of society (Brisenden, 1986).

Within this frame of reference the primary aims of day centres must be to provide users with access to a range of facilities, including 'social rehabilitation' (Henshall, 1985) and careers opportunities which enable people with impairments to live in the community and promote integration. Consequently, day services would have a specified positive role and day centre attendance a specified purpose.

Such an approach does not, however, ignore the fact that within the present societal context complete rehabilitation may not be possible for all day centre users. But while some may be rehabilitated and use the centres as a jumping-off point for a fuller integration, those who remain would be encouraged to promote the needs of people with disabilities in able-bodied society and thus work toward changing that society.

While 'horticulturalism' places an emphasis on skill acquisition, participation and a definite shift away from passive inactivity, it does not deny users access to social or leisure pursuits. This is an important point considering the level of loneliness experienced by many people with impairments. The incorporation of social pursuits follows firstly from the fact that social interaction occurs in most forms of human activity and the debilitating effects of social isolation can just as easily be offset by activities with a didactic content as they can by those without, secondly, that leisure pursuits are appreciated far more if they are experienced in conjunction with non-leisure activities, and finally, that many so-called leisure activities have an implicitly therapeutic content, particularly for those whose education was lacking and whose experience is limited. On the other hand, 'horticulturalism' may involve a number of problems associated with the helper/helped relationship. But I believe they are less apparent within the context of the day centre.

Critics of 'horticulturalism' might contend that professional intervention impedes individual adaptation and innovation and compounds disability. But in view of the fact that day centres are generally viewed as 'dumping grounds' for the 'no hopers', it is difficult to see how this argument applies, unless it is related to professional non-involvement. It is generally acknowledged that there is a paucity of professionals specifically concerned with rehabilitation in the day centre service. In keeping with other research in this field, the findings of this study suggest that there is an urgent need for more professional involvement rather than less, particularly from the careers services.

Because day centre personnel and the users live in the local community, staff are not subject to the same level of emotional pressure as those in other sections of the caring industry such as residential institutions. Moreover, since the overwhelming majority of day centre workers are from similar socio-economic backgrounds to those of day centre users, there is usually less of a social barrier between the two. With only two exceptions, this is clearly evident in this study. In addition, since day centre use is explicitly voluntary there is an element of interdependence and reciprocity between the helper and the helped in the day centre context, which might not be present in other institutional settings. Staff are less able to exert excessive pressure on users in order to achieve.

However, due to external factors such as poor education and limited opportunities user motivation is likely to be a problem for realization of the horticultural approach. This might diminish if day centre attendance is able to offer more than simply child-like dependence and semi-confinement. Motivation would probably also increase if users participate in the services they use. As Brimblecomb has suggested, 'if there is participation by the consumers in the running and development of services, motivation is likely to be higher' (Brimblecomb et al., 1985, p. 120). Consequently, participation in the general running of day services must be a necessary prerequisite of attendance. Moreover, since participation often stimulates a desire for control, 'horticulturalism' is far more likely to stimulate 'disabled action' than either 'warehousing' or 'enlightened guardianship'. Consequently, it is likely that in many cases the dominance of the 'horticultural' approach will be relatively short-lived.

However, because of the emphasis placed on self-determination and independence by 'horticulturalism' there is an inherent danger that debilitating psychological consequences might ensue for those people who cannot achieve them. While this is an important and valid point, much of the problem can be averted by adequate and appropriate consultation between the helper and the helped, where realistically attainable goals are mutually agreed, and if day services have sufficient resources, both human and material, to achieve them.

Due to the degree of oppression faced by people with impairments, it may be argued that any serious thoughts of their complete rehabilitation are futile. I believe that this view is unacceptable within the day centre context. Moreover, while at the present juncture there is little cause for optimism in this regard, particularly at the national level and that many policies which pursue this aim are limited, there is some light at the end of the tunnel. This takes the form of the unprecedented politicization of some sections of the 'disabled' population and the recent rapid expansion of self-help groups, and their subsequent achievements at the local level (see Chapter Six). Any philosophy of rehabilitation must generate this type of self-help and political involvement. As this study has clearly shown, 'enlightened guardianship' is incapable of doing this. 'Horticulturalism', on the other hand, is not.

The following section outlines a number of recommendations which I believe are necessary if day services for the younger physically impaired are to move in this direction. They draw on the observations made during this study and the work of other writers in the field, notably Carter (1981) and Kent *et al.* (1984).

Recommendations

As noted earlier there is a need for a clear national policy and planning framework for day services for the physically impaired. If this framework is to adopt the general approach outlined above then it must include the following objectives.

1. Day centres must provide the facilities and services for 'social rehabilitation' (Henshall, 1985) for those who require it.

    The appropriate facilities should be available for users to learn the practical skills needed to cope with impairment themselves rather than depend on others. Staff should encourage and assist users to develop necessary social and intellectual skills, including the ability to organize their own lives, make their own decisions, and function within the community.

2. Day centre users can and should be encouraged to participate in the general running and organization of the facilities and services they use within the day centre environment.

    This should include self-help and mutual support, routine

maintenance, preparation of food, stock control, finance, and the organization and deployment of staff. Opportunities for users to become helpers should be enthusiastically supported by the sponsors of the day services, and there should be a clearly defined, appropriate training programme and promotion ladder for users to rise within the system for those who seek it.

3. User participation and mechanisms for user participation in day centre policy making should be mandatory, and should be organized around a formal constitution which stipulates users' rights as well as their responsibilities.

    The contents of this document should be arrived at by mutual agreement between users and staff. It should be based on democratic principles which guard against factionalism, misrepresentation and excessive paternalism by those with authority. Representative bodies should be periodically elected and accountable to the users as well as the management.

4. Day centres must provide information, advice and counselling services, both for users and their families.

    There is an increasing tendency for local authorities to view day centres as resource centres for people with disabilities (Jordan, 1986). The importance of this function was clearly evident in this study. However, users should be encouraged to take responsibility for the collection and delivery of these services.

5. There should be effective and efficient cooperation between day centre staff and agencies concerned with rehabilitation.

    This proposal will require a radical reappraisal of professional perceptions of day services and their primary function. It is apparent from most of the literature as well as the data provided by this study that most agencies, particularly careers services, view day centres as 'dumping grounds' for the 'cabbages' and 'no hopers' who are forgotten once attendance begins. This is clearly not in the users' best interests. If individually structured programmes geared toward independence training are to be provided within a day centre setting then it is essential that professional involvement, if and when required, is properly planned and coordinated.

6. Day services must identify and try to break down the barriers to integration which confront people with impairments in the local area.

    Day centres must become more outward looking and actively promote understanding and integration within the local community (Kent *et al.*, 1984). Where possible this should include (a) the adoption of an open door policy, (b) the regular provision of practical services for other sections of the community, (c) active opposition by users and staff to localized barriers to integration, and (d) facilities within units for educating families and other informal carers to the needs of individuals with physical impairments.

(a) Day services should not be exclusive to one section of the local community.

The idea that day centres for the impaired should be used by the non-impaired has been suggested by several authorities on this subject (for example Tuckey and Tuckey, 1981) and was enthusiastically endorsed by all the user respondents and all the care assistants who took part in this study. Senior staff, however, took a more cautious approach, arguing that if day centres adopted this policy then care must be taken to ensure that the needs of users with impairments were not overlooked. This could be achieved by the inclusion of written safeguards in the formal constitution similar to those adopted by the Stonehouse at Corby in 1985 (Carr, 1987).

While there is general agreement that the needs of younger users are different to those of the elderly, user status should not be dependent on age. But care must be taken to avoid swamping by one particular age group.

Although admission policies dependent on age have definite advantages in terms of user induction and heightened social interaction, there are latent disadvantages to this policy which were apparent during this study. Some users did not wish to leave the Contact group when they reached the prerequisite age limit. And there is no reason to suppose that this would not occur at the new Resource Centre.

(b) If the status of people with impairments is to change then they must be seen to be making a practical contribution to the local community rather than simply consumers of resources (Kent *et al.*, 1984).

To help achieve this, and also enhance user self-esteem, day services and day centre users should seek to provide practical services for other sections of the community. Users at the Stonehouse, for example, ran a toy library for users and local residents (Tuckey and Tuckey, 1981).

Many of the users in the Contact group, both males and females, expressed a desire to work with children and/or animals. With a little help and training there is no reason why they should not be involved in a day-centre-based childminding service or creche or short-term pets' boarding kennels. It is important to note that the primary motivation behind these activities should not be economic, but any income generated from these or similar enterprises could be used to supplement the centre's funds.

(c) If environmental, economic and social obstacles to integration at the local level are to be overcome, users and staff must promote programmes designed to change public perceptions of day services and those who use them.

More emphasis must be placed on activities which go out into the community and change people's attitudes and understanding (Kent and Massie, 1981). The music and drama group's successful attempt to entertain children in a local nursery provides a good example of this type of strategy. Users should also be encouraged to form self-help groups which take a more active role in local affairs and lobby local authorities and other institutions for the removal of barriers which preclude people with impairments.

(d) Facilities should be provided by and within centres to educate families and other informal carers to the needs of people with impairments.

This is particularly important with reference to the problem of parental over-protectiveness, a problem which was so apparent for many of the users in this study. It is pointless people learning social and life skills for use outside the centres if they only get the chance to practice them in an institutional setting.

7. Sponsoring agencies should ensure that buildings used for day centres are an integral part of the local community rather than apart from it.

Large centres situated close to, or in the grounds of, other segregated institutions such as the Alf Morris complex or the Resource Centre should be abandoned in favour of smaller centrally located units similar to Dortmund Square which are close to local amenities and shops. While there are clear advantages in large centres because of the range of services they offer there is the danger that over-provision discourages users from using facilities available to the general public (Carter, 1981). This is contrary to the general principle of integration.

8. Day centre staff should receive a salary in accordance with their skills and responsibilities.

In accord with trends in other areas of social provision this study shows that the level of professional training among senior day centre personnel was relatively high and the training programme for CAs has been recently improved. Although all these workers were happy with the work they were doing, they were concerned about the inadequacy of their salaries. This was particularly applicable to the CAs, whose gross income during the study period was less than the net income of the average day centre user. If day services are to recruit and maintain a dedicated and proficient workforce then they should receive the appropriate re-muneration for the job.

9. Day centre transport should be flexible and subject to users' needs, rather than those of a central authority.

The policy of transporting users to and from day centres in large specially adapted stigmatizing vehicles at specific times of the day should be abandoned in favour of policies which transfer control to the individual user. To some degree this had been achieved in the Contact group by the policy of using a local taxi firm, although the choice of taxi was determined by the Local Authority. Alternatively users could be given a grant for transport which gave them complete freedom of choice.

If large specially adapted vehicles are required for group outings, then control must rest with day centre management committees and not with a centralized transport office. This control should include the type of vehicle chosen as well as its appearance.

In areas where public transport facilities include the smaller 'Access' type minibuses which offer a far more flexible service because they have no specific routes or timetables, day centre management committees should liaise with bus companies so that users reliant on public transport are adequately catered for in terms of getting to and from the centres.

10. In accordance with the recommendation of the Griffiths report on community care (Griffiths, 1988) sufficient funding should be provided by central government to enable local authorities to provide adequate and appropriate day services within the local community.

Whether or not local authorities run the services themselves or look to the private sector for this function, they should take a broad view

> when evaluating the cost effectiveness of day care provision and recognise that it makes good economic sense as well as being socially desirable to provide services which encourage personal autonomy for disabled individuals (Kent *et al.*, 1984, p. 24).

Conclusion

Considering the unprecedented demographic changes which will almost certainly affect Britain over the next two or three decades, notably the rapid expansion in numbers of the elderly and the envisaged acute shortage of labour — especially in the lower age ranges, the need for a radical reappraisal of societal attitudes and social policies regarding children and young people with impairments has never been more acute. Existing policies which successfully disable many children and young adults with impairments by not providing them with the confidence, practical and intellectual skills, and opportunities necessary to live outside institutional settings are no longer simply morally reprehensible, they are likely to prove economically disastrous. Any provision, such as the type of day services proposed here, which holds out the possibility of circumventing the profoundly negative social and financial consequences of existing policies must be supported and expanded without delay, at both the national and local level. Society can no longer afford the social construction of the 'cabbage syndrome'.

Appendix: Interview Schedules

It is important to note that these interview schedules were used as discussion guides and conversation openers rather than as straightforward standardized questionnaires (see Chapter Three).

INTERVIEW SCHEDULE USED FOR THE CONTACT USERS

1. How old are you?
2. What is the nature of your impairment?
3. (As appropriate.) Are you able to walk outside your home?
4. Can you travel by bus, train or car by yourself?
5. Who do you live with?
6. What is the occupation of the head of the household?
7. Have you ever lived away from home, in a residential home, hospital or boarding school for example?
8. (As appropriate.) How long ago and for how long?
9. How old were you when you left school?
10. What type of school did you attend?
11. Did you gain any academic qualifications at school?
12. Do you feel school prepared you for adulthood?
13. (As appropriate.) If so, how? If not, why not?
14. Have you had any form of further education?
15. (As appropriate.) If so, where and for how long?
16. (As appropriate.) Did you gain any academic qualifications from further education and if so what were they?
17. (As appropriate.) Do you feel that further education has been beneficial since you left and if so how?
18. Have you had any form of paid employment before you started using the day centres?
19. (As appropriate.) What kind, how long did it last and why did you leave?
20. How did you begin coming to the day centres? Did you arrange to come yourself or did someone else arrange it for you and if so who?
21. How long have you been coming to the centres?

22. Do you feel that coming to the centres has been beneficial to you?
23. (As appropriate.) If so, how? If not, why not?
24. How often do you attend?
25. Would you like to attend more or less?
26. Are you happy with the present system of using different centres on different days of the week?
27. (As appropriate.) If so, why? If not, why not?
28. Which centre do you prefer and why?
29. Are you happy with your present travel arrangements to and from the centres?
30. (As appropriate.) If not, why not?
31. Would you say you get on well with the staff in the centres?
32. (As appropriate.) If so, why? If not, why not?
33. Do you feel you could discuss personal problems with a member of the staff?
34. (As appropriate.) If so, who? If not, why not?
35. Has any member of staff ever discussed rehabilitation or training with you?
36. (As appropriate.) If so, who?
37. Do you think there are enough staff in the centres?
38. (As appropriate.) If not, why not?
39. Would you say you get on well with the other users in the centres?
40. (As appropriate.) If so, why? If not, why not?
41. Do you have a best friend in the day centres and if so who is s/he?
42. Are you happy with the activities/facilities offered at the centres?
43. (As appropriate.) If not, why? What type of activities/facilities would you like to see offered at the centres?
44. Are you free to choose what you do while at the centres?
45. (As appropriate.) If not, why not?
46. How do you spend most (75 per cent) of your time while at the centres? (a) arts and crafts, (b) formal discussion groups, (c) further education, (d) games and activities organized by staff, (e) games and activities organized by users, (f) sitting chatting?
47. Why do you choose this/these activity/ies instead of the others offered?
48. Do you have any complaints about the centres and the way they are run?
49. (As appropriate.) If so, what are they?
50. If you wanted to make a complaint how would you go about it?
51. Do you feel you have any say in how the centres are run? For example, do you feel you have any say in what activities/services are provided?
52. (As appropriate.) If so, how are users able to say what they want in the centres? If not, why not?
53. Is there a users' committee or elected body representing the users in the centres?
54. (As appropriate.) If there is, who sits on it, when was the last time it met and what effect does it have on internal policy?
55. Do you think users' committees are a good idea?
56. (As appropriate.) If so, why? If not, why not?
57. Are users free to come and go as they please while the centres are open?

58. (As appropriate.) Why aren't users free to come and go as they please? Should users be free to come and go as they choose?
59. Are there any rules concerning users' behaviour in the centres?
60. (As appropriate.) What are they?
61. (As appropriate.) Who makes the rules?
62. (As appropriate.) Do you think there should be more or less rules in the centres and why?
63. (As appropriate.) What happens if the rules are broken?
64. Do you think users should assist in the general running of the centres?
65. (As appropriate.) If so, why? If not, why not?
66. How can the present day centre system be improved?
67. What are the main advantages/disadvantages for Contact users from the present policy of mixing different user groups in the same centre?
68. Do you think the day centres should be open to other non-impaired sections of the community at the same time as the present users?
69. (As appropriate.) If so, why? If not, why not?
70. Are you likely to be leaving the day centres in the foreseeable future?
71. Have you any hobbies and if so what are they?
72. Are you a member of a club or similar organization?
73. (As appropriate.) If so, which one/s and how often do you attend?
74. How often do you go out socially — say in an average fortnight?
75. Where do you usually go — youth club (able-bodied), clubs for the physically impaired, out for a meal, pub, disco/night club, social/working men's club, cinema/theatre/pop concert?
76. Who do you usually go with — friends your own age, younger/older, impaired or non-impaired, siblings, relatives, parents?
77. Do you have a boy/girlfriend?
78. (As appropriate.) Is s/he impaired or non-impaired?
79. What are your plans/ambitions for the future?
80. How do you think society generally treats people with impairments?

INTERVIEW SCHEDULE USED FOR DIRECT SERVICE STAFF (CARE ASSISTANTS/VOLUNTARY WORKERS).

1. How old are you?
2. Are you married?
3. Have you any children?
4. At what age did you leave formal education?
5. Have you any academic qualifications?
6. Have you had any other type of employment before your present job?
7. How long have you been in your present post?
8. Why did you choose this type of work?
9. Have you ever had any contact or experience of work with people with impairments, before you began working in the centres?

10. What is your official job title?
11. Is there a written formal job description of your duties?
12. How would you describe your duties?
13. How did you feel when you began doing this type of work?
14. Do you think that the centres are adequately staffed?
15. (As appropriate.) If not, why not, and what type of staff do you think are needed in the centres?
16. What qualities do you think are necessary for this type of work?
17. What type of training did you receive for your present job?
18. Do you think that this training was adequate?
19. (As appropriate.) If not, why not, and how could this training be improved?
20. Is there a staff committee or similar forum where staff (all levels) can exchange ideas operating in this centre?
21. (As appropriate.) Who sits on it? How often does it meet? Does it have any effect on internal policy?
22. (As appropriate.) Do you think staff committees are a good idea?
23. (As appropriate.) If so, why? If not, why not?
24. Do you think there are any advantages/disadvantages for the users arising from the present policy of recruiting care staff via government-sponsored youth employment schemes?
25. Are you happy with the way staff are currently organized in the centres?
26. (As appropriate.) If not, why?
27. What is the primary aim of the day centre service with reference to the Contact users? (As appropriate.) Is it (a) to promote rehabilitation, self-determination and independence, (b) to provide a social atmosphere for social activity?
28. Do you think that the needs of the Contact group are distinct from those of the other user groups in the centres?
29. (As appropriate.) If so, why? If not, why not?
30. Do you think that the activities/facilities offered in the centres are appropriate for the needs of the Contact users?
31. (As appropriate.) If so, why? If not, why not?
32. What are the advantages/disadvantages of using different centres on different days of the week for the same user group?
33. (As appropriate.) Which centre do you prefer and why?
34. Do you know of any Contact users who have left the centres in the past year?
35. (As appropriate.) Why did they leave?
36. Do users' families play any part in the organization or general running of the day centres?
37. (As appropriate.) If so, how?
38. How would you say you get on with the Contact users?
39. Would you describe the Contact users as (a) physically impaired, (b) mentally impaired, (c) both?
40. Do you think that most (75 per cent) of the Contact users are (a) likely to stay in the day centres for one year or less? (b) likely to stay in the day centres for

one to five years? (c) likely to need some form of institutional care for the rest of their lives?

41. How do you come to this conclusion?
42. Are there any discussions in the centres between staff and Contact users concerning rehabilitation or training?
43. (As appropriate.) How often are they held and what form do they take?
44. Who decides what activities are offered in the centres?
45. (As appropriate.) Do users have any say in the activities offered?
46. (As appropriate.) If so, how? If not, why not?
47. Are the users free to choose what they want to do in the centres?
48. What do most (75 per cent) Contact users do for most (75 per cent) of the time while they are in the centres? — (a) arts/crafts, (b) formal discussion groups, (c) further education, (d) games and activities organized by staff, (e) games and activities organized by users, (f) sit chatting?
49. Why do you think this/these is/are the most popular activity/ies?
50. Do you think users have any say in how the centres are run?
51. (As appropriate.) If so, why? If not, why not?
52. Is there a users' committee operating in the centre?
53. (As appropriate.) If so, who sits on it? How often does it meet? Does it have any influence on internal policy?
54. Do you think a users' committee is a good idea?
55. Are users free to come and go as they choose while the centre is open?
56. (As appropriate.) If not, why not?
57. (As appropriate.) Do you think users should be free to come and go as they please while the centres are open?
58. Are there any rules concerning users' behaviour in the centres?
59. (As appropriate.) Who makes the rules?
60. (As appropriate.) Do users have any say in the rule-making process?
61. (As appropriate.) Do you think that the rules are appropriate for the needs of the users?
62. (As appropriate.) What happens if users break the rules?
63. Do you think that the users assist in the general organization and running of the day centres?
64. (As appropriate.) If so, how? If not, why not?
65. Do you think users should assist in the general organization and running of the centres?
66. How can the present day centre service be improved?
67. What are the main advantages/disadvantages for Contact users from the present policy of mixing different user groups in the same centre?
68. Do you think that the day centres should be open to other non-impaired sections of the community at the same time as the present users?
69. (As appropriate.) If so, why? If not, why not?
70. Do you think you are likely to stay in the caring industry in the foreseeable future?
71. (As appropriate.) If so, why? If not, why not?

72. How do you think society generally treats people with impairments?

INTERVIEW SCHEDULE USED FOR SENIOR DAY CENTRE STAFF

1. How old are you?
2. Are you married?
3. Do you have any children?
4. At what age did you leave formal education?
5. Have you any academic qualifications?
6. Have you had any other type of employment before your present job?
7. How long have you been in your present job?
8. Why did you chose this type of work?
9. Have you ever had any contact or experience of work with people with impairments, before you began working in the centres?
10. What is your official job title?
11. Is there a written formal job description of your duties?
12. How would you describe your duties?
13. What qualities do you think are necessary for this type of work?
14. What type of training did you receive for your present job?
15. Do you think that this training was adequate?
16. (As appropriate.) If not, why not, and how could this training be improved?
17. (As appropriate.) Is there an official policy on staff levels in the centres and if so what is it?
18. Do you think that the centres are adequately staffed?
19. (As appropriate.) If not, why not, and what type of staff do you think are needed in the centres?
20. Do you think there are any advantages/disadvantages for the users arising from the present policy of recruiting care staff via government-sponsored youth employment schemes?
21. How long and what type of training do these workers and care staff in general receive?
22. Do you think that this training is adequate for the job they do?
23. (As appropriate.) If not, why not, and how could this training be improved?
24. Are you happy with the way staff are currently organized in the centres?
25. Is there a staff committee, or a similar forum for staff (all levels) to exchange ideas, operating in this centre?
26. (As appropriate.) Who sits on it? How often does it meet? Does it have any effect on internal policy?
27. (As appropriate.) Do you think staff committees are a good idea?
28. (As appropriate.) If so, why? If not, why not?
29. What is the primary aim of the day centre service with reference to the Contact users? (As appropriate.) Is it (a) to promote rehabilitation, self-determination and independence, (b) to provide a social atmosphere for social activity?

30. Do you think that the needs of the Contact group are distinct from those of the other user groups in the centres?
31. (As appropriate.) If so, why? If not, why not?
32. Do you think that the activities/facilities offered in the centres are appropriate for the needs of the Contact users?
33. (As appropriate.) If so, why? If not, why not?
34. What are the advantages/disadvantages of using different centres on different days of the week for the same user group?
35. (As appropriate.) Which centre do you prefer and why?
36. Do you know of any Contact users who have left the centres in the past year?
37. (As appropriate.) Why did they leave?
38. Is there any contact maintained with users if they leave and if so how?
39. Do users' families play any part in the organization or general running of the day centres?
40. (As appropriate.) If so, how?
41. How are users introduced to the service?
42. Do you receive any background information on users when they are introduced into the centres?
43. If so, from whom?
44. Is there any information concerning users you do not have which you feel would be helpful in your work?
45. If so, what is it, and how would it be helpful?
46. Do users have access to the information you have which concerns them?
47. Do you think you have sufficient contact with other agencies concerned with the problems associated with disability such as physiotherapists, social workers, careers officers for example?
48. (As appropriate.) If not, how could this situation be improved and how would improved communication benefit Contact users?
49. Would you describe the Contact users as (a) physically impaired, (b) mentally impaired, (c) both?
50. Do you think that most (75 per cent) of the Contact users are (a) likely to stay in the day centres for one year or less? (b) likely to stay in the day centres for one to five years? (c) likely to need some form of institutional care for the rest of their lives?
51. How do you come to this conclusion?
52. Are there any discussions in the centres between staff and Contact users concerning rehabilitation or training?
53. (As appropriate.) How often are they held and what form do they take?
54. Who decides what activities are offered in the centres?
55. (As appropriate.) Do users have any say in the activities offered?
56. (As appropriate.) If so, how? If not, why not?
57. Are users free to choose what they want to do in the centres?
58. What do most (75 per cent) Contact users do for most (75 per cent) of the time while they are in the centres? — (a) arts/crafts, (b) formal discussion groups, (c) further education, (d) games and activities organized by staff, (e)

games and activities organized by users, (f) sit chatting?

59. Why do you think this/these is/are the preferred activity/ies?
60. Do you think users have any say in how the centres are run?
61. (As appropriate.) If so, how? If not, why not?
62. Is there a users' committee operating in the centre?
63. (As appropriate.) If so, who sits on it? How often does it meet? Does it have any influence on internal policy?
64. Do you think a users' committee is a good idea?
65. Are users free to come and go as they please while the centre is open?
66. (As appropriate.) If not, why not?
67. (As appropriate.) Do you think users should be free to come and go as they choose while the centres are open?
68. Are there any rules concerning users' behaviour in the centres?
69. (As appropriate.) Who makes the rules?
70. (As appropriate.) Do users have any say in the rule-making process?
71. (As appropriate.) Do you think that the rules are appropriate for the needs of the users?
72. (As appropriate.) What happens if users break the rules?
73. Do you think that the users assist in the general organization and running of the day centres?
74. (As appropriate.) If so, how? If not, why not?
75. Do you think users should assist in the general organization and running of the day centres?
76. How can the present day centre service be improved?
77. What are the main advantages/disadvantages for Contact users from the present policy of mixing different user groups in the same centre?
78. Do you think that the day centres should be open to other non-impaired sections of the community at the same time as the present users?
79. (As appropriate.) If so, why? If not, why not?
80. Do you think you are likely to stay in the caring industry in the foreseeable future?
81. (As appropriate.) If so, why? If not, why not?
82. How do you think society generally treats people with impairments?

Table 18 Dates when interview data were collected

Respondent's name	Status	Date
Margaret	User	29.12.86
Tony	User	29.12.86
Joyce	User	31.12.86
Billy	User	3.1.87
Andy	User	5.1.87
Mrs H	Parent	9.1.87
Richard	User	11.1.87
John	User	12.1.87
Sheila	User	16.1.87
Jamie	User	19.1.87
Sally	User	22.1.87
Karen	User	26.1.87
Molly	User	27.1.87
Matthew	User	28.1.87
Paul	User	4.2.87
Gavin	User	6.2.87
Norman	User	9.2.87
Henry	User	16.2.87
Marilyn	User	17.2.87
Bruce	User	18.2.87
Nancy	User	23.2.87
Elizabeth	User	25.2.87
Millie	User	27.2.87
Barry	User	2.3.87
Wendy	User	6.3.87
Curt	User	8.3.87
James	User	13.3.87
Roger	User	15.3.87
Charles	User	15.3.87
Spike	User	17.3.87
Philip	User	23.3.87
Robert	User	29.3.87
Clive	User	1.4.87
Angela	User	14.4.87
Jayne	SAO	2.1.87
Sally	CA	15.3.87
Annie	CA (GS)	22.3.87
Pete	CA (GS)	27.3.87
Tracy	VW/CA (GS)	6.4.87
Barbara	VW	10.4.87
Andrea	CA	14.4.87
Maria	CA	22.4.87
Jessica	CO	23.4.87
Bob	AO	24.4.87
Vera	CA	27.4.87
Rick	AO	28.4.87
Janis	VW	1.5.87
Jimmy	CA	6.5.87
Denise	AO	8.5.87
Mary	CA (GS)	13.5.87
Hilary	Tutor	12.5.87
Mrs W	OIC	15.5.87
Sandra	OIC	18.5.87
Sean	VW/CA (GS)	27.5.87
David	Tutor	28.5.87
Tracy A	VW	29.5.87

Table 18 Continued

Respondent's name	Status	Date
Prudence	Tutor	3.6.87
Patrick	AO	5.6.87
Maggie	Tutor	9.6.87
Andrew	OIC	11.6.87
Jackie	AO/SAO	16.6.87
Gef	Transport manager	17.6.87
Jennifer	Specialist social worker	19.6.87
Mrs B	RDCO	22.6.87

Key
OIC   = Officer in Charge
SAO   = Senior Activity Organizer
AO   = Activity Organizer
CA   = Care Assistant
GS   = Government-Sponsored Employment Scheme
VW   = Voluntary Worker
CO   = Clerical Officer
RDCO = Residential and Day Care Officer

Note: In the interests of confidentiality respondents' names are fictitious.

Bibliography

ABBERLEY, P. (1987) 'The concept of oppression and the development of a social theory of disability', *Disability, Handicap and Society*, 2, 1, pp. 5–21.

ALASZEWSKI, A. (1986) *Instituional Care and the Mentally Handicapped: The Mental-Handicap Hospital*, Croom Helm, London.

ALBRECHT, G. (1976) *The Sociology of Physical Disability and Rehabilitation*, University of Pittsburgh Press, Pittsburgh.

ANDERSON, E., and CLARKE, L. (1982) *Disability and Adolescence*, Methuen, London.

ANSPACH, R. (1979) 'From stigma to identity politics', *Social Science and Medicine*, 134, pp. 765–73.

BALDWIN, S. (1985) *The Cost of Caring*, Routledge and Kegan Paul, London.

BARTON, L. (1986) 'The politics of special educational needs', *Disability, Handicap and Society*, 1, 3, pp. 273–90.

BARTON, L. and TOMLINSON. S. (Eds) (1984) *Special Education and Social Interests*, Croom Helm, London.

BARTON, W. R. (1959) *Institutional Neurosis*, John Wright and Sons, Bristol.

BATTYE, L. (1966) 'The Chatterly syndrome', in HUNT, P. (Ed.) *Stigma*, Geoffrey Chapman, London.

BAYLEY, M. (1973) 'Mental handicap and community care', quoted in JONES, K. 'People in institutions: Rhetoric and reality,' in JONES, C., and STEVENSON, J. (Eds) (1982) *The Yearbook of Social Policy in Britain*, Routledge and Kegan Paul, London.

BECKER, H. S. (1963) *Outsiders*, Free press, New York.

BECKER, H. S. (1986) *Writing for the Social Sciences*, University of Chicago Press, Chicago.

BELL, C. and NEWBY, H. (1980) *Doing Sociological Research*, George Allen and Unwin, London.

BIERENBAUM, A. (1970) 'On managing a courtesy stigma', *Journal of Health and Social Behaviour*, 11, pp. 196–206.

BLACK REPORT (1981) *Inequalities in Health, Report of a Research Working Group*, DHSS, London.

BLAXTER, M. (1981) *The Meaning of Disability*, 2nd edn, Heinemann, London.

BLAXTER, M. (1984) 'Letter in response to Williams', *Social Science and Medicine*, 17, 15, p. 1014.

BLOOMFIELD, R. (1976) 'Younger chronic sick units: A survey and critique', unpublished paper (discussed in Oliver, M., 1983a op. cit.).

BLOOR, M. (1983) 'Notes on member validation', in EMERSON, R. M. (Ed.) *Contemporary Field Research: A Collection of Readings*, Little, Brown, Boston.

BLOOR, M. (1987) 'Social control in a therapeutic community, Re-examination of a critical case', *Sociology of Health and Illness*, March 1987, pp. 305–24.

BLUM, A. F. (1970) 'Theorizing', in DOUGLAS, J. D. (Ed.) *Deviance and Respectability*, Basic Books, New York.

BLUMER, H. (1954) 'What is wrong with social theory', *American Sociological Review*, 19.

BOOTH, T. A. (1978) 'From normal baby to handicapped child', *Sociology*, 12, 2, pp. 203–21.

BOOTH, T. (1981) 'Demystifying integration', in SWANN, W. (Ed.) *The Practice of Special Education*, Basil Blackwell in Association with the Open University, Oxford.

BORSEY, A. (1986) 'Personal trouble or public issue? Towards a model of policy for people with disabilities', *Disability, Handicap and Society* 1, 2, pp. 179–95.

BOWE, F. (1978) *Handicapping America*, Harper and Row, New York.

BRADSHAW, J. (1980) *The Family Fund*, Routledge and Kegan Paul, London.

BRAKE, M. (1980) *The Sociology of Youth Culture and Youth Subculture*, Routledge and Kegan Paul, London.

BRECHIN, A. and LIDDIARD, P. (1981) *Look at it This Way*, Hodder and Stoughton in association with the Open University, Milton Keynes.

BRIMBLECOMB, F. S. W., *et al.* (1985) *The Needs of Handicapped Young Adults*, Paediatric Research Unit, Royal Devon and Exeter Hospital, Exeter.

BRISENDEN, S. (1986) 'Independent living and the medical model of disability', *Disability, Handicap and Society*, 1, 2, pp. 171–8.

BROWN, J. (1980) 'The Normonsfield Enquiry', in BROWN, M. and BALDWIN, S. (Eds) *The Yearbook of Social Policy*, Routledge and Kegan Paul, London.

BULMER, M. (1987) *The Social Basis of Community Care*, Allen and Unwin, London.

BURY, M. B. (1979) 'Disablement in society', *International Journal of Rehabilitation Research*, 2, 1, pp. 34–40.

BURY, M. B. (1982) 'Chronic illness as biological disruption', *Sociology of Health and Illness*, 4, pp. 167–87.

CAMPLING, J. (1979) *Better Lives for Disabled Women*, Virago, London.

CAMPLING, J. (1981) *Images of Ourselves, Women with Disabilities Talking*, Routledge and Kegan Paul, London.

CANTRELL, T., *et al.* (1985) *Prisoners of Handicap*, RADAR, London.

CARR, R. (1987) personal communication.

CARTER, J. (1981) *Day Centres For Adults; Somewhere To Go*, George Allen and Unwin, London.

CARTER, J. (1988) *Creative Day Care for Mentally Handicapped People*, Basil Blackwell, London.

CCETSW (1974) *Social Work; People with Handicaps Need Better Trained Workers*, Central Council for Education and Training in Social Work, London.

CLODE, D., *et al.* (1987) *Towards the Sensitive Bureaucracy*, Gower, London.

COOK, J. and MITCHELL, P. (1982) *Putting Teeth in the Act. A History of Attempts to Enforce the Provision of Section 2 of the Chronically Sick and Disabled Persons Act 1970*, RADAR, London.

COOPER, D. (1986) '2 year YTS and young disabled people, factoral information', *Educare*, 26, November, pp. 6–9.

CORAD (1982) *Report by the Commission on Restrictions Against Disabled People*, HMSO, London.

COURT REPORT (1975) *Fit for the Future; Report of the Committee in Child Health Services*, HMSO, London.

CRAWLEY, B. (1988) *The Growing Voice*, CMH, London.

DARLING, R. B. (1979) *Families Against Society*, Sage, Beverly Hills, California.

DARTINGTON, T., MILLER, E. J. and GWYNNE, G. V. (1981) *A Life Together*, Tavistock, London.

DAVIS, F. (1963) *Passage Through Crisis, Polio Victims and Their Families*, Bobbs Merrill, Indianapolis.

DAVIS, F. (1964) 'Deviance disavowal, The management of strained interaction by the visibly handicapped', in BECKER, H. S. (Ed.) *The Other Side*, Free Press, New York.

DAVIS, K. (1984) 'The politics of independent living; Keeping the movement radical', extract from *DCDP News*, July.

DAVIS, K. (1985) 'Co-ordinators Annual Report', in *'Welcome to the Coalition'*, pp. 7–11, *DCDP News*, Derbyshire.

DAVIS, K. (1986) 'Report to the Members', 'Equality, integration, participation', *DCDP News*, Derbyshire, pp. 8–11.

DE JONG, G. (1979) *The Movement for Independent Living, Origins, Ideology and Implications for Disability Research*, University Centre for International Rehabilitation, Michigan State University, USA.

DENZIN, N. (1970) *The Research Act in Sociology*, Butterworth, London.

DES (1978) *Special Educational Needs, Report of the Committee of Enquiry into the Education of Children and Young People*, (The Warnock Report) HMSO, London.

DISABILITY ALLIANCE (1986/7) *Disability Rights Handbook*, Disability Alliance, London.

DORNER, S. (1976) 'Adolescents with spina bifida — How they see their situation', *Archives of Diseases in Childhood*, 51, pp. 439–44.

DOUGLAS, M. (1966) *Purity and Danger*, Routledge and Kegan Paul, London.

DOWNES, D. (1978) 'Promise and performance on British criminology', *British Journal of Criminology*, 29, pp. 483–502.

DURRANT, P. (1983) 'Personal social work', in BRECHIN, A., *et al.* (Eds) *Handicapped in a Social World*, Hodder and Stoughton in Association with the Open University, Milton Keynes.

EDWARDS, C. and CARTER, J. (1980) *The Data on Day Care*, National Institute for Social Work, London.

ERNTSTOFF, S. and HOWE, S. (1988) 'The divided borough', *New Statesman and Society*, 1, 9, pp. 12–13.

ERIKSON, E. H. (1968) *Identity, Youth and Crisis*, Norton, New York.

FAGIN, L., and LITTLE, M. (1984) *The Foresaken Families*, Penguin, Harmondsworth.

FINER REPORT (1974) *Report of Committee on One Parent Families*, DHSS, London.

FINKELSTEIN, V. (1980) *Attitudes and Disabled People*, World Rehabilitation Fund.

FINKELSTEIN, V. (1990) *Disability. The Capitalist Contribution to Society. A Marxist Interpretation of Disablement*, Pluto, London.

FORESHAW, G., *et al.* (1981) 'Pooling community resources', *Health and Social Sercives Journal*, 30 January 1981, pp. 101–103.

FOUCAULT, M. (1977) *Discipline and Punish, the Birth of the Prison*, Allen Lane, London.

FRY, E. (1986) *An Equal Chance for Disabled People*, Spastics Society, London.

GLENDINNING, C. (1986) *A Single Door*, Allen and Unwin, London.

GOFFMAN, E. (1961) *Asylums*, Penguin, Harmondsworth.

GOFFMAN, E. (1968) *Stigma, Notes on the Management of Spoiled Identity*, Penguin, Harmondsworth.

GOODALL, J. (1988) 'Living options for physically disabled adults, A review', *Disability, Handicap and Society*, 3, 2, pp. 173–93.

GORDON, G. (1966) *Role Theory and Illness, A Sociological Perspective*, Connecticut College and University Press, New Haven, USA.

GOUGH, I. (1979) *The Political Economy of the Welfare State*, Macmillan, London.

GRIFFITHS REPORT (1988) *Agenda For Action, A Report to the Secretary of State for Social Services by Sir Roy Griffiths*, DHSS, London.

HABER, L., and SMITH, R. (1971) 'Disability and deviance, normative adaptation and role behaviour', *American Sociological Review*, 36, pp. 87–97.

HANKS, J. R. and HANKS, L. M. (1948) 'The physically handicapped in certain non-occidental societies', *Journal of Social Issues*, 4, pp. 11–20.

HARGREAVES, D. (1967) *Social Relations in a Secondary School*, Routledge and Kegan Paul, London.

HARGREAVES, D. (1975) *Interpersonal Relations and Education*, Routledge and Kegan Paul, London.

HARRIS, A. (1971) *Handicapped and Impaired in Great Britain*, HMSO, London.

HELLER, F. (1987) 'The forgotten science', *New Society*, 80, 127, pp. 18–20.

HENSHALL, A. (1985) *Prospect Hall, An Introduction to Social Rehabilitation*, Prospect Hall Ltd., Birmingham.

HIRST, M. (1982) 'Young adults with disabilities and their families', *University of York, Social Policy Research Unit, Working Papers*, DHSS, 112/7/82MH.

HIRST, M. (1984) 'Moving on: Transfer of young people with disabilities to adult services', *University of York, Social Policy Research Unit, Working Papers*, DHSS 190/6/84MH.

HIRST, M. (1987) 'Careers of young people with disabilities between the ages of 15 and 21', *Disability, Handicap and Society*, 2, 1, pp. 61–74.

HMSO (1971) *Better Services for the Mentally Handicapped*, HMSO, London.

HUCHINSON, J. (1987) personal communication.

HUGHES, J. A. (1981) *Sociological Analysis, Methods of Discovery*, Nelson, London.

HUNT, P. (Ed.) (1966) *Stigma*, Geoffrey Chapman, London.

HUNT, P. (1981) *Settling Accounts with the Parasite People, A Critique of A Life Apart by Miller and Gwynne*, Disability Challenge, UPIAS, London.

HURST, A. (1984) 'Adolescence and physical disability, An interactionist view', in BARTON, L. and TOMLINSON, S. (Eds) *Special Education and Social Interests*, Croom Helm, London.

INGELBY, D. (1983) 'Mental health and social order', in COHEN, S. and SCULL, A. (Eds) *Social Control and The State*, Basil Blackwell, London.

JEWELL, P. (1973) 'Self management in day centres', in HATCH, S. *Towards Participation in Social Services*, Fabian Tract, 419, Fabian Society, London.

JONES, K. (1972) *A History of the Mental Health Services*, Routledge and Kegan Paul, London.

JONES, K. (1975) *Opening the Door*, Routledge and Kegan Paul, London.

JONES, K. (1982) 'People in institutions; Rhetoric and reality', in JONES, C. and STEVENSON, J. (Eds) *The Yearbook of Social Policy in Britain*, Routledge and Kegan Paul, London.

JONES, K. and FOWLES, A. (1984) *Ideas on Institutions*, Routledge and Kegan Paul, London.

JONES, K. and SIDEBOTHAM, R. (1962) *Mental Hospitals at Work*, Routledge and Kegan Paul, London.

JONES, K., *et al.* (1983) *Issues in Social Policy*, (2nd edn) Routledge and Kegan Paul, London.

JORDAN, D. (1986) *Moving Forward, An Evaluative Study of Day Centre Provision for the Younger Physically Handicapped; With Recommendations*, Kent DHSS, Kent.

JOWETT, J. (1982) *Young Disabled People, Their Further Education, Training and Education*, NFER, Nelson, Windsor.

KASSEBAUM, G., and BAUMANN, B. (1960) 'Dimensions of the sick role in chronic illness', *Journal of Health and Social Behaviour*, 1, pp. 35–42.

KENT, A., and MASSIE, B. (1981) 'Significant Living Without Work', *Educare*, 12, pp. 31–5.

KENT, A., *et al.* (1984) *Day Centres For Young Disabled People*; RADAR, London.

KING, R., RAYNES, N., and TIZARD, J. (1971) *Patterns of Residential Care*, Routledge and Kegan Paul, London.

KITTRIE, N. (1971) *The Right to be Different*, Johns Hopkins University Press, USA, Cited in WILDING, P. (1982) *Professional Power and Social Welfare*, Routledge and Kegan Paul, London.

KREBS, D. L. (1970) 'Altruism, an examination of the concept and a review of the literature', *Psychological Bulletin*, 73, 4, pp. 258–312.

KUH, D., *et al.* (1988) 'Work and work alternatives for disabled young people', *Disability, Handicap and Society*, 3, 1, pp. 4–26.

KUHN, T. (1962) *The Structure of Scientific Revolutions*, University of Chicago Press, Chicago.

LEMERT, E. (1962) *Human Deviance, Social Problems and Social Control*, Prentice Hall, Englewood Cliffs, New Jersey.

LONES, J. (1985) 'Who Cares'? *Contact*, 37, pp. 11–13.

LONDON BOROUGH OF HAMMERSMITH (1979) *'Clients' Views on Day Centres for the Elderly and the Physically Handicapped in Hammersmith*, Clearing House for Local Authority Social Services Research, University of Birmingham.

LUKES, S. (1974) *Power: A Radical View*, Macmillan, London.

LYNES, T. (1988) 'A guide to the social fund', *New Society*, 8 April 1988, 83, 1319, pp. 19–20.

MANNING, N. and OLIVER, M. (1985) 'Madness, epilepsy and medicine', in MANNING, N. (Ed.) *Social Problems and Welfare Ideology*, Gower, London.

MARTIN, J., MELTZER, H. and ELLIOT, D. (1988) *The Prevalence of Disability Among Adults*, HMSO, London.

MARTIN, J. and WHITE, A. (1988) *The Financial Circumstances of Disabled People Living in Private Households'*, HMSO, London.

MECHANIC, D. (1964) *Mental Health and Social Policy*. Prentice Hall, Englewood Cliffs, New Jersey.

MENZIES, I. E. P. (1960) 'A case study in the functioning of social systems as a defence against anxiety', *Human Relations*, 13, pp. 95–121.

MEREDITH DAVIES, B. (1982) *The Disabled Child and Adult*, Bailliere Tindall, London.

MERTON, R. K. (1957) *Social Theory and Social Structure*, Free Press, New York.

MILLER, E. J. and GWYNNE, G. V. (1972) *A Life Apart*, Tavistock, London.

MILLS, J. (1988) 'An uncaring community', *New Society*, 11 February 1988, 83, 1311, pp. 20–22.

MINDE, K. S. (1972) 'How they grow up: Forty-one physically handicapped children and their families', *American Journal of Psychiatry*, 128, pp. 1154–60.

MORRIS, T., and MORRIS, P. (1962) *Pentonville Prison*, Routledge and Kegan Paul, London.

MUSGROVE, F. (1977) *Margins of the Mind*, Methuen, London.

NATIONAL FOUNDATION FOR EDUCATION RESEARCH (1973) *The Child With Spina Bifida*, NFER-Nelson, Windsor.

OCPS (1980) *Classification of Occupations*, HMSO, London.
OLIVER, M. (1983a) *Social Work with Disabled People*, Macmillan, London.
OLIVER, M. (1983b) 'The Politics of Disability', paper given at the annual general meeting of the Disability Alliance, 15 April 1983.
OLIVER, M. (1986) 'Social policy and disability; Some theoretical issues', *Disability, Handicap and Society*, 1, 1, pp. 5–18.
OLIVER, M. (1987a) 'Redefining disability; A challenge to research', *Research, Policy and Planning*, 5, pp. 9–13.
OLIVER, M. (1987b) 'From strength to strength', *Community Care*, 19 February 1987, pp. 17–20.
OWENS, P. (1987) *Community Care and Severe Physical Disability*, Bedford Square Press, London.
PARKER, G. (1984) 'Into Work. A Review of the Literature About Disabled Young Adults' Preparation for and Movement into Work,' *University of York, Department of Social Administration and Social Work, Occasional Papers*, York.
PARKER, G. (1985) *With Due Care and Attention*, Social Policy Studies Centre, London.
PARKER, R. (1981) 'Tending and social care, Divisions of responsibility', in GOLDBERG, E. M. and HATCH, S. (Eds) *A New Look at the Personal Social Services*, London Policies Institute Discussion Paper, 4, pp. 17–34.
PARKER, S. (1975) 'The sociology of leisure, progress and problems', *British Journal of Sociology*, 26, pp. 91–101.
PARSONS, T. (1951) *The Social System*, Routledge and Kegan Paul, London.
PEARSON, G. (1987) *The New Heroin Users*, Basil Blackwell, London.
REDDING, D. (1989) 'A private function', *Community Care*, 5 January 1989, pp. 15–16.
REES, S. (1978) *Social Work, Face to Face*, Arnold, London.
ROBB, B. (1967) *Sans Everything, A Case to Answer*, Nelson, London.
ROITH, A. (1974) 'The myth of parental attitudes', in BOSWELL, D. M. and WYNGROVE, J. M. (Eds) *The Handicapped Person in the Community*, Tavistock, London.
ROTH, M., and KROLL, J. (1986) *The Reality of Mental Illness*, Cambridge University Press, Cambridge.
ROWE, B. (1973) 'A Study of Social Adjustments in Young Adults with Cerebral Palsy', unpublished B.Sc. dissertation, University of Newcastle upon Tyne.
RUTTER, M. (1979) *Changing Youth in a Changing Society*, Nuffield Provincial Hospital Trust, London.
RYAN, J. and THOMAS, F. (1980) *The Politics of Mental Handicap*, Penguin, Harmondsworth.
SAFILIOS-ROTHSCHILD, C. (1970) *The Sociology and Social Psychology of Disability and Rehabilitation*, Random House, New York.
SCHLESINGER, H. and WHELAN, E. (1979) *Industry and Effort*, Spastics Society, London.
SCOTT, R. (1970) 'The construction of conceptions of stigma by professional experts', in DOUGLAS, J. D. (Ed.) *Deviance and Respectability*, Basic Books, New York.
SCULL, A. (1978) *Museums of Madness*, Allen Lane, London.
SCULL, A. (1984) *Decarceration*, (2nd edn), Polity Press, London.
SEEBOHM REPORT (1968) *Report of the Committee on Local Authority and Allied Personal Social Services*, HMSO, London.
SEGAL, A. (1986) 'Push for power', *New Society*, 25 April 1986, 79, 1217, pp. 16–17.
SELFE, L. and STOW, L. (1981) *Children with Handicaps*, Hodder and Stoughton, London.
SHARPE, V. (1975) *Social Control in a Therapeutic Community*, Saxon House, Farnborough.

SIEGLAR, M. and OSMOND, M. (1974) *Models of Madness, Models of Medicine*, Collier Macmillan, London.

SILVERMAN, D. (1985) *Qualitative Methodology and Sociology*, Gower, Aldershot.

SIMPKINS, J. and TICKNER, Y. (1978) *Whose Benefit*, RADAR, London.

STONE, D. A. (1985) *The Disabled State*, Macmillan, London.

STOWELL, R. (1987) *Catching Up*, National Bureau for Handicapped Students and the Department of Education and Science, London.

STRAUSS, A. L., *et al.* (1964) *Psychiatric Ideologies and Institutions*, The Free Press, New York.

STUBBINS, J. (1983) 'Resettlement services of the employment services, Manpower Services Commission, Some observations', in BRECHIN, A., *et al.* (Eds) *Handicap in a Social World*, Hodder and Stoughton in Association with the Open University Press, Milton Keynes.

SUTHERLAND, A. T. (1981) *Disabled We Stand*, Souvenir Press, London.

SYMONDS, J. (1982) *Day Care Centres: Some Developments in England*, London.

TESTER, S. (1989) *Caring by Day. A Study of Day Care Services for Older People*, Centre for Policy Studies on Ageing, London.

THOMAS, D. (1982) *The Experience of Handicap*, Methuen, London.

TITMUS, M. R. (1970) *The Gift Relationship: From Human Blood To Social Policy*, Allen and Unwin, London.

TOMLINSON, S. (1981) *Educational Subnormality — A Study in Decision Making*, Routledge and Kegan Paul, London.

TOMLINSON, S. (1982) *The Sociology of Special Education*, Routledge and Kegan Paul, London.

TOMLINSON, S. (1985) 'The expansion of special education', *Oxford Review of Education*, 11, pp. 157–65.

TOOLEY, M. (1983) *Abortion and Infanticide*, Oxford University Press, New York.

TOPLISS, E. (1979) *Provision for the Disabled*, Basil Blackwell with Martin Robertson, Oxford.

TOPLISS, E., and GOULD, B. (1981) *A Charter for the Disabled*, Basil Blackwell, Oxford.

TOWNSEND, P. (1967) *The Last Refuge*, Routledge and Kegan Paul, London.

TOWNSEND, P. (1979) *Poverty in the United Kingdom*, Penguin, Harmondsworth.

TOWNSEND, P., *et al.* (1987) *Health and Deprivation, Inequality and the North*, Croom Helm, London.

TREVELYAN, G. M. (1944) *English Social History*, Pitman, London.

TUCKEY, L. and TUCKEY, B. (1981) *An Ordinary Place*, NFER, Nelson, Windsor.

TWADDLE, A. (1969) 'Health decisions and sick role variations', *Journal of Health and Social Behaviour*, 10, pp. 195–215.

UPIAS (1976) *Fundamental Principles of Disability*, Union of Physically Impaired Against Segregation, London.

UPIAS (1981) *Policy Statement; Disability Challenge*, Union of Physically Impaired Against Segregation, London.

VOYSEY, M. (1975) *A Constant Burden*, Routledge and Kegan Paul, London.

WALKER, A. (1981) *Community Care, the Family, the State and Social Policy*, Basil Blackwell and Martin Robertson, Oxford.

WALKER, A. (1982) 'Why we need a social strategy', *Marxism Today*, March 1982.

WARREN, M. D. (1979) *Changing Capabilities and Needs of People with Handicaps*, Health Research Unit, University of Kent.

WEBER, M. (1948) *From Max Weber: Essays in Sociology*, (Edited with an introduction by H. GERTH and C. W. MILLS), Routledge and Kegan Paul, London.

WEST, P. (1979) 'An Investigation into the Social Construction and Consequences of the Label "Epilepsy" ', unpublished Ph.D thesis, University of Bristol.

WEST, P., *et al.* (1984) 'Public Preferences for the Care of Dependent Groups', *Social Science and Medicine*, 18, 4, pp. 287–95.

WHELAN, E. and SPEAKE, B. R. (1978) *Adult Training Centres in England and Wales*, National Association of Teachers of the Mentally Handicapped, Manchester.

WILDING, P. (1982) *Professional Power and Social Welfare*, Routledge and Kegan Paul, London.

WILLIAMS, G. H. (1984) 'The movement for independent living, An evaluation and critique,' *Social Science and Medicine*, 17, 15, pp. 1000–12.

WILLIS, P. (1977) *Learning to Labour*, Saxon House, London.

WILLIS, P. (1985) *The Social Condition of Young People in Wolverhampton in 1984*, Wolverhampton Borough Council, Wolverhampton.

Index